Prophesy Deliverance!

40th Anniversary Expanded Edition

Prophesy Deliverance!

An Afro-American Revolutionary Christianity

40th Anniversary Expanded Edition

Cornel West

Edited and with a foreword
by Jonathan Lee Walton

WESTMINSTER
JOHN KNOX PRESS
LOUISVILLE • KENTUCKY

© 1982, 2002, 2022 Cornel West
Foreword and response essays © 2022 Westminster John Knox Press

40th Anniversary edition
Published by Westminster John Knox Press
Louisville, Kentucky

22 23 24 25 26 27 28 29 30 31—10 9 8 7 6 5 4 3 2 1

Scripture quotations marked RSV are from the Revised Standard Version of the Bible, copyright © 1946, 1952, 1971, and 1973 by the Division of Christian Education of the National Council of the Churches of Christ in the U.S.A., and are used by permission.

Book design by Drew Stevens
Cover design by Nita Ybarra

Library of Congress Cataloging-in-Publication Data is on file
at the Library of Congress, Washington, DC.

ISBN-13: 978-0-664-26565-6

Contents

Foreword

There are few grand intellectuals whose work shapes several fields across multiple generations. Think of W. E. B. Du Bois, Simone de Beauvoir, Reinhold Niebuhr, and Toni Morrison. The corpus of Cornel West clears this incredibly high bar.

Over the past four decades, the name Cornel West has become synonymous with philosophical nuance and a signifier for progressive cultural criticism. His genius is undeniable. His influence is unmistakable. For those who have read any of his many published books, experienced one of his spellbinding lectures, or witnessed his grace and gravitas while debating with interlocutors on the political right or left, you know that his vocation rests upon three interrelated principles: defend the personhood and rights of the most vulnerable, challenge the supremacist logics of empire, and encourage democratic dialogue across categories of difference.

Herein lies the power and continued importance of the book that you now hold in your hands, *Prophesy Deliverance! An Afro-American Revolutionary Christianity*. This wholly original and enduring text did more than inaugurate Cornel West's eminent and illustrious academic career in which he has held distinguished appointments at Yale, the University of Paris, Harvard, and Princeton. Of his many published works, *Prophesy Deliverance!* best conveys Cornel West's prophetic call and courageous Christian witness.

Prophesy Deliverance! proposes a Christian response to the dehumanizing and degrading tendencies of the late capitalist, postmodern age. The author mines the rich diversity of the Black experience in America to offer what he calls an Afro-American revolutionary Christianity. This particular form of Black critical thought is informed by the best of the Black evangelical tradition blended with what he deems the most usable dimensions of academic philosophy, namely neo-pragmatism and critical Marxism. This book captures this then twenty-nine-year-old professor's historical, philosophical, and theological dexterity.

At the time of the book's publication, Cornel West had recently become the first African American to earn a PhD from the philosophy department at Princeton University. His dissertation focused on the ethical dimensions of Marxist thought. The project identifies early Christian influences that had a profound, though often unacknowledged, influence on Karl Marx, namely Marx's identification with human suffering and the poor. Thus, West sought to identify an indisputable link between Marxism and Christianity.

West had also recently begun his teaching career on the faculty at Union Theological Seminary in New York City (where he now holds the distinguished Dietrich Bonhoeffer Chair in Philosophy and Christian Practice). Here, West was immersed in some of the best liberal and liberationist theologies. His influences included not only the neo-orthodox legacy of Paul Tillich and Reinhold Niebuhr, whose work took human suffering and catastrophe seriously considering the horrors of the twentieth century, but also the liberation and emerging feminist theologies that were coming to shape Union and the broader progressive wing of the church and academy. Being in regular dialogue with deep thinkers like James Cone, James Melvin Washington, Katie Geneva Cannon, and Michele Wallace enriched the spiritual imagination of this philosopher who was as comfortable quoting Hegel, Barth, and Kierkegaard as he was Matthew, Mark, Luke, and John.

These are some of the significant intellectual trends Cornel West brings together in *Prophesy Deliverance!* Like the Black musicians who animate and narrate his life, this work embodies analytic freedom and creativity. This self-professed "bluesman in the life of the mind" builds on the best intellectual contributions toward analyzing the present. *Prophesy* blends genres and transverses traditional categories, often placing otherwise isolated academic frameworks in creative tension. Thus, like the blues, his ideas come across as a dialectic exercise that tracks the human condition—joy and pain, hope and doubt, faith and despair.

From a historical perspective, the book aims to address the specificity of the African American predicament. Since 1619, Black people have faced the perennial challenges of self-conception and self-determination in North America. Nevertheless, Cornel West argues in the first chapter that one cannot address the specificity of the African American predicament without interrogating the conditions that produced a particular white American subject in the modern world.

West appeals to double consciousness—a category first introduced by Ralph Waldo Emerson and popularized by W. E. B. Du Bois's description of Black life in America—to argue that the first stage of American culture was defined by intensely self-conscious insecurity vis-à-vis European culture. White Americans were essentially incomplete and alienated Europeans who obscured their self-professed intellectual inferiority regarding the Old World with an obsession with wealth and material expansion in the New World. Herein lie the roots of the American bourgeois capitalist order. Whites of the colonial period experienced their own double consciousness of being culturally provincial yet financially prosperous, or, as West states, "genteel Brahmin[s] amid uncouth conditions" (p. 17).

Philosophically, *Prophesy Deliverance!* leverages the insights of poststructuralist thought to trace the emergence of white supremacy in the modern West. The author appeals to the insights of French philosophers like Michel Foucault and Jacques Derrida to identify and unpack gestures of exclusion that pushed Black identity outside of "enlightened" possibility. Chapter 2, "A Genealogy of Modern Racism," invites us to consider the prevailing metaphors and controlling categories that established the intellectual and discursive norms of our society. Cornel West uncovers the ways that this "structure of modern discourse" essentially excludes the idea of Black freedom and equality.

Contrary to popular liberal opinion, ideas of freedom and racism were not developed in opposition. West argues that notions of freedom and white supremacy are conceptual allies. The scientific revolution of the seventeenth century established the classical aesthetic and cultural norms of beauty, intelligence, and knowledge. These included the valorization of the Greek body and mind as epitomes of beauty and brilliance. Enlightenment thinkers of the eighteenth century built upon these ideas to further concretize conceptions of empirical validation and authority. Nineteenth-century thinkers appealed to these categories to encode natural history with scientifically authorized racism. The accepted view became that Black and Brown people could not meet the rational capacity that freedom necessitates. Such "enlightened" and "scientific" discourses foreclosed the possibility of equality in Black intelligence, culture, or character. As a result, any concept of Black freedom becomes unintelligible in the modern West.

Prophesy Deliverance! thus provides the genealogical account of modern racism that has now become the standard historical chronology among intellectual historians. Four decades before Tyler Stovall's masterful text *White Freedom: The Racial History of an Idea,* Cornel West interrogated the symbiotic relationship between freedom and race as a central theme of modern society born of the Enlightenment.

This is no small point. As Professor Brandon Terry points out in his reflection on chapter 3, "The Four Traditions of Response," it is easy for today's students of intellectual history and philosophical theories of race to underappreciate the importance and originality of *Prophesy*'s interventions. Not just in terms of the racialized history of the Enlightenment but also regarding West's avant-garde treatment of African American political response. That a despised and degraded people would have such valuable moral and ethical treasures to enrich both the Christian faith and the larger American body politic was, and largely remains, a revolutionary idea. Nevertheless, West combs through the most influential cultural and political resources of the African American experience toward providing a usable history.

Another feature of *Prophesy Deliverance!* is how it displays Cornel West's unapologetic, Christian-informed worldview. Like the philosophical tradition of pragmatism to which Cornel West is intellectually indebted, *Prophesy* displaces epistemology (a concern with the origins and methods of knowledge) as the ultimate goal of philosophy in favor of ethics (a concern with the right, just, and fitting moral responses). For West, however, social and political notions of freedom should not be confused with a more fundamental existential freedom. Here we see the indelible imprint of Afro-Protestant evangelical piety that shapes so much of Cornel West's moral imagination.

By existential freedom, West refers to a conception of freedom not measured by one's material conditions. Nor is one's sense of self reducible to prevailing views. The adage that best sums up existential freedom is, "It's not what folk call you. But rather what you answer to." This is Cornel West's understanding of Christian freedom. Long before he started reading Jean-Paul Sartre or wrestling with Søren Kierkegaard's understanding of subjective truths, it was at Shiloh Baptist Church in Sacramento where Clifton and Irene B. West reared their children into this spiritual tradition. Thus, West's rhythmic, tripartite writing style is just one reflection of Afro-Protestantism's profound influence. The other is a faith community, led by Cornel West's childhood pastor Reverend Willie P. Cooke, who could approximate visions of hope and possibility despite obvious external constraints.

Such a capacious view of freedom expands the terrain of justice in *Prophesy Deliverance!* Like his progressive Afro-Protestant influences— Jarena Lee, George Washington Woodbey, Martin Luther King Jr., and Pauli Murray—Cornel West uses *Prophesy* to champion a radical notion of democracy that provides a preferential option to those who are most likely excluded from any liberal consensus. A narrow focus on freedom circumscribed by flat conceptions of individuality should not obscure or erase the dignity of those society has deemed different or even deviant. Jesus's powerful parable in Matthew 25 best captures this point. How we treat the most vulnerable, violated, and victimized is how we treat God.

Cornel West's philosophical approach is certainly informed by progressive Afro-Protestantism, but is not exclusive to Christianity. West makes it clear in *Prophesy* that a progressive and prophetic Christian witness must be willing to reach across socially and intellectually constructed barriers. Tribes, ideologies, and uncritical commitment to any doctrine or dogma amount to crass idolatry, particularly when it blinds us to human suffering. Racial, religious, or national identity cannot trump moral affinity. Nor ought class, gender expression, sexuality, and any other social construct delimit or overdetermine human personality. Each of us has a moral responsibility to see and affirm the divine in each other, namely those that our cultural patterns and social structures have rendered most vulnerable.

As a result of this latter point, *Prophesy Deliverance!* moves toward a conclusion in its final two chapters with a challenge to what West considered the major limitations of the Black theology project at the time: its inability to account for the varying forms of oppression plaguing Black communities, that is, economic exploitation, gender discrimination, and intra-racial class hierarchies. West argued that if Black theologians were genuinely committed to a progressive approach to social change, they must take class conflict and intraracial class hierarchies more seriously. West used *Prophesy* to extend Martin Luther King Jr.'s critique of capitalism and labor exploitation. As King often asked while increasingly expanding his voice from desegregation to economic injustice, "What good is having the right to sit at a lunch counter if you can't afford to buy a hamburger?"

West thus appeals to progressive Marxism as a sobering corrective that offers prophetic Christian thought a more robust social analysis. Pulling baby Moses from the Nile River is one thing. Identifying, interrogating, and undoing Pharoah-like structures that foreclose futures is another. Similarly, at its best, prophetic Christianity offers progressive Marxism a sobering corrective to what Cornel West considers its naive utopianism and narrow focus on socioeconomic conditions at the expense of existential and cultural realities. All the while he recognizes that both traditions could use a more robust view of the tragic dimensions of life: disease, dread, and despair. Acknowledging historical and human limits can temper the twin temptations of romantic sentimentality on the one hand and pessimistic cynicism on the other.

These are just a few of the reasons why religious progressives still have much to learn from *Prophesy Deliverance!* In an age where, unfortunately, evangelical piety has essentially become indistinguishable from a rabid will to unbridled power, *Prophesy Deliverance!* strikes a different note. Idolatrous jingoism is out of key for this moral musician who views the world through the suffering of those perennially crushed by the weight of unfettered capitalism, imperialism, and market-based morality. He offers an inclusive, radically democratic, and antidogmatic vision of society at a time when our communities need less certainty and more faith. In this regard, this powerful text is not only a bold proclamation. It is also a humble plea. *Prophesy Deliverance!* is a sincere prayer.

Jonathan Lee Walton
Wake Forest University School of Divinity
Winston-Salem, North Carolina

Preface to the Fortieth Anniversary Expanded Edition

A Prophetic and Poetic Approach to Catastrophe

Two decades ago, in the preface for the twentieth-anniversary edition of this text, I professed my abiding love for this book that lays bare my fundamental moral commitments. Forty years have now passed since I put pen to paper. Now, more than ever, I can still say that *Prophesy Deliverance!* remains my favorite work.

I am thankful to Westminster John Knox Press and my dear brother, former student, and forever friend Jonathan Lee Walton for pulling together an exemplary group of brilliant minds to discuss this book's lasting import. That *Prophesy Deliverance!*—despite its youthful ambition and unapologetic urgency born of the "Reagan revolution"—still speaks to subsequent generations is both humbling and heartbreaking. It is humbling insofar as human hope grounded in Christian love is the central tenet of the text. To God be the glory that *Prophesy Deliverance!* continues to offer intellectual, spiritual, and political resources to those who seek existential and sociopolitical freedom divorced from cruelty and cynicism. Though it is heartbreaking that despite the gains of a privileged Black elite in all spheres of American society, to view Black people as fully human modern subjects worthy of honor, dignity, and respect continues to be a largely novel idea in 2022.

As I look back on this work forty years later, I see one major shift in my thinking. It has to do with my embrace of the tragicomic. The sense of the tragic was undoubtedly present in my thinking in 1982. Yet, like the tradition of philosophy, I deployed pragmatism to wrestle with the problematic. Since then, I have embraced the tragicomic to confront better what I now regard as the catastrophic. It began in the mid-1990s. For one, I've always known that no true philosopher can avoid wrestling with death. What was once abstract became real on May 26, 1994, when my beloved father, Clifton L. West, died of pancreatic cancer. Never had I felt such grief and loss. During this same period, my grief was coupled with political outrage. As reflected in the Clinton administration's mendacious welfare and unconscionable crime bills, the meanness directed toward America's working people sickened me. So for someone like myself, shaped by US culture, I fell back to a different language of love—the blues. It's a tradition that says that I want to be unflinchingly honest about catastrophe, not just in the sense of extreme moments in life. It is a tradition that reminds us that there is no deep love without deep sorrow. There is no hope without deep despair.

In *Prophesy Deliverance!* I acknowledged my indebtedness to the blues. But I had not begun thinking of myself as what I now refer to as a Chekhovian Christian, based on the tragicomic genius of Anton Chekhov. I first discovered Chekhov studying philosophy, grand figures like Kierkegaard, Nietzsche, Karl Jaspers, Heidegger, Sartre, and Camus. Yet when I read Chekhov, I found a kindred spirit with the blues. Like the blues, Chekhov confronts the narrative of catastrophe head-on. What I saw in Chekhov was precisely a democratizing of the catastrophic—the steady ache of misery in everyday life, the inescapability and ineluctability of coming to terms with the catastrophic effects. And this is very important because the catastrophic is not to be reduced to the problematic, a prominent feature of *Prophesy Deliverance!* Philosophers, like the philosophical pragmatists and Marxist tradition that I juxtapose in this text, are interested in solving problems. Whereas with the blues and Anton Chekhov's writings, there's no resolution at all. Fundamentally life is about the quality of your stamina, your perseverance. And since my initial encounter with Chekhov, I have come to consider him even more profound than the blues and thus instructive to my own Christian faith in recent decades.

Now, why would Chekhov be deeper than the blues? Three reasons. The first reason is that the blues itself is not just American but profoundly Romantic. One limitation of *Prophesy Deliverance!* is the way such romanticism might constitute a backdrop for the concluding chapter. There's no Romantic backdrop in Chekhov. He's both attuned to catastrophe and driven by profound compassion and empathy. There's no utopian projection there, no easy solutions, no solutions at all—no projection of a future of fundamental transformation that can be realized. But he still refuses to yield to cynicism or to paralyzing despair.

There's also Chekhov's critical approach to the faith that could not eradicate its indelible impact. Anton Chekhov was a former choirboy who endured great pain. Like the great American sage James Baldwin, he suffered paternal abuse, became alienated from religion, yet remained informed by the biblical text. And like Baldwin, though he left the church, he was still a love warrior. The dogma, hierarchy, and hypocrisies of institutional religion became too much to bear. Just as Shatema Threadcraft points out in her wonderful reflections on gender hierarchies and masculinist forms of abuse within the Black evangelical tradition, these are religious realities of which we must be truth-tellers. Chekhov was one such truth-teller, and we cannot understand his commitment to such truth-telling without acknowledging the productive backdrop of his religious formation. Like Baldwin and the unmistakable genius of Toni Morrison, Anton Chekhov's writings are religiously musical. Which is to say, if you are profoundly religious, these writers are still for you. Because his words resonate with religious folk. He's not going to flatten them out in the name of some secular positivistic sensibility. Nevertheless, as I understand both Baldwin and Morrison as representatives of a grand marginalist tradition of Black political response, if you try to enlist such thinkers into your religious army, it's not going to happen. These are free artists.

Finally, Chekhov is what I would call an existential democrat— somebody who, above all else, emphasizes the dignity of ordinary people in all of their wretchedness and in all of their sense of possibility. This means he's highly suspicious, as ought to be every small-*d* democrat, of the arbitrary power deployment. He demands accountability with regard to the most vulnerable. But we know it's not just a matter of speaking truth to power. You also have to speak truth to the relatively powerless. So it's a human thing across the board for Chekhov. That's why for him, ideology is too Manichaean. It's too adolescent. It's too easy to think that somehow your own side is not also corrupted by some of the things that you're struggling against. But that doesn't in any way mean that his fundamental solidarity is not with the most vulnerable. That's what he writes in his will to his sister: help the poor, take care of the family.

His solidarity goes deeper. It's no accident that he's the greatest Russian writer who sided with Dreyfus in the Dreyfus affair. All the great Russian writers were shot through with the anti-Jewish prejudice and hatred that had been part and parcel of the history of the Russian Empire. Chekhov lost his best friend Suvorin over this issue. Suvorin said, you're making the biggest mistake of your career, you're going to lose your Russian readers; Chekhov said, I don't give a damn. That's solidarity based on integrity. There's a certain moral witness there, along with the tragicomic complexity that we see in his work. So he's going to be highly suspicious of consolidated forms of power wherever they are.

This is the sort of solidarity and prophesying deliverance that aligns with the most vulnerable that I sought to express in this text forty years ago. This book acknowledged the blue note that Black people gifted to modernity that engenders a steely resolve that is unconquerable, unstoppable, and unsuffocatable in the face of dread and despair. The blues is the raw material of hope. But as a Chekhovian Christian, I now better understand the difference between talking about hope and being a hope. Being a hope is a matter of movement, not a virtue in an abstract way but an activity. And to prophesy—identifying concrete evils and staring them in the face—is not just an activity but a spiritual orientation informed by a tragicomic sensibility. In a market-driven America that is obsessed with overnight panacea, push-button solutions, so utilitarian, so consequentialist, my Chekhovian-informed faith is what pushes me to keep prophesying deliverance for all God's people.

Cornel West

Preface to the Twentieth Anniversary Edition

The Tragicomic and the Political in Christian Faith

After two decades of detours and digressions—as a part of painful development, this book remains my favorite work. Despite its over-reaching ambition and adolescent aggression, this text lays bare the fundamental concerns of my corpus: to plumb the depths of Afro-American experiences in order to disclose the terrifying truths of our modern human predicament. My writings rest upon two revolutionary assumptions of modern times—that Black people are full-fledged human beings, and that their doings and sufferings have something distinctive to say about what it means to be modern, American, and human. Yet this work is not simply interpretive, analytical, or poetic in aim; it also seeks to be political in its attempt to enrich and enable the struggle for freedom.

Although my explicit intention in this book was to put forward a prophetic interpretation of the Christian tradition rooted in the Afro-American struggle against white supremacy, informed by progressive Marxist theory and fallibilist pragmatic thought and tempered by a profound tragic sense of life, my underlying motivation was to understand the complexities and ambiguities of modernity through the lens of an enslaved, Jim-Crowed, and hated people of African descent in the United States of America. In other words, I tried to reconceive modern Western civilization in the light of its weak will to conceive of Black people as either modern, Western, or civilized (or even civilizable!). Needless to say, all of us are more than simply modern, Western, or civilized. But the bold attempt in 1982 to view Black people in the United States as the primary agents through which we interpret Western modernity and civilized humanity was relatively novel—building on the pioneering work of W. E. B. Du Bois, Ralph Ellison, and especially the great Black musicians. My effort to articulate an Afro-American philosophy was predicated on the notion that Black voices—mediated through European languages and American realities—had significant insights for the human quest for wisdom and the struggle for freedom.

Like much of my work, this book is primarily a historical interpretation—shot through with dialogical encounters and democratic
ends—that tries to illuminate the past and present in order to inspire
courageous action for a better future. To prophesy is not to predict an
outcome but rather to identify concrete evils. To prophesy deliverance
is not to call for some otherworldly paradise but rather to generate
enough faith, hope, and love to sustain the human possibility for more
freedom. For me, to be a Christian is not to opt for some cheap grace,
trite comfort, or childish consolation but rather to confront the darker
sides, and the human plights, of societies and souls with the weak armor
of compassion and justice. The fundamental human mystery is how
and why this weak armor—in a cold and cruel world—is not snuffed
out just as the Christian mystery is, how and why love so thoroughly
crushed by evil forces is not fully extinguished. Afro-American quests
for wisdom and freedom provide some crucial insight and inspiration
regarding these unfathomable mysteries.

DEATH AND DESIRE

Modern Black existence is not simply circumscribed by concrete forms
of death; it is obsessed with dealing with varieties of death. American slavery—the dominant form of social death in Western modernity—not only imposed severe limits on Black lives; it also promoted
distinctive kinds of psychic and spiritual death that constituted lived
presuppositions for Black people. Needless to say, it also assured premature physical death for many Afro-Americans. Like Russian and
Spanish cultures (for complex reasons), Afro-American life spawned
forms of death-obsessions unprecedented in American civilization. Yet,
as Leo Tolstoy and Federico García Lorca bear witness, this obsession
may yield intense engagement with life, its joys and sorrows, ecstasies
and pains. Those who read my book primarily as an attempt to provide
a tension-ridden synthesis of prophetic Christianity and progressive
Marxism through the prism of Black oppression and resistance have a
point, but they miss my deeper point: to transform abstract talk about
God and suffering into concrete enactments of existential and political struggles with no human guarantee for ultimate victory. In short,
the human dialectics of death and desire, extinction and eros, failures
and foibles are the basic movement and notion in *Prophesy Deliverance!* Hence, hope—human hope—is the basic theme of the text. But

it is a hope severed from bitterness and bigotry, cruelty and cynicism, revenge and resentment. To put it bluntly, it is a hope grounded in Christian love (often far removed from Christian practices and quite different from Nietzsche's misguided genealogies).

The Black prophetic Christian tradition—from Frederick Douglass to Martin Luther King Jr. and Fannie Lou Hamer—exemplifies a courage to hope in the face of undeniably desperate circumstances rooted in a love that refuses to lose contact with the humanity of others or one's self. And the Black musical tradition—from the spirituals and blues to jazz and hip-hop—embodies a desire for freedom and a search for joy in the face of death-dealing forces in America. My book tries to make explicit this quest for hope and freedom, love and joy in Black life. Needless to say, Black people have no monopoly on such quests. Yet, as with all human beings, these quests are filtered through the arts, culture, and politics. The human cry for help and the mortal effort to find a way out of one's trapped predicament always bear the mark of one's cultural, political, and economic contexts. Since the weight of white supremacy has shaped distinctive Black cries and efforts, Black desires in the face of forms of Black death require serious probing. *Prophesy Deliverance!* was one such inquiry. My bedrock conclusion was that the Black creative appropriation of Christianity has disproportionately shaped the form and content of these Black cries and efforts—for good and bad. Good, because Christian faith has sustained a hope against hope for despised people with severely limited options in an American civilization that prides itself on its liberties, opportunities, and possibilities. Bad, because Christian outlooks have downplayed the fundamental role of economic structures and institutions in subjugating peoples and individuals in an American society that views itself as the land of upward mobility and social experimentation. To put it crudely, my aim in *Prophesy Deliverance!* was to Afro-Americanize the profound insights of Kierkegaard's critique of bourgeois Christendom and Marx's critique of bourgeois capitalism in order to enhance the human quest for wisdom and freedom. "Afro-Americanization" here means roughly to show that Kierkegaardian and Marxist insights were reached by key prophetic Christian and progressive leftist figures in Black history. This operation is unabashedly circular and, at worst, self-serving. Yet it is useful in that it sparks a serious challenge to Black prophetic religion and Black progressive politics. I remain a card-carrying Kierkegaardian—with a strong Chekhovian twist—and a Marxist-informed radical democrat with a tragicomic sense of life. The relative absence of the great Chekhov and the grand Coltrane—whose shadows color my later work—loom large in *Prophesy Deliverance!* Yet small bits of them are discernible.

DOGMATISM AND DIALOGUE

Prophesy Deliverance! is also a call for dialogue—not simply between Christians and Marxists—but more fundamentally in the face of all forms of dogmatism, including those of Christians and Marxists. In fact, my self-styled allegiance to American pragmatism and American jazz is first and foremost a commitment to polyphonic inquiry and improvisational conversation. For me, prophetic Christianity is a deep suspicion of any form of idolatry—of any human effort to evade or deny the contingency and fragility of any human construct (including religious ones). Modern attempts to ossify, petrify, or freeze human creations of method, technique, rationality, sexuality, nationality, race, or empire are suspect. The best of progressive Marxism simply reveals the operations of power and forms of subordination beneath such idolatries (including Marxist ones). The centrality of dialogue in my text—and subsequent work—puts a premium on imaginative narratives and dynamic stories that connect subversive memories and inseparable traditions to lived experiences. Hence, the crucial presence of nuanced voices and delicate bodies—that is, the tone, texture, tempo, and timbre of the arts—in my work. I try to highlight the creative tensions—without reducing the complexities—between the poetic, political, and philosophic dimensions of intellectual reflections, especially those in the humanities. I tend to highlight music—as in the Afro-American humanist tradition—because it takes seriously transfigured human cries and transforming eloquent moments of silence. Again, my Kierkegaardian sensibility gives existential issues of death, dread, despair, and disappointment a crucial—though not exclusive—weight in serious and substantive dialogue. And my Marxist heritage calls for a revolutionary patience in the face of an ice age that aborts any immediate chance for fundamental social change.

DOMINATION AND DEMOCRACY

If there is a master term in my text—and work—it is democracy. I understand democracy as a mode of being, a way of life, a disposition toward the world that is a flexible, protean, and improvisational existential practice. Courage, freedom, and experimentation are inseparable in my philosophic outlook. Yet the relentless self-criticism and self-correction of this outlook preclude viewing democracy as an idol. So even my existential democratic ideal may be wrong—or inappropriate for some contexts. The keys here are humility and empathy—the need to remain vigilant in the face of any form of domination that may trump the quest for wisdom and freedom (including forms of democracy). The obstacles are arrogance and indifference that stifle Socratic self-examination and societal critique.

Existential democratic practice is fueled by the comic. All systems of domination—be they religious, political, social, or economic—fear the incongruity disclosed by the comic. And any subversive program suspicious of the comic reveals its tendencies toward domination. So any attempt to eliminate—or even tame—the comic is antidemocratic, a cowardly effort to hide and conceal the mendacity and hypocrisy of a system of domination. And since all traditions, hierarchies, and systems attempt to do so, including democratic ones, all existential democratic practices are fugitives in history—surfacing at select moments only to be thwarted. Like love in Christian narratives, existential democratic practices are perennially crucified only to be resurrected and again betrayed by false prophets and grand inquisitors. Hence, democracy in history is a tragicomic phenomenon—a sad yet sweet dialectic of courageous agency and historical constraints, a melancholic yet melioristic interplay of freedom and limitations that identifies and confronts social misery only to see its efforts to overcome such misery often fall short of their mark. Hence, it is neither sentimental nor cynical. Rather it is relentless and resilient—with compassion—yet usually disappointed with its results.

This tragicomic conception of existential democracy—linked to the ecstasies and erosions of the body and body politic—is alien to much of *Prophesy Deliverance!* Yet it is central to my present Chekhovian Christian view of radical democratic being and doing. Needless to say, the relative absence of the comic in the Christian and Marxist traditions (and pragmatism too!) delayed the move to my present outlook. Now Lucian means as much or more to me than Socrates, Erasmus much more than Luther, Chekhov far more than Du Bois. This outlook enables me to embrace the best of the prophetic Christian and progressive Marxist traditions—their anti-idolatrous and compassionate praxis—and also affirm the Beckett-like character of love and justice in human history.

In some ways, I arrive where I began—with the blue note that Black people injected into modernity that accents dissonance in the midst of sentimental harmony and defiance against social misery (or private agony). This blue note, or tragicomic gesture, does not preclude revolutionary agency or even collective insurgency; it simply requires that we thoroughly scrutinize ourselves so that we preserve the intellectual honesty and existential humility necessary for any quest for wisdom and freedom. To then prophesy deliverance is to link our wit to any wisdom and our funk to any freedom—it is to connect a loving Jesus who laughs to an inquiring Du Bois who breakdances.

Acknowledgments (1982)

This book was supported by neither foundation funds nor institutional grants. Yet many people provided me with provocative comments and penetrating criticisms. My faithful Black colleagues at Union Theological Seminary in New York City—Professors James Cone, James Forbes, and James Washington—as well as my fellow interlocutors in the New York Society of Black Philosophers—gave themselves unselfishly in the form of close textual scrutiny and intellectual encouragement. Stanley Aronowitz also read the whole manuscript with care and caution. My editor, Dr. James Heaney at Westminster Press, is greatly responsible for the appearance of the book.

For parts of the introduction and all of chapter 3, I am especially indebted to Daniel Aaron, Walter Jackson, Steve Jamison, Martin Kilson (to whom I owe more than mere gratitude), Meredith Langberg, Robert Moses, Larry Morse, Nellie McKay, Ronald Potter, Eugene Rivers, Donald Barfield, Preston Williams, Robert McAfee Brown, Stanley Browne, Marx Wartofsky, Glenn Jordan, and Hilda Holloman West; chapter 2, to Paul Bove, Anders Stephanson, Curtis Banks, Fredric Jameson, Howard McGary, Al Prettyman, and Samuel Roberts; sections of chapter 4, to Dean Carmelo Alvarez and the faculty and students at Seminario Biblico Latinoamericano in San José, Costa Rica; and chapter 5, to my friend and comrade Darryl Mitchell, though he surely disagrees with much of its content.

Major portions of this manuscript were presented during my yearlong seminar at House of the Lord Church in Brooklyn, New York. I wish to thank Rev. Herbert Daughtry, Albert Miller, and the church ministers and missionaries for this rich opportunity—and for their inspirational support. Lastly, I would like to thank my doctoral student in philosophy, Anthony Edwards, presently incarcerated at Greenhaven Correctional Facility in Stormville, New York, for his stimulating conversations with me.

This work was made possible—as are all of my writings—by my precious family: my inimitable parents, Clifton L. West Jr. and Irene Bias West; my steadfast brother, Clifton L. West III; my supportive sisters, Cynthia West Cole and Cheryl West Gaston; my gracious stepson Nelson Hernandez and my wonderful son Clifton Louis West. Needless to say, without the patience and perseverance of my lovely wife, Ramona Santiago, this book may have never been written.

CW

I believe that philosophy in America will be lost between chewing a historic cud long since reduced to woody fiber, or an apologetics for lost causes, or a scholastic, schematic formalism, unless it can somehow bring to consciousness America's own needs and its own implicit principle of successful action.

John Dewey
"The Need for a Recovery of Philosophy"

What had an old slave to do with humanity? Perhaps it was something that Woodridge had said in the literature class back at college. I could see him vividly, half-drunk on words and full of contempt and exaltation, pacing before the blackboard chalked with quotations from Joyce and Yeats and Sean O'Casey; thin, nervous, neat, pacing as though he walked a high wire of meaning upon which no one of us would ever dare venture. I could hear him: "Stephen's problem, like ours, was not actually one of creating the uncreated conscience of his race, but of creating the *uncreated features of his face*. Our task is that of making ourselves individuals. The conscience of a race is the gift of its individuals who see, evaluate, record . . . We create the race by creating ourselves and then to our great astonishment we will have created something far more important: We will have created a culture.

Ralph Ellison
Invisible Man

Introduction

The Sources and Tasks of Afro-American Critical Thought

The object of inquiry for Afro-American critical thought is the past and the present, the doings and the sufferings of African people in the United States. Rather than a new scientific discipline or field of study, it is a genre of writing, a textuality, a mode of discourse that interprets, describes, and evaluates Afro-American life in order comprehensively to understand and effectively to transform it. It is not concerned with "foundations" or transcendental "grounds" but with how to build its language in such a way that the configuration of sentences and the constellation of paragraphs themselves create a textuality and distinctive discourse which are a material force for Afro-American freedom.[1]

FIRST SOURCE: PROPHETIC CHRISTIAN THOUGHT

Afro-American thought must take seriously the most influential and enduring intellectual tradition in its experience: evangelical and pietistic Christianity. This tradition began the moment that African slaves, laboring in sweltering heat on plantations owned and ruled primarily by white American Christians, tried to understand their lives and servitude in the light of biblical texts, Protestant hymns, and Christian testimonies.[2] This theological reflection—simultaneously building on and breaking with earlier African non-Christian theological reflection—is inseparable from the Black church.[3] This "church," merely a rubric to designate Black Christian communities of many denominations, came into being when slaves decided, often at the risk of life and limb, to "make Jesus their choice" and to share with one another their common Christian sense of purpose and Christian understanding of their circumstances. Like the tradition of other Christian communities, this took many forms, some more prophetic than others, and its multiplicity of streams made possible the rich diversity of contemporary Black theological reflection which encompasses both prophetic and priestly streams, the visionary and quotidian components, of the tradition. Afro-American critical thought must focus on the former of these streams, the prophetic. This has been guided by a profound conception of human nature and human history, a persuasive picture of what one is as a person, what one should hope for, and how one ought to act.[4] It also proposes the two fundamental moral norms of individuality and democracy as the center of Afro-American thought. I will not stress here the obvious opposition of prophetic Black Christianity to racism, but rather its character as an underlying prophetic worldview.

The basic contribution of prophetic Christianity, despite the countless calamities perpetrated by Christian churches, is that every individual regardless of class, country, caste, race, or sex should have the opportunity to fulfill his or her potentialities.[5] This first and fundamental norm is the core of the prophetic Christian gospel. A transcendent God before whom all persons are equal thus endows the well-being and ultimate salvation of each with equal value and significance. I shall call this radical egalitarian idea *the Christian principle of the self-realization of individuality within community.* This is often interpreted as simply the salvation of *individual* souls in heaven, an otherworldly community. But such a truncated understanding of the core of the Christian gospel accents its otherworldly dimension at the expense of its this-worldly possibilities. The fuller prophetic Christian tradition must thus insist upon both this-worldly liberation and otherworldly salvation as the proper loci of Christianity.

The quite similar fundamental thrust of Marxism, despite the numerous brutalities perpetrated by Marxist regimes, is the self-fulfillment, self-development, and self-realization of harmonious personalities.[6] Marxism is a child of nineteenth-century Romanticism to the extent that it subscribes to a steadfast hope in an earthly paradise and invests in politics a passion previously monopolized by Christianity. Since Romanticism was, as M. H. Abrams demonstrated, a naturalization of the Christian worldview, a secularization of the Christian gospel, it is no accident that Marxism and Christianity share a similar moral impulse.[7] Socioeconomic well-being has remained at the center of Marxist dogma, but the political liberties and diverse cultural activities of individuals have, for the most part, been ignored by it. Thus, the historical roots of the notion of individuality are found in the Christian gospel and the Romantic worldview, a moral core which Marxism has also appropriated. The norm of individuality reinforces the importance of community, common good, and the harmonious development of personality. And it stands in stark contrast to those doctrinaire individualisms which promote human selfishness, denigrate the idea of community, and distort the holistic development of personality. The norm of individuality conceives persons as enjoyers and agents of their uniquely human capacities, whereas doctrinaire individualism views them as maximizers of pleasure and appropriators of unlimited resources.[8]

Two further fundamental elements in the Christian gospel are the dignity of persons and, likewise, the depravity of persons: human beings possess the capacity to transform prevailing realities for the better, and yet are prone to do so imperfectly. The dignity of persons is their ability to contradict what is, to change and be changed, and to act in the light of that which is not-yet. The depravity of persons is their proclivity to cling to the moment, to refuse to transform and to be transformed. The Christian gospel accents decision, commitment, engagement, and action which transform what is in the light of that which is to be. The Christian gospel also acknowledges that such contradiction and transformation are circumscribed by human imperfection.

Contradiction and transformation are at the heart of the Christian gospel. The former always presupposes what presently is; the latter, the prevailing realities. For Christians, this "what is" and these "prevailing realities" are products of fallen, finite creatures, products that bear the stamp of imperfection. *This dialectic of imperfect products and transformative practice, of prevailing realities and negation, of human depravity and human dignity, of what is and the not-yet constitutes the Christian dialectic of human nature and human history.* Each element of the dialectic is inextricably bound to the other, as are human nature and human history.

This emphasis on process, development, discontinuity, and even disruption precludes the possibility of human perfection and human utopias. Human beings possess the capacity to change their conditions and themselves, but not to perfect either their conditions or themselves. Human history dooms human beings to problems and problematics, obstacles and obstructions, to relative achievements and relative accomplishments.

For Christians, the realm of history is the realm of the pitiful and the tragic.[9] It serves as the context for passive persons who refuse to negate and transform what is and for active persons who reject and change prevailing realities. The pitiful are those who remain objects of history, victims manipulated by evil forces; whereas the tragic are those persons who become subjects of history, aggressive antagonists of evil forces. Victims are pitiful because they have no possibility of achieving either penultimate liberation or ultimate salvation; aggressive antagonists are tragic because they fight for penultimate liberation, and in virtue of their gallant struggle against the limits of history they become prime candidates for ultimate salvation. In this sense, to play a tragic role in history is positive: to negate and transform what is, yet run up against the historical limits of such negation and transformation, is candidacy for transcending those limits.

Penultimate liberation is the developmental betterment of human-kind, the furtherance of the uncertain quest for human freedom in history. Ultimate salvation hopes for the transcendence of history, the deliverance of humankind from the treacherous dialectic of human nature and human history. The process of penultimate liberation can culminate within history, whereas the process of ultimate salvation is grounded in history but promises to proceed beyond it.

For prophetic Christianity, the two inseparable notions of freedom are existential freedom and social freedom. Existential freedom is an effect of the divine gift of grace which promises to sustain persons through and finally deliver them from the bondage to death, disease, and despair. Social freedom is the aim of Christian political practice, a praxis that flows from the divine gift of grace; social freedom results from the promotion and actualization of the norms of individuality and democracy. Existential freedom empowers people to fight for social freedom, to realize its political dimension. Existential freedom antici-pates history and is ultimately transhistorical, whereas social freedom is thoroughly a matter of this-worldly human liberation.

The prophetic Christian dialectic of human nature and human his-tory produces *democracy* as its second fundamental norm. Democracy requires that accountability—of institutions to populace, of leaders to followers, of preachers to laity—be the center of any acceptable social vision. This accountability exists when people have control over the leaders and institutions that serve them. Democratic participation of people in the decision-making processes of institutions that regulate and govern their lives is a precondition for actualizing the Christian principle of the self-realization of human individuality in community. The norms of individuality and democracy are in this way inseparable. The former rests upon the moral core of the Christian gospel, the latter upon its historical realism.

The prophetic Christian norm of democracy reflects the dignity of persons in that it accents potential for human betterment. It recognizes the depravity of persons in that it acknowledges human disabilities. The Christian dialectic of human nature and human history makes the norm of democracy necessary and possible; yet only the praxis of imperfect human beings renders it desirable and realizable.

As with the Christian gospel, negation and transformation lie at the heart of Marxism. What is must be overcome; prevailing realities must be changed. Instead of a dialectic of human nature and human history, Marxism posits a dialectic of human practice and human history: human nature is nothing other than human practice under specific historical conditions, conditions which themselves are both results of past human practice and preconditions for it in the present. This *collapse* of human nature into human practice and into human history—as opposed to a dialectical relation of human nature to human practice and to human history—is the distinctive difference between Christianity and Marxism. The Christian espouses a dialectical historicism which stresses the dignity and the depravity of persons, whereas the Marxist puts forward a full-blown historicism in which the eventual perfectability of persons within history is inevitable. The Christian worldview is a clandestine complaint against history, the Marxist an avowed apotheosis of it.

The contribution of prophetic Christian thought as a source for Afro-American critical thought is twofold. First, it confronts candidly the tragic character of human history (and the hope for ultimate transhistorical triumph) without permitting the immensity of what is and must be lost to call into question the significance of what may be gained. In this way, it allows us to sidestep what Baudelaire called "the metaphysical horror of modern thought" and take more seriously the existential anxiety, political oppression, economic exploitation, and social degradation of actual human beings. Second, prophetic Afro-American Christian thought elevates the notion of struggle (against the odds!)—personal and collective struggle regulated by the norms of individuality and democracy—to the highest priority. To be a prophetic Afro-American Christian is to negate what is and transform prevailing realities against the backdrop of the present historical limits. In short, prophetic Afro-American Christian thought imbues Afro-American thinking with the sobriety of tragedy, the struggle for freedom, and the spirit of hope.

SECOND SOURCE: AMERICAN PRAGMATISM

The basic notions in American philosophy that ought to play a significant role in the formation of Afro-American critical thought are primarily the products of the reforming orientation of the pragmatic movement.[10] This began with a series of papers that Charles Peirce wrote in 1872, continued in a more visible manner after 1898 in William James, and was elaborated in detail by George Mead and, above all, by John Dewey. The pragmatic movement questioned the subjectivist turn in European philosophy, the idea that knowledge requires philosophical foundations in direct personal awareness, through intuition or unmediated insight. For American pragmatists, the quest for such certainties and foundations could only be misguided.

John Dewey recognized that philosophy is inextricably bound to culture, society, and history.[11] For Dewey, an autonomous philosophy would be culturally outmoded. Like its first cousin, theology, philosophy was once an autonomous discipline with its own distinct set of problems, most of which now lie at the mercy of psychology, sociology, history, and anthropology.

Despite this, however, the normative function of philosophy remains. It becomes the critical expression of a culture and the critical thought of a society, sacrificing in the process its delusions of autonomy. Philosophy is, thus, the interpretation of a people's past for the purpose of solving specific problems presently confronting the cultural way of life from which the people come. For Dewey, philosophy is critical in that it constantly questions the tacit assumptions of earlier interpretations of the past. It scrutinizes the norms these interpretations endorse, the solutions they offer, and the self-images they foster.

American pragmatism rejects the idea of knowledge as a private affair where one begins with uninterpreted givens, theory-free entities, self-authenticating episodes, or intrinsically credible beliefs, and builds all other knowledge upon them. Rather, it conceives of knowledge as within the conceptual framework of intersubjective, communal inquiry. Of course, some norms, premises, and procedures must be taken for granted, but these are never immune to revision. For American pragmatists, the myth of the given must be demythologized. Knowledge should not be a rummaging for foundations but a matter of public testing and open evaluation of consequences. Knowledge claims are secured by the social practices of a community of inquirers, rather than the purely mental activity of an individual subject. The community understands inquiry as a set of social practices geared toward achieving and warranting knowledge, a perennial process of dialogue which can question any claim but never all at once. This self-correcting enterprise requires neither foundations nor grounds. It yields no absolute certainty. The social or communal is thus the central philosophical category of this pragmatist conception of knowledge. It recognizes that in knowledge the crucial component is not intuition but social practice and communal norm.

The pragmatist movement also bursts the narrow conception of experience of the Cartesian tradition and its historical successors. In contrast to the narrowness of Cartesian individualism, the pragmatic conception of experience is broader in scope and richer in content. And, lastly, pragmatism's primary aim is to discern, delineate, and defend particular norms through highlighting desirable possibilities present in the practices of a specific community or society. The goal of reflection is amelioration, and its chief consequence is the transformation of existing realities. This process is guided by moral convictions and social norms, and the transformation is shaped by the interpretation and description of the prevailing communal practices.

Afro-American thought recognizes, of course, the major shortcomings of the pragmatist movement: its relative neglect of the self, its refusal to take class struggle seriously, and its veneration of scientific method and the practices of the scientific community.[12] And, in contrast to this, Afro-American Christian thought must, for its part, emphasize the uniqueness of human personality, the centrality of the class struggle, and the political dimensions of knowledge. But pragmatism's contributions are still enormous. Through its historicist orientation, for example, Afro-American thought can avoid both absolutist dogmatism and paralysis in action. Pragmatism also dethroned epistemology as the highest priority of modern thought in favor of ethics: not the professional discipline of ethics but the search for desirable and realizable historical possibilities in the present. Despite its limitations, pragmatism provides an American context for Afro-American thought, a context that imparts to it both a shape and a heritage of philosophical legitimacy.

Following its sources, I shall define Afro-American critical thought as an interpretation of Afro-American history, especially its cultural heritage and political struggles, which provides norms for responding to challenges presently confronting Black Americans. The particular historical phenomena interpreted and justified by it consist in religious doctrines, political ideologies, artistic expressions, and unconscious modes of behavior. These serve as raw ingredients to be utilized to interpret the Afro-American past and defend the existence of particular norms within it.

THE TASKS

The two basic challenges presently confronting Afro-Americans are self-image and self-determination. The former is the perennial human attempt to define who and what one is, the issue of self-identity. The latter is the political struggle to gain significant control over the major institutions that regulate people's lives. These challenges are abstractly distinguishable, yet concretely inseparable. In other words, culture and politics must always be viewed in close relationship to each other.[13]

The major function of Afro-American critical thought is to reshape the contours of Afro-American history and provide a new self-understanding of the Afro-American experience which suggests guidelines for action in the present.[14] It attempts to make theoretically explicit what is implicit in history, to describe and demystify cultural and social practices and offer solutions to urgent problems besetting Black Americans.

Afro-American thought is thus critical in character and historical in content. It is an interpretive activity which reveals new insights and uncovers old blindnesses about the complexity and richness of the Afro-American experience. Its first task is to put forward an over-arching interpretive framework for the inescapable problematic of any such inquiry: What is the relationship between the African, American, and European elements in this experience? The prerequisite for a sophisticated response to this is an understanding of the emergence, development, and end of European modernity, the complex variation of it which evolved as American culture, and the intricate transactions between marginalized Africans—for the most part effectively excluded from the behavioral modes and material benefits of European life— and the American culture in which these dark bastard people were both participants and victims. I will attempt to tackle this enormous problematic in chapter 1.

The second task of an Afro-American religious philosophy is to engage in a genealogical inquiry into the cultural and linguistic roots—in addition to the economic, political, and psychological roots—of the idea of white supremacy which has shaped the Afro-American encounter with the modern world. What is the complex configuration of controlling metaphors, categories, and norms which shape and mold this idea in the modern West? I try to put forward some plausible answers to this in chapter 2.

The third task of Afro-American thought is to provide a theoretical reconstruction and evaluation of Afro-American responses to white supremacy. In chapter 3 this takes the form of delineating four fundamental traditions in Afro-American thought and practice. I will endorse one of them.

The fourth task of Afro-American religious thought is to present a dialogical encounter between prophetic Afro-American Christian thought and progressive Marxist social analysis. The aim of this dialogue—put forward in chapter 4—is to demystify the deep misunderstanding and often outright ignorance each side has of the other. And since in Christianity and Marxism we are dealing with the most distorted traditions in the modern world, we have a difficult task before us. In my view, this effort is warranted by the fact that in an alliance between prophetic Christianity and progressive Marxism—both castigated remnants within their own worlds—lies the hope of Western civilization. The destiny of Afro-Americans is inextricably bound—as is most of the world—with the fate of this civilization.

The last task of Afro-American religious philosophy is to provide a political prescription for—or strategic intervention into—the specific praxis in the present historical moment of the struggle for liberation. Therefore I bring the book to a close in chapter 5 by articulating practical and programmatic dimensions. Afro-American critical thought begins in a broad theoretical mode by situating the life-worlds of Africans in the United States and ends in a narrow practical mode steeped in those same life-worlds. This philosophical journey is mediated by value-laden interpretations of the Afro-American struggle for freedom; the major bias of this inquiry is the desire for freedom.

The articulation of an Afro-American religious philosophy presupposes access to and acquisition of certain kinds of skills, training, and knowledge. The skills, interpretive and descriptive, make use of

imagination, self-reflection, and logical analysis. The training requirements are open-ended and may range from those of a classical humanist
to those of an autodidactic street philosopher. The crucial element is the
ability for rigorous thought, clear exposition, and investment of one's
whole self in one's thinking. Afro-American thought must also remove
itself from the uncritical elements of mainstream Afro-American life.
This is not a geographical or existential removal, but an intellectual one
which acknowledges the demands of the discipline. Any critical and creative activity requires a certain degree of marginality. Intellectual activity
certainly flourishes best when one is on the margin, not in an ivory
tower but resolutely outside the world of aimless chitchat and gossip.

Afro-American philosophy expresses the particular American variation of European modernity that Afro-Americans helped shape in this
country and must contend with in the future. While it might be possible
to articulate a competing Afro-American philosophy based principally
on African norms and notions, it is likely that the result would be theoretically thin. Philosophy is cultural expression generated from and existentially grounded in the moods and sensibilities of a writer entrenched
in the life-worlds of a people. The life-worlds of Africans in the United
States are conceptually and existentially neither solely African, European, nor American, but more the latter than any of the former. In fact,
ironically, the attempt by Black intellectuals to escape from their Ameri-
canness and even go beyond Western thought is itself very *American*.

Any who would fashion a theory of American Negro culture while ignoring the intricate network of connections which binds Negroes to the larger society . . . is to attempt a delicate brain surgery with a switch-blade. And it is possible that any viable theory of Negro American culture obligates us to fashion a more adequate theory of American culture as a whole. The heel bone is, after all, connected, through its various linkages, to the head bone.

Ralph Ellison
Shadow and Act

When it is acknowledged that under the disguise of dealing with ultimate reality, philosophy has been occupied with the precious values embedded in social traditions, that it has sprung from a clash of social ends and from a conflict of inherited institutions with incompatible contemporary tendencies, it will be seen that the task of future philosophy is to clarify men's ideas as to the social and moral strifes of their own day. Its aim is to become so far as is humanly possible an organ for dealing with these conflicts.

John Dewey
Reconstruction in Philosophy

1

American Africans in Conflict

Alienation in an Insecure Culture

MODERNITY, COLONIAL PROVINCIALITY, LOCALISM

The Age of Enlightenment, from 1688 to 1789—roughly from the Glorious Revolution in England to the tumultuous French Revolution—constitutes the emergence of European modernity.[1] This occurred within an embryonic capitalist global economy that supported absolutist monarchies. It throve, mostly because of Black slavery in the Western Hemisphere and the exploitation of working men, women, and children in the rural household industry of western Europe. The most populous European country, France, was the chief industrial center. Holland, especially the vivacious city of Amsterdam, maintained its two-century dominance in commerce and shipping as the major financial center in Europe.

The basic features of early modern European culture were the increasing acceptance of the authority of science, the appearance of a new kind of pagan neoclassicism, and the subjectivist turn in philosophy. The intellectual defense and institutional support of the practices of scientists became more and more persuasive to the literate population. These practices were guided by an adherence to a new paradigm of knowledge, an experimental method that attempted to test hypotheses and yield objective conclusions by appealing to evidence and observation. The increasing acceptance of the authority of science resulted in assaults on the authority of the church and on its theology and religious practices.

This Enlightenment revolt against the prestige of the church was part of a search for models of uncensored criticism. It led to a recovery of classical antiquity and especially a deep appreciation and appropriation of the artistic and cultural heritage of ancient Greece. This classical revival—or neoclassical movement in eighteenth-century Europe—was partly the result of a four-hundred-year European love affair with Greece and Rome. This affair began in the Early Renaissance (1300–1500), intensified in the High Renaissance (1500–1530), cooled in the Mannerist era (1530–1600), and appeared again in full force during the Baroque period (1600–1750). In short, early modern European culture promoted a new, modern type of paganism.

The emergence of European modernity also witnessed a subjectivist turn in philosophy. This quest, initiated by Descartes, gave first place to concepts of the subject, the ego, or the self, and preeminence to the notion of representative knowledge. The subject, ego, or self constituted the starting point for philosophical inquiry, and mental representations by the subject, ego, or self supplied the principal means for subjects to make contact with objects, ideas to copy things, or concepts to correspond to the external world. Philosophy became the queen of the emerging scientific disciplines within this new paradigm as a metadiscipline which provided objective and valid grounds for knowledge claims put forward in the newer disciplines, especially physics. This turn in philosophy granted science a monopoly on truth in the marketplace of ideas, to the dismay of both artists and theologians. As Hans-Georg Gadamer has noted in our own time, this monopoly on truth entails a prejudice against prejudice, a supposed transcendence of prejudice through objectivity.

Immanuel Kant deepened Descartes's subjectivism by erecting new formal foundations upon a transcendental subject which builds an objective world by means of a universal conceptual scheme. In one grand stroke, he thus legitimated Newtonian science, vindicated Protestant morality, and set art in a realm of its own. The ultimate consequence of this architectonic endeavor was to isolate early modern European culture into separate spheres of goodness, truth, and beauty—and morality, science, and art—reinforcing meanwhile the role of philosophy as a tribunal of pure reason for the claims of culture.

Between 1776 and 1782 texts appeared and events occurred that were representative of this early modern period. These included Adam Smith's *The Wealth of Nations* (1776), Edward Gibbon's *The History of the Decline and Fall of the Roman Empire* (1776), the American

Revolution (1776), David Hume's *Dialogues Concerning Natural Religion* (1779), Gotthold Lessing's *Nathan the Wise* (1779), Immanuel Kant's *Critique of Pure Reason* (1781), and the first part of Jean Jacques Rousseau's *Confessions* (1781). In these are the intellectual agenda of the period: the rise of the bourgeois capitalist order, the struggle between Christianity and neoclassical paganism, the widening gaps between philosophy, ethics, and art, and the increasing alienation of the individual.

The end of this period was marked by the birth of the United States, the first new nation, through a colonial, not a social revolution. After a century and a half of the reconciling of self-imposed exile with a well-developed European social and political consciousness, the problem of provinciality had become central in the development of American culture.[2] It resulted primarily from the geographical displacement of European peoples from that European civilization whose superiority they openly acknowledged. Adding to this, an antagonism to the indigenous American peoples and an unwillingness to mingle with unchristian African slaves created an alienated, intensely self-conscious, and deeply anxiety-ridden society.

The first stage of American culture was thus saturated with colonial provinciality. The first Americans looked to their parent civilization for intellectual and cultural resources, applying these to very un-European conditions principally by means of crude imitation. The most provocative commentators on the problematic of provinciality in American culture have been Alexis de Tocqueville, George Santayana, and Van Wyck Brooks.[3] On de Tocqueville's view, American culture smothered intellectual life in pursuit of democracy and equality, thereby vitiating the aristocratic requisites for cultural vitality. To Santayana, the agonized conscience of Calvinism and the metaphysical comfort of transcendentalism weighted like a genteel incubus upon the American mind, partly explaining the odd American juxtaposition of intellectual conservatism with technological inventiveness. For Van Wyck Brooks, American vacillation between Puritan purity and vulgar materialism, echoing William James's "angelic impulses" and "predatory lusts," fragmented the intellectual tradition and generated an unrestrained quest for wealth.[4]

Colonial provinciality reached its zenith in the first major figure of the Genteel tradition, Jonathan Edwards. The most profound of European-American thinkers, he constructed his defense of Calvinism from a sophisticated blend of the empiricism of Locke, the determinism of Newton, and the idealism of Plato.

Edwards's valorizing of Newton bespoke his attitude toward the authority of science, an attitude close to that of his own lesser contemporary and rival, Cadwallader Colden.[5] Yet Edwards distinguished the domain of science from the special arena of religious knowledge, the intuitive realm where the sixth sense, that of the heart, reserved for the elect, reigns. His fierce struggle against the voluntaristic Arminians likewise defended complex versions of original sin and predestination familiar from European Calvinism.

The Enlightenment left a comparable European stamp on the area of political thought. Jefferson's doctrine of natural rights and theory of moral sentiments revealed his debts both to classical antiquity and to Locke, Shaftesbury, and Frances Hutchinson.[6] The anti-clericalism of Thomas Paine, and its concomitant defense of the freedom of conscience and speech, further exemplified the critical spirit of the European Enlightenment in America. Lastly, the radical environmentalism of Benjamin Rush and his humanitarian advocacy of the abolition of slavery and the rehabilitation of criminals revealed an Enlightenment belief in the unlimited possibilities of individuals in society when guided by reason.

American culture during the provincial period culminated in the Calvinist pietism, Enlightenment rationalism, and liberal republicanism of William Ellery Channing.[7] The vernal American Schleiermacher, Channing is the pivotal figure of the Genteel tradition, in its transition from Calvinism to transcendentalism, at the turning point between the colonial provinciality and the postcolonial provinciality in American culture. His revolutionary humanitarianism, bordering on utopian socialism, condemned slavery, bigotry, and pagan worldliness. He proposed to overcome these through Christian pietism, moral use of scientific knowledge, and the perfection of human nature through self-realization in democratic communities.

Channing's humanitarianism unfortunately did not serve either as guide or as norm for American practice toward Africans during the provincial period. The non-Christianity and black skin color of the dark pagan peoples threatened the self-identity of Puritan colonists inextricably bound to Christianity.[8] Since the absence of or even novel interpretation of Christian beliefs could often bring about mistreatment or banishment, the growing idea of white supremacy legitimated still harsher treatment for Africans.

In *The Souls of Black Folk* (1903), W. E. B. Du Bois eloquently described a double consciousness in Black Americans, a dual lens through which they saw themselves.[9] For Du Bois, the dialectic of

Black self-recognition oscillated between being *in* America but not *of* it, from being Black natives to Black aliens. Yet Du Bois overlooked the broader dialectic of being American yet feeling European, of being provincial but yearning for British cosmopolitanism, of being at once incompletely civilized and materially prosperous, a genteel Brahmin amid uncouth conditions. Black Americans labored rather under the burden of a triple crisis of self-recognition. Their cultural predicament was comprised of African appearance and unconscious cultural mores, involuntary displacement to America without American status, and American alienation from the European ethos complicated through domination by incompletely European Americans.

This predicament was qualitatively different from that of other Africans in the diaspora, in the Caribbean, Canada, and Central and South America. Africans in the United States confronted a dominant Protestant European population whose own self-identity suffered from an anxiety-ridden provinciality. The Black American struggle for self-identity has always contributed constructively to the American struggle for self-identity, though the latter has only exacerbated and complicated it in return.

During the colonial provincial stage of American culture, Africans were worse than slaves; they were also denuded proto-Americans in search of identity, systematically stripped of their African heritage and effectively and intentionally excluded from American culture and its roots in European modernity. Their search for identity focused principally on indigenous African practices, rituals, religions, and worldviews they had somehow retained.[10]

The process of cultural syncretism which combined indigenous African practices and provincial American culture generated a unique variant of American life, one far removed from, yet still tied to, European modernity. Added ingredients in this were the distinctly antimodern values and sensibilities of the southern United States, the geographic cradle of Black America.

The first stage of African practice in America was neither barbarian nor provincial. Africans valued human life and sustained in their alien environment a religious cosmology which gave meaning to human existence. And it was not provincial, because it worshiped neither at the altar of British nor at the altar of American cultural superiority. Black people were relatively uninformed about British culture and not yet fully American. More pointedly, they had not yet arrived at a synthetic Afro-American identity.

HEYDAY OF MODERNITY, POSTCOLONIAL
PROVINCIALITY, CHRISTIAN PRACTICES

The heyday of modernity, the golden age of the modern period, fell roughly between 1789 and 1871—that is, from the French Revolution to the unification of the German Empire. During it, early modern European culture took root and flowered in the authority of science, in modern paganism, and in the historicizing of philosophical subjectivism. The industrializing capitalist world order consolidated at this time, and nation-states emerged, both phenomena enjoying the confidence of the new bourgeoisie. The dominated classes—factory workers and the rural labor force—began to grumble, but since they had limited organization and vision, this yielded minimal results.

This was, above all, the German Age, and the year 1807 alone witnessed the completion of Hegel's *The Phenomenology of Spirit,* Goethe's *Faust,* Part 1, and Beethoven's Fifth Symphony.

Yet despite the romantic reply to the bland universality, glib generality, and monotonous uniformity of the Enlightenment, the authority of science emerged with flying colors. Romanticism attacked scientific arrogance and pretense, yet the brunt of its assault fell not on science per se but rather on the crudely mechanistic model of Newton's popular imitators. The conceptions of the mind and the world characteristic of this model repelled the Romantics. Disgusted with superficial distinctions, they relegated the dissective power of the mind to the understanding (*Verstand*) and its integrative activities to reason (*Vernunft*), replacing mechanistic models with organic ones.[11]

The Romantics venerated a reason very different from that of the Enlightenment, which appealed ultimately to the experimental method and aimed to keep the imagination at bay. Romantic reason, on the other hand, is the epitome of a free creative imagination transcending the limits of the world of sense.

The Romantic movement, the golden age of European modernity, conveyed a sense of novelty.[12] The French Revolution, which in one stroke replaced feudal institutions with bourgeois capitalism, embodied the possibilities of social reconstruction and revolutionary transformation. The European exploration of other cultures and societies likewise buttressed curiosity about the unknown and brought to light distinctive features of its own emerging constituent national cultures. Lastly, widespread technological innovation and the increase of wealth in the early stages of the Industrial Revolution reinforced belief in the capacity of humankind to master nature and enjoy its fruits.

With Napoleon, the Romantic dream of transforming the social order mellowed to temperate efforts at self-realization.[13] The fascination with exotic and primitive peoples illustrated by the popular myth of the noble savage persisted, yet it soon revealed the repressive imperialist regimes that often evolve in interaction with foreigners. The tremendous energies generated by the early Industrial Revolution continued, but alienations and the formation of new class antagonisms revealed unforeseen instabilities in bourgeois capitalism.

Hegel's historicizing of the subjectivism cast would-be academic philosophers into the social, political, and cultural struggles of the period. His grand project took, in some sense, however, the form of a Christian Christology gone mad. In place of Kant's presupposed subject of knowledge, Hegel put a transindividual subject that externalized itself in the world and progressively evolved within it in a dialectical fashion. This development can be discerned, of course, only by the most adroit philosopher, namely, Hegel himself. This development is simultaneously the freedom march of humankind and the progressive self-consciousness of that transindividual subject, what Hegel called the *Weltgeist,* or world spirit.

The year 1859 was momentous for cultural works that portrayed the central themes and concerns of the golden age: Darwin's *The Origin of the Species,* Mill's *On Liberty,* Marx's *Critique of Political Economy,* Wagner's *Tristan und Isolde,* George Eliot's *Adam Bede,* Dickens's *A Tale of Two Cities,* Meredith's *The Ordeal of Richard Feverel,* Tennyson's *The Idylls of the King,* FitzGerald's *Rubaiyat of Omar Khayyam,* and Turgenev's *A Nest of Gentlefolk.* The dominant themes and concerns in these are the historical and evolutionary character of human existence, the scope of freedom and democracy in the prevailing order, and the emerging sentiments of European nationalism and of racism and sexism.

European hegemony over the life of the mind proved to be a major preoccupation of American culture during its provincial period. American artists and writers strove consciously to establish an autonomous national culture no longer dependent on that of Europe. American ought to sing its own songs, write its own poems, novels, and philosophy. America must look deep down within itself without using the lens of the parent civilization to do so.

The most important product of this self-absorptive mood in America was Ralph Waldo Emerson. In his famous lecture of 1837, "The American Scholar," Emerson portrayed Europe as the symbol of the dead past. The present task of American thinkers was to liberate themselves from slavish dependence on Europe. His message of self-reliance was not merely a reflection of a democratic and intuitive philosophy or a Jeffersonian vision of the self-sufficient yeoman farmer, but an attack on the prevailing provincialism of America in his day. Of course, without the idealism of Plato, the natural law theory of the Stoics, and the romanticism of Coleridge and Carlyle, there was little of intellectual substance left to "the sage of Concord," save his energetic spirit, charismatic style, and piercing wit. The postcolonial agenda of American culture called for homespun originality and indigenous inventiveness, despite the eclecticism and pretense this might entail.

Eclecticism and pretentiousness mark the most significant literary products of the American renaissance, as seen in the major works of Edgar Allan Poe, James Fenimore Cooper, Walt Whitman, Nathaniel Hawthorne, Herman Melville, Emily Dickinson, and Henry David Thoreau.[14] It is not that the works are artistic failures, but rather that they are products of a culture under the grip of provincialism, of a culture proud yet not solidified, boastful but not self-confident, eager to flex its muscles without agile flexibility.

Edgar Allan Poe, for example, with his English childhood and Parisian sensibilities, cared neither to imitate English literary models nor to write an authentic American tale. Instead, he created fantasies in which European aristocracy roamed about in bone-chilling German castles. James Fenimore Cooper's mythology loomed too large and his debt to the Scottish Sir Walter Scott was too pronounced. Walt Whitman, the effervescent American Goethe, was penetrating and provocative but hardly profound, a master of rhythmic and colorful language never able to attain a natural or comfortable idiom of expression. Though Whitman was, without a doubt, the most influential American poet of the period, his songs of himself and his democratic vistas of America seem too fabricated—or simply fail to ring true at all.

Postcolonial American culture's preoccupation with breaking away from Europe was far removed from the situation among Africans in the United States at the time. The initial tenacity with which Africans held on to their indigenous practices and the reluctance of many southern white slaveholders to teach Christianity to the slaves limited the Christianizing process in the early period. Even the Great Awakening of the

1740s, which swept the country like a hurricane, failed to reach the masses of slaves. Only with the Great Western Revival at the turn of the nineteenth century did the Christianizing process gain a significant foothold among Black people.[15]

The central questions at this juncture are: Why did large numbers of American Black people become Christians? What features of Protestant Christianity persuaded them to become Christians?

The Baptist separatists and the Methodists, religious dissenters in American religious culture, gained the attention of the majority of slaves in the Christianizing process. The evangelical outlook of these denominations stressed individual experience, equality before God, and institutional autonomy. Baptism by immersion, practiced by the Baptists, may indeed have reminded slaves from Nigeria and Dahomey of African river cults, but this fails fully to explain the success of the Christianizing process among Africans.[16]

Black people became Christians for intellectual, existential, and political reasons. Christianity is, as Friedrich Nietzsche has taught us and liberation theologians remind us, a religion especially fitted to the oppressed. It looks at the world from the perspective of those below. The African slaves' search for identity could find historical purpose in the exodus of Israel out of slavery and personal meaning in the bold identification of Jesus Christ with the lowly and downtrodden. Christianity also is first and foremost a theodicy, a triumphant account of good over evil. The intellectual life of the African slaves in the United States—like that of all oppressed peoples—consisted primarily of reckoning with the dominant form of evil in their lives. The Christian emphasis on against-the-evidence hope for triumph over evil struck deep among many of them.

The existential appeal of Christianity to Black people was the stress of Protestant evangelicalism on individual experience, and especially the conversion experience. The "holy dance" of Protestant evangelical conversion experiences closely resembled the "ring shout" of West African novitiate rites: both are religious forms of ecstatic bodily behavior in which everyday time is infused with meaning and value through unrestrained rejoicing.[17]

The conversion experience played a central role in the Christianizing process. It not only created deep bonds of fellowship and a reference point for self-assurance during times of doubt and distress; it also democratized and equalized the status of all before God. The conversion experience initiated a profoundly personal relationship with God, which gave slaves a special self-identity and self-esteem in stark contrast with the roles imposed upon them by American society.

The primary political appeal of the Methodists and especially of the Baptists for Black people was their church polity and organizational form, free from hierarchical control, open and easy access to leadership roles, and relatively loose, uncomplicated requirements for membership. The adoption of the Baptist polity by a majority of Christian slaves marked a turning point in the Afro-American experience.

On the one hand, the major organization among Black Americans, the Christian churches, followed a polity farthest removed from modern bureaucratic and hierarchical forms of organization.[18] In this sense, the organizational form of most Afro-American churches, charismatic and often autocratic in leadership, neither promoted nor encouraged widespread respect for and acquisition of bureaucratic skills requisite for accountable leadership and institutional longevity. In short, the Christian churches' organizational form imposed considerable constraints on the administrative capabilities and institutional capacities of Black people.

On the other hand, this organizational form ensured autonomous control over the central institution in the Afro-American community, which set Blacks in the United States apart from other Africans in the diaspora. Independent control over their churches promoted the proliferation of African styles and manners within the Black Christian tradition and liturgy. It also produced community-minded political leaders, polished orators, and activist journalists and scholars. In fact, the unique variant of American life that we call Afro-American culture germinated in the bosom of this Afro-Christianity, in the Afro-Christian church congregations.

DECLINE OF MODERNITY, INDUSTRIAL PROVINCIALITY, INCLUSIONARY PRACTICES

The decline of European modernity between 1871 and 1950—from the unification of the German Empire to the emergence of the United States as the unquestioned supreme world power—occurred within the political and socioeconomic contours of an increasingly crisis-ridden monopoly capitalist world economy. This yielded devastating world wars, holocaust-producing fascist regimes, and sharp reaction against repressive communist governments. The dominated classes in industrial nations—including victims of racist and sexist oppression—flexed their political muscles more in this period and embarked on various courses toward inclusion in and ineffective opposition to the liberal capitalist order. The proliferation of mass culture, especially luxury consumer goods, effected a prolonged entree of significant segments of the dominated classes into the bourgeois world of educational and occupational opportunities, middlebrow culture, and comfortable living.

In this modernist period, it seemed as if, for the West, "things fell apart; the center could not hold," to revise William Butler Yeats, the greatest English poet of the period. For science, a crisis set in. János Bolyai, N. I. Lobachevski, Karl F. Gauss, and Bernhard Riemann had already called into question the omnipresence of Euclidean geometry by discovering three-dimensional space and thereby making possible new, non-Euclidean geometries. Einstein's theory of special relativity undermined the prevailing Newtonian physics. Niels Bohr and Werner Heisenberg promoted the indeterministic character of quantum phenomena, which subsequently threatened classical laws of logic such as the law of distribution. Kurt Gödel demonstrated the incompleteness of mathematics, and L. E. J. Brouwer rejected two-value logic and the law of excluded middle, hence paving the way for intuitionist mathematics.

For modern paganism, despair also set in. This revealed itself most clearly in 1922. That year, the modernist year par excellence, witnessed within twelve months the appearance of the most profound and probing works in the history of the modern West. These included T. S. Eliot's *The Waste Land,* James Joyce's *Ulysses,* Hermann Hesse's *Siddhartha,* Osip Mandelstam's *Tristia,* Eugene O'Neill's *Anna Christie,* Bertolt Brecht's *Baal,* e. e. cummings's *The Enormous Room,* Sinclair Lewis's *Babbitt,* Jean Toomer's "Song of the Sun," Wallace Stevens's "The Comedian as the Letter C," Max Weber's *Economy and Society,* I. A. Richards's (with C. K. Ogden and James Wood) *Foundations of Aesthetics,* and Sigmund Freud's essay on jealousy, paranoia, and homosexuality. These were published in the same year that Mussolini's Blackshirts marched on Rome; and less than a year after Lenin and Trotsky's suppression of the Kronstadt rebellion, a suppression that soured the hopes of many sympathizers of the Russian Revolution.

In philosophy during the modernist period, major attacks were also made upon the primacy of the subject. Despite Hegel's historicizing of the subjectivist turn in philosophy, academic philosophers managed to overthrow Hegelianism and replace it either with analytical realism in Britain, neo-Kantianism in Germany, and phenomenology in France, themselves later attacked by structuralism, existentialism, and analytical behaviorism.

During the decline of European modernity the most precious ideals of science, politics, philosophy, and the arts were radically called into question. This period was thus well disposed toward apocalyptic, crisis-centered views of history which stressed shock, the violation of expected continuities, and a deep sense of futility. Lionel Trilling—with his Arnoldian outlook and tactful candor—suggests that the modernist element signifies nihilism, "a bitter line of hostility to civilization," "a disenchantment with culture itself."[19]

This modernist temper projects the sense of an abrupt break with all tradition, a radical disruption from the past which implies not so much a revolution but rather a devolution or dissolution. Virginia Woolf reflected this modernist temper when she wrote, "On or about December 1910 human character changed."[20]

The industrial provincial stage of American culture neither escaped nor engulfed the modernist temper.[21] New attempts appeared to extend the Genteel tradition—or provide metaphysical comfort for agonized consciences—in the form of highly sophisticated idealist philosophical systems, as in the works of Borden Parker Bowne, James Edwin Creighton, and, above all, Josiah Royce. The monumental literary achievement of the expatriate Henry James subjected the Genteel tradition to close scrutiny and detailed analysis, appraising it as a mere interesting habit of mind among a host of others. The Genteel tradition no longer survived as a holistic worldview, but rather as a subterranean sensibility upon which to build anew.[22]

During the modernist period, industrial provincial American culture presented clear-cut alternatives to its artists: either indigenize or become European. This dilemma was illustrated most graphically by the two exemplary American literary artists of the era, the seminal Mark Twain and the supercilious T. S. Eliot. For Twain, the aim was neither to resort to the eclectic strategies of Whitman or Melville nor to imitate the models and manners of Europe. Rather, it was to create the first genuine American idiom in literature. Similar to his fellow colleague and critic Ezra Pound, Eliot did not imitate Europeans, but rather became one. Although he expatriated to London, he had Paris on his mind and wrote his mature poetry under the influence of French symbolists and the classical European tradition of Homer, Ovid, and Dante. In this sense, Eliot was no longer from St. Louis and Pound no longer from Idaho. Both rested outside the gravity of industrial provincial American culture, not simply because they removed themselves from it, but rather because they discarded it.

On the philosophical front, this either-or dilemma took the form of a choice between warmed-over idealism and indigenous pragmatism, between updating the Genteel tradition and promoting a new reformist orientation.[23] Just as a dialogue between the Twain and Eliot streams never materialized, so a debate between Royce and Dewey never occurred. Both streams avoided each other, partly because of the divergent roads they chose and possibly because of their fundamental incompatibility.

The either-or dilemma of industrial provincial American culture is found only in the trained and talented artists and intellectuals of the rising Afro-American petite bourgeoisie, such as Alexander Crummell, W. E. B. Du Bois, Jean Toomer, Henry Ossawa Tanner, Alain Locke, Richard Wright, Laura Wheeler Waring, and others. The almost exclusive priority of African practices in the United States in this period was to gain inclusion within the rapidly expanding American capitalist order. With the increase of xenophobic sentiments and movements, the escalation of crypto-fascist terror in the southern part of the United States, and the vast immigration of eastern and southern European laborers to urban centers in the northern section of the United States, achieving Afro-American inclusion within the mainstream of American society proved difficult.

Public discourse within the Afro-American community concerning this inclusion was shaped by the debate that took place between the early W. E. B. Du Bois and Booker T. Washington—the two major spokesmen of the Afro-American petite bourgeoisie.[24] There were, of course, other interlocutors in the debate, including William Monroe Trotter of the Niagara Movement, Rev. James Bowen of the Methodist Episcopal clergy, and Rev. George Washington Woodbey of the Socialist Party, but the privileged positions and voices of Du Bois and Washington drowned them out.

For both Du Bois and Washington, the pressing issues were neither impractical ones such as the redistribution of wealth, a more humane mode of production, or opposition to American imperialism (in Puerto Rico and the Philippines) nor impertinent ones such as the undesirability of miscegenation or the removal of the Christian taint on Afro-American culture. Rather, these two petit bourgeois leaders directed their attention to the form and content of Afro-American inclusion in American society.

Both agreed on the form: nonviolent reform within the legal, political, and economic channels of American life. They differed on the content: Washington favored self-help initiatives in the economic sphere and promoted a slow agrarian proletarianization process tied to increased Afro-American property holdings and wealth acquisition, whereas Du Bois opted for upward social mobility in the social and political spheres and supported a protest movement that would achieve equal legal, social, and political status for Afro-Americans in American society. They violently clashed, not simply because of their divergent viewpoints but, more important, because their limited access to resources and talent forced them to struggle for power on overlapping terrain.

The Du Bois–Washington debate set the framework for inclusionary African practices in the United States in this century. The numerous Black ideological battles between integrationism and nationalism, accommodationism and separatism are but versions and variations of the Du Bois–Washington debate.[25] For example, Marcus Garvey, the great Jamaican leader of the first mass movement among Africans in the United States, simply gave Washington's self-help orientation a nationalist slant and back-to-Africa twist; his personal admiration of Washington is indisputable.

The first minor attempt to burst out of the framework of the Du Bois–Washington debate was the socialist viewpoint set forth in the pages of *The Messenger,* edited by the Young Turks, Chandler Owen and A. Philip Randolph.[26] This perspective, which echoed George Washington Woodbey's position more than a decade earlier, not only called into question the procapitalist assumption circumscribing the Du Bois–Washington debate but also linked the enhancement of Afro-Americans to the radical elements of the labor movement. This valuable addition proved to be premature at the time, especially given the racist character of the labor movement. But in decades to come, this perspective proved to be portentous. Randolph's long and distinguished yet flawed career bears out the depths of his foresight. In short, he was the pioneer on the frontier of Afro-American labor relations.

A second minor attempt to step outside the confines of the Du Bois–Washington debate consisted of the African Blood Brotherhood's amalgam of revolutionary Black nationalism and scientific socialism.[27] Its principal figures—Cyril Briggs, Richard B. Moore, W. A. Domingo, Harry Haywood—were the first African communists in the United States. Their major contribution was that they put imperialist issues on the agenda of the Afro-American liberation movement. Yet such issues—along with untimely revolutionary rhetoric—remained on the back burner for petit bourgeois intellectuals and entrepreneurs, proletarian preachers and parishioners in urban centers, and sharecroppers, tenants, and yeoman farmers in rural areas throughout Afro-America.

The major vehicles by which Black progress occurred in this period were patronage relationships with white elites and bosses in city machines, organized protest and boycott efforts (usually church-based) against discrimination, labor shortages during the two world wars, participation in the progressive labor movement (especially in the unionization of industrial workers), and achievements in athletics and entertainment. These diverse means of Afro-American upward social mobility constituted ad hoc measures which presupposed political oppression, economic exploitation, and social degradation as the prevailing realities and posited inclusion within the American liberal capitalist order as the desirable goal. Such inclusionary measures signified the Afro-American encounter with the modern world on a significant scale for the first time; they revealed the difficulties presented by racist American society, the desperation of a bastard people in hostile circumstances, and the determination of Africans in the United States, despite limited organization and vision, to be free.

END OF MODERNITY, POSTINDUSTRIAL COSMOPOLITANISM, DISPERSIVE PRACTICES

We live now three decades after the end of European modernity. The very term "postmodernism" reflects fear of the future; it is a backward-looking term. We witness the nuclear and ideological stand-off between the capitalist (not necessarily free) United States and the communist (definitely unfree) Soviet Union, both imperialist powers suffering immense internal decay. The dominated classes in industrial and postindustrial nations have accelerated the speed of their inclusion within the liberal capitalist regimes, accompanied by widespread tranquilizing and depoliticizing by mass culture. Poor, developing nations have launched successful political, anticolonial revolutions, yet often lapse into a neocolonial dependence on developed capitalist countries. A few developing nations even have had successful social revolutions, though they usually fall into the neocolonial Soviet orbit.

The recent stirrings of postmodernism can be illustrated in the following ways:

First, the crisis in science which emerged in European modernism is now becoming a more widespread crisis in the authority of science, in many ways similar to the crisis in the authority of the church in the Age of Enlightenment. This rudimentary state of demythologizing science relegates scientific descriptions and theories of the self, world, and God alongside rather than above religious, artistic, and moral descriptions and theories of the self, world, and God. This demythologizing process is promoted (usually unintentionally) by major figures in the philosophy of science, such as N. R. Hanson, Michael Polanyi, Thomas Kuhn, Imre Lakatos, and, above all, Paul Feyerabend.[28] This process signifies a deep authority crisis in knowledge, a kind of demonopolizing of science on truth and reality in the marketplace of ideas. It raises the prospect of a possible plurality of epistemic authorities on truth and reality as well as a frightening full-blown relativism or laissez-faire policy regarding access to truth and reality.

Second, the despair of modern paganism during the European modernist period has degenerated into various forms of cynicism, fatalism, hedonism, and narcissism in the lowbrow, middlebrow, and highbrow cultures of postmodernism. These attitudes and sensibilities—recently studied by Ihab Hassan, Raymond Olderman, Christopher Lasch, Heinz Kohut, Jerome Klinkowitz, and others—can be glimpsed in mass consumer culture, in popular movies, in television programs, and through disco records.[29] Postmodernist sentiments also can be found in such literary works as Jorge Borges's *Labyrinths* (1964), William Burroughs's *Naked Lunch* (1962), Donald Barthelme's *Snow White* (1967), Ishmael Reed's *The Free-lance Pallbearers* (1967), John Barth's *Lost in the Funhouse* (1968), Ronald Sukenick's *The Death of the Novel* (1969), Kurt Vonnegut Jr.'s *Slaughterhouse-Five* (1969), Raymond Federman's *Double or Nothing* (1972), Thomas Pynchon's *Gravity's Rainbow* (1973), and Philip K. Dick's *A Scanner Darkly* (1977). This degeneration—in mass culture and sophisticated literary texts—reveals, to a certain extent, the dead end to which modern paganism has come: impotent irony, barren skepticism, and paralyzing self-parody.

Third, philosophical attacks on the primacy of the subject are deepened and extended in postmodernism. In short, postmodernism is an accentuation and acceleration of the major developments and processes in European modernism. It is a deepening of the decline of modernity, with little sense of what is to follow, if anything at all. It bears the birth pains of slow epoch transition, the ironic excesses of prolonged historical suspension, and the ecstatic anticipations of a new, though not necessarily better, era.

The postindustrial cosmopolitan stage of American culture—the prevailing situation with its avant-garde domesticated by absorption into the marketable mainstream, its artists as professors, academic critics as artists, and philosophers as technicians—witnesses the emergence of the United States as the cultural vanguard in postmodernism. For the first time, European audiences look to the United States for artistic and cultural leadership. This leadership is not simply a result of the hegemony of US world power or its supreme nuclear capacity. More important is the fact that it is an effect of a nation that has steadily gained cultural self-confidence while other leading European countries flounder in either self-pity (Germany), self-defeat (England), or self-obsession (France).

The point is not so much that the United States has come of age, but rather that the United States has seized Western cultural leadership in a declining and decadent age.[30] Of course, the United States has no Jean-Paul Sartre or Martin Heidegger, no Samuel Beckett or even Gabriel García Márquez. Yet cultural leadership in the West no longer requires such stellar figures; productive academic figures now suffice.

In postindustrial cosmopolitan American culture, the either-or dilemma of the previous period evaporates. Taking their cues from William Faulkner—without the size of his canvass, the complexity of his vision, and the depths of his talent—postmodern American artists are able to learn from Europe without a feeling of inferiority and of digging deep into American life without a sense of provinciality. In philosophy, the choice is no longer between the last of the Genteel tradition and the reformist orientation—idealism or pragmatism, Royce or Dewey—or even between the reformist orientation and the new realism. The very framework of such a choice has been eclipsed by the linguistic turn in philosophy, with its analytical rigor and technical argumentation.[31] Philosophy in the United States is no longer an arena in which comprehensive worldviews are adopted and intellectual attitudes cultivated, but rather a professional field of study where intricate puzzlelike problems are solved, resolved, or dissolved.

The professionalization and specialization at work in post-industrial cosmopolitan American culture find their counterparts in the process of differentiation currently proceeding in the Afro-American experience. This differentiation generates dispersive practices among

Afro-Americans; heretofore untouched intellectual territories, secular outlooks, business ventures, occupational positions, geographic locations, and even sexual experimentations are now being discovered and enacted by Afro-Americans. This differentiation—though an index of progress—has rendered the collective enhancement of Afro-Americans even more problematic.

The paradox of Afro-American history is that Afro-Americans fully enter the modern world precisely when the postmodern period commences; that Afro-Americans gain a foothold in the industrial order just as the postindustrial order begins; and that Afro-Americans procure skills, values, and mores efficacious for survival and sustenance in modernity as the decline of modernity sets in, deepens, and yearns to give birth to a new era and epoch. The Afro-American petite bourgeoisie make significant gains in such circumstances, but even they have a fragile economic position and vulnerable political status, and they experience cultural atrophy. At the same time, the Afro-American underclass and the poor working class exhibit the indelible traces of their oppression in modernity and their dispensability in postmodernity: relative political powerlessness and perennial socioeconomic depression, cultural deterioration reinforced by devastated families and prefabricated mass culture, and subversive subcultures dominated by drugs and handguns which surface as civil terrorism in Black ghettos and American cities.

The postmodern period has rendered the framework of the Du Bois–Washington debate obsolete, but presently there is little theory and praxis to fill the void. We shall focus directly on these urgent and pressing issues in chapter 5, but we have much territory to cover before we do so. Let it suffice to say that a noteworthy product of the dispersive practices of Afro-Americans in postindustrial cosmopolitan American culture is the advent of Afro-American philosophy.

The fact that, excepting some passages in John C. Calhoun, none of our important philosophic writings mentions the existence of slavery or of the Negro race, that liberal democratic philosophers like Jefferson could continue to own and even sell slaves and still fervently believe that all men are created free and equal, ought to serve as a reminder of the air-tight compartments into which the human mind is frequently divided, and of the extent to which one's professed philosophy can be entirely disconnected from the routine of one's daily occupation.

Morris R. Cohen
American Thought: A Critical Sketch

For the history of the American Negro is unique also in this: that the question of his humanity, and of his rights therefore as a human being, became a burning one for several generations of Americans, so burning a question that it ultimately became one of those used to divide the nation. It is out of this argument that the venom of the epithet *Nigger!* is derived.

James Baldwin
"Stranger in the Village"

2

A Genealogy of Modern Racism

The notion that Black people are human beings is a relatively new discovery in the modern West. The idea of Black equality in beauty, culture, and intellectual capacity remains problematic and controversial within prestigious halls of learning and sophisticated intellectual circles. The Afro-American encounter with the modern world has been shaped first and foremost by the doctrine of white supremacy, which is embodied in institutional practices and enacted in everyday folkways under varying circumstances and evolving conditions.[1]

My aim in this chapter is to give a brief account of the way in which the idea of white supremacy was constituted as an object of modern discourse in the West, without simply appealing to the objective demands of the prevailing mode of production, the political interests of the slaveholding class, or the psychological needs of the dominant white racial group. Despite the indispensable role these factors would play in a full-blown explanatory model to account for the emergence and sustenance of modern racism in the West, I try to hold these factors constant and focus solely on a neglected variable in past explanatory models—namely, the way in which the very structure of modern discourse *at its inception* produced forms of rationality, scientificity, and objectivity as well as aesthetic and cultural ideals which require the constitution of the idea of white supremacy.

This requirement follows from a logic endemic to the very structure of modern discourse. This logic is manifest in the way in which the controlling metaphors, notions, and categories of modern discourse produce and prohibit, develop and delimit, specific conceptions of truth and knowledge, beauty and character, so that certain ideas are rendered incomprehensible and unintelligible. I suggest that one such idea that cannot be brought within the epistemological field of the initial modern discourse is that of Black equality in beauty, culture, and intellectual capacity. This act of discursive exclusion, of relegating this idea to silence, does not simply correspond to (or is not only reflective of) the relative powerlessness of Black people at the time. It also reveals the evolving internal dynamics of the structure of modern discourse in the late seventeenth and eighteenth centuries in western Europe—or during the Enlightenment. The concrete effects of this exclusion and the intellectual traces of this silence continue to haunt the modern West: on the nondiscursive level, in ghetto streets, and on the discursive level, in methodological assumptions in the disciplines of the humanities.

I shall argue that the initial structure of modern discourse in the West "secretes" the idea of white supremacy. I call this "secretion"— the underside of modern discourse—a particular logical consequence of the quest for truth and knowledge in the modern West. To put it crudely, my argument is that the authority of science, undergirded by a modern philosophical discourse guided by Greek ocular metaphors and Cartesian notions, promotes and encourages the activities of observing, comparing, measuring, and ordering the physical characteristics of human bodies. Given the renewed appreciation and appropriation of classical antiquity, these activities are regulated by classical aesthetic and cultural norms. The creative fusion of scientific investigation, Cartesian epistemology, and classical ideals produced forms of rationality, scientificity, and objectivity which, though efficacious in the quest for truth and knowledge, prohibited the intelligibility and legitimacy of the idea of Black equality in beauty, culture, and intellectual capacity. In fact, to "think" such an idea was to be deemed irrational, barbaric, or mad.

THEORETICAL CONSIDERATIONS:
THE GENEALOGICAL APPROACH

I call this inquiry a "genealogy" because, following the works of Friedrich Nietzsche and Michel Foucault, I am interested in the emergence (*Entstehung*) or the "moment of arising" of the idea of white supremacy within the modern discourse in the West.[2] This genealogy tries to address the following questions: What are the discursive conditions for the possibility of the intelligibility and legitimacy of the idea of white supremacy in modern discourse? How is this idea constituted within the epistemological field of modern discourse? What is the complex configuration of metaphors, notions, categories, and norms which produces and promotes such an object of modern discourse?

My genealogical approach subscribes to a conception of power that is neither simply based on individual subjects—e.g., heroes or great personages as in traditional historiography—nor on collective subjects—e.g., groups, elites, or classes as in revisionist and vulgar Marxist historiography. Therefore I do not believe that the emergence of the idea of white supremacy in the modern West can be fully accounted for in terms of the psychological needs of white individuals and groups or the political and economic interests of a ruling class. I will try to show that the idea of white supremacy emerges partly because of the powers within the structure of modern discourse—powers to produce and prohibit, develop and delimit, forms of rationality, scientificity, and objectivity which set perimeters and draw boundaries for the intelligibility, availability, and legitimacy of certain ideas.

These powers are subjectless—that is, they are the indirect products of the praxis of human subjects. They have a life and logic of their own, not in a transhistorical realm but within history alongside yet not reducible to demands of an economic system, interests of a class, or needs of a group. What I am suggesting is not a history without a subject propagated by the structuralist Marxist Louis Althusser, but rather a history made by the praxis of human subjects which often results in complex structures of discourses which have relative autonomy from (or is not fully accountable in terms of) the intentions, aims, needs, interests, and objectives of human subjects.[3]

I am further suggesting that there is no direct correspondence between nondiscursive structures, such as a system of production (or, in Marxist terms, an economic base), and discursive structures, such as theoretical formations (or, in Marxist terms, an ideological superstructure). Rather, there are powers immanent in nondiscursive structures and discursive structures.[4] Traditional, revisionist, and vulgar Marxist types of historiography focus primarily on powers within nondiscursive structures—e.g., powers of kings, presidents, elites, or classes—and reduce the powers within discursive structures to mere means for achieving the intentions, aims, needs, interests, and objectives of subjects in nondiscursive structures. This reductionism is not wrong; it is simply inadequate. It rightly acknowledges noteworthy concrete effects generated by the relationship between powers in discursive structures and those in nondiscursive structures, but it wrongly denies the relative autonomy of the powers in discursive structures and hence reduces the complexity of cultural phenomena.

The primary motivation behind such reductionism (such as personalistic analyses of race prejudice or orthodox Marxist accounts of racism) is to ensure an easy resolution of a highly complex problem, without calling into question certain fundamental assumptions that inform such resolutions. These fundamental assumptions, such as the subject-based conception of power, and easy resolutions, such as the elimination of race prejudice by knowledge or the abolition of racism under socialism, preclude theoretical alternatives and strategic options. In this way, these fundamental assumptions and hypothetical resolutions illustrate the effects of the powers immanent in certain liberal and Marxist discourses.

THE STRUCTURE OF MODERN DISCOURSE

I understand "the structure of modern discourse" to be the controlling metaphors, notions, categories, and norms that shape the predominant conceptions of truth and knowledge in the modern West. These metaphors, notions, categories, and norms are circumscribed and determined by three major historical processes: the scientific revolution, the Cartesian transformation of philosophy, and the classical revival.[5]

The scientific revolution is usually associated with the pioneering breakthroughs of Copernicus and Kepler in astronomy, Galileo and Newton in physics, and Descartes and Leibnitz in mathematics. These breakthroughs were pre-Enlightenment, most of them occurring during the seventeenth century, the so-called Age of Genius. The scientific revolution is noteworthy (to say the least) primarily because it signified the authority of science. This authority justified new modes of knowledge and new conceptions of truth and reality; it arose at the end of the era of pagan Christianity and set the framework for the advent of modernity.

The originary figures of the scientific revolution went beyond the Renaissance problematic—of finding a compromise formula which reconciled Christian and classical modes of thinking and living—yet stopped short of drawing thoroughly secular conclusions from their breakthroughs, that is, of waging intellectual war on natural religion and dogmatic theology. Galileo's Platonism and Newton's Socinianism illustrate this peculiar protomodern worldview of making peace between science and religion.[6]

For our purposes, the scientific revolution is significant because it highlights two fundamental ideas: *observation* and *evidence*. These two ideas have played, in an isolated manner, a role in previous paradigms of knowledge in the West (since the times of Aristotle and Aristarchus). But the scientific revolution brought these ideas together in such a way that they have become the two foci around which much of modern discourse evolves. The modern concepts of hypothesis, fact, inference, validation, confirmation, and verification cluster around the ideas of observation and evidence.

The major proponents of the scientific revolution, or, more specifically, of the authority of science, were two philosophers, Francis Bacon and René Descartes. Bacon is noteworthy primarily because of his metaphilosophical honesty. For him, the aim of philosophy was to give humankind mastery over nature by means of scientific discoveries and inventions. He then promoted the philosophical importance of the inductive method as a means of arriving at general laws to facilitate this human mastery. Despite Bacon's acceptance of orthodox religion, his rejection of Copernican theory, and his lack of acquaintance with some of the major scientific discoveries of his time—e.g., the work of Andreas Vesalius on modern anatomy, William Gilbert on magnetism, or William Harvey (Bacon's own medical attendant) on the circulation of blood—Bacon's writings, especially *The Advancement of Learning*, did much to promote the authority of science.[7]

Descartes is highly significant because his thought provided the controlling notions of modern discourse: *the primacy of the subject and the preeminence of representation*. Descartes is widely regarded as the founder of modern philosophy not simply because his philosophical outlook was profoundly affected by the scientific revolution but, more important, because he associated the scientific aim of predicting and explaining the world with the philosophical aim of picturing and representing the world. In this view, the fruits of scientific research do not merely provide more useful ways for human beings to *cope* with reality; such research also yields a true *copy* of reality. Descartes's conception of philosophy as a tortuous move from the subject to objects, from the veil of ideas to the external world, from immediate awareness to extended substances, from self-consciousness to things in space, and ultimately from doubt to certainty was motivated primarily by an attempt to provide a theoretical basis for the legitimacy of modern science. Martin Heidegger made this crucial connection between Cartesian philosophy and modern science in his famous essay "The Age of the World View":

We are reflecting on the nature of modern science in order to find its metaphysical basis. What conception of the existent and what concept of truth cause science to become research?

Understanding as research holds the existent to account on the question of how and how far it can be put at the disposal of available "representation." Research has the existent at its disposal if it can either calculate it in advance, in its future course, or calculate it afterwards as past. Nature and history become the object of expository representation. . . .

This objectification of the existent takes place in a re-presentation which aims at presenting whatever exists to itself in such a way that the calculating person can be secure, that is, certain of the existent. Science as research is produced when and only when truth has been transformed into such certainty of representation. In the metaphysics of Descartes the existent was defined for the first time as objectivity of representation, and truth as certainty of representation.[8]

Bacon and Descartes had basic differences: Bacon inductive orientation and Descartes the deductive viewpoint; Bacon the empiricist outlook and Descartes the rationalist (mathematical) perspective. Despite these differences, both of these propagandists of modern science agreed that scientific method provides a new paradigm of knowledge and that observation and evidence is at the center of scientific method. In *The New Organon,* Bacon likened his ideal natural philosopher to the bee, which collects "its material from the flowers of the garden and of the field" and digests it "by a power of its own." In his *Discourse on Method,* Descartes set forth as a rule that "observations" become "the more necessary the further we advance in knowledge." And, as D'Alembert acknowledged in *The Encyclopedia,* both Bacon and Descartes "introduced the spirit of experimental science."[9]

The last major historical process that circumscribed and determined the metaphors, notions, categories, and norms of modern discourse was the classical revival. This classical revival—in response to medieval mediocrity and religious dogmatism—was initiated in the Early Renaissance (1300–1500), principally with humanist studies in Roman art and Latin literature, such as Giotto in painting, Petrarch in letters, and Dufay in music. This revival intensified during the High Renaissance (1500–1530), with Da Vinci, Raphael, Bramante, and the early Michelangelo in the arts; Ariosto, Rabelais, and Erasmus in literature; and Josquin and Lassus in music. The revival mellowed in the Mannerist era (1530–1600), as illustrated by El Greco, Tintoretto, and the later Michelangelo in the arts; Montaigne, Cervantes, and Shakespeare in literature; and Marenzio, Gabrieli, and Frescobaldi in music. The revival was strengthened in the Baroque period (1600–1750), as seen in the works of Velasquez and Rembrandt in the arts; Racine, Milton, and Vondel in literature; and Bach and Handel in music. The classical revival culminated in the neoclassical movement in the middle of the eighteenth century, with the paintings of David and Ingres, the lyrics of Hölderlin, the tragedies of Alfieri, the verse and prose of Landor, and the music of Haydn and Mozart. The Enlightenment revolt against the authority of the church and the search for models of unrestrained criticism led to a highly charged recovery of classical antiquity, and especially to a new appreciation and appropriation of the artistic and cultural heritage of ancient Greece.

For our purposes, the classical revival is important because it infuses Greek ocular metaphors and classical ideals of beauty, proportion, and moderation into the beginnings of modern discourse. Greek ocular metaphors—Eye of the Mind, Mind as Mirror of Nature, Mind as Inner Arena with its Inner Observer—dominate modern discourse in the West.[10] Coupled with the Cartesian notion of knowledge as inner representation, modern philosophical inquiry is saddled with the epistemological model of intellect (formerly Plato's and Aristotle's Nous, now Descartes's Inner Eye) inspecting entities modeled on retinal images, with the Eye of the Mind viewing representations in order to find some characteristic that would testify to their fidelity.

The creative fusion of scientific investigation, Cartesian philosophy, Greek ocular metaphors, and classical aesthetic and cultural ideals constitutes the essential elements of modern discourse in the West. In short, modern discourse rests upon a conception of truth and knowledge governed by an ideal value-free subject engaged in observing, comparing, ordering, and measuring in order to arrive at evidence sufficient to make valid inferences, confirm speculative hypotheses, deduce error-proof conclusions, and verify true representations of reality.

THE EMERGENCE OF MODERN RACISM: THE FIRST STAGE

The recovery of classical antiquity in the modern West produced what I shall call a "normative gaze," namely, an ideal from which to order and compare observations. This ideal was drawn primarily from classical aesthetic values of beauty, proportion, and human form and classical cultural standards of moderation, self-control, and harmony.[11] The role of classical aesthetic and cultural norms in the emergence of the idea of white supremacy as an object of modern discourse cannot be underestimated.

These norms were consciously projected and promoted by many influential Enlightenment writers, artists, and scholars, of whom the most famous was J. J. Winckelmann. In his widely read book, *History of Ancient Art,* Winckelmann portrayed ancient Greece as a world of beautiful bodies. He laid down rules—in art and aesthetics—that should govern the size of eyes and eyebrows, of collarbones, hands, feet, and especially noses. He defined beauty as noble simplicity and quiet grandeur.[12] In a celebrated passage he wrote:

> As the depth of the ocean always remains calm however much the surface may be agitated, so does the expression in the figures of the Greeks reveal a great and composed soul in the midst of passions.[13]

Although Winckelmann was murdered in middle life, never set foot in Greece, and saw almost no original Greek art (only one exhibition of Greek art in Munich), he viewed Greek beauty and culture as the ideal or standard against which to measure other peoples and cultures.

Winthrop Jordan and Thomas Gossett have shown that there are noteworthy premodern racist viewpoints aimed directly and indirectly at nonwhite, especially Black, people.[14] For example, in 1520 Paracelsus held that Black and primitive peoples had a separate origin from Europeans. In 1591, Giordano Bruno made a similar claim, but had in mind principally Jews and Ethiopians. And Lucilio Vanini posited that Ethiopians had apes for ancestors and had once walked on all fours. Since theories of the separate origin of races were in disagreement with the Roman Catholic Church, Bruno and Vanini underwent similar punishment: both were burned at the stake. Of course, biblically based accounts of racial inferiority flourished, but the authority of the church prohibited the proliferation of nonreligious, that is, protomodern, accounts of racial inferiority.

What is distinctive about the role of classical aesthetic and cultural norms at the advent of modernity is that they provided an acceptable authority for the idea of white supremacy, an acceptable authority that was closely linked with the major authority on truth and knowledge in the modern world, namely, the institution of science. In order to see how this linkage took place, let us examine the categories and aims of the major discipline that promoted this authority, that is, those of natural history.

The principal aim of natural history is to observe, compare, measure, and order animals and human bodies (or classes of animals and human bodies) *based on visible, especially physical, characteristics.* These characteristics permit one to discern identity and difference, equality and inequality, beauty and ugliness among animals and human bodies.

The governing categories of natural history are preeminently *classificatory* categories—that is, they consist of various taxonomies in the form of tables, catalogs, indexes, and inventories which impose some degree of order or representational schema on a broad field of visible characteristics. *Observation* and *differentness* are the essential guiding notions in natural history. Foucault wrote:

> Natural history has as a condition of its possibility the common affinity of things and language with representation; but it exists as a task only in so far as things and language happen to be separate. It must therefore reduce this distance between them so as to bring language as close as possible to the observing gaze, and the things observed as close as possible to words. Natural history is nothing more than the nomination of the visible. . . .
>
> Natural history . . . covers a series of complex operations that introduce the possibility of a constant order into a totality of representations. It constitutes a whole domain of empiricity as at the same time describable and orderable.[15]

The initial basis for the idea of white supremacy is to be found in the classificatory categories and the descriptive, representational, order-imposing aims of natural history. The captivity of natural history to what I have called the "normative gaze" signifies the first stage of the emergence of the idea of white supremacy as an object of modern discourse. More specifically (and as Ashley Montagu has tirelessly argued), the genealogy of racism in the modern West is inseparable from the appearance of the classificatory category of race in natural history.

The category of race—denoting primarily skin color—was first employed as a means of classifying human bodies by François Bernier, a French physician, in 1684. He divided humankind into basically four races: Europeans, Africans, Orientals, and Lapps.[16] The first authoritative racial division of humankind is found in the influential *Natural System* (1735) of the most preeminent naturalist of the eighteenth century, Carolus Linnaeus. For Linnaeus, species were fixed in number and kind; they were immutable prototypes. Varieties, however, were members of a species that might change in appearance. The members of a species produced fertile offspring; interfertility was the test for the division of species. There were variations of kind within a species; the races were a prime example. For Linnaeus, there were four races: Homo Europaeus, Homo Asiaticus, Homo Afer, and Homo Americanus.

Winthrop Jordan has argued that Linnaeus did not subscribe to a hierarchical ranking of races but rather to "one chain of universal being." Jordan states:

> It was one thing to classify all living creation and altogether another to arrange it in a single great hierarchy; and when Linnaeus undertook the first of these tasks he was not thereby forced to attempt the latter. In the many editions of the *Systema Naturae* he duly catalogued the various kinds of men, yet never in a hierarchic manner.[17]

Yet it is quite apparent that Linnaeus implicitly evaluated the observable characteristics of the racial classes of people, especially those pertaining to character and disposition. For example, compare Linnaeus's description of the European with the African:

> European. White, Sanguine, Brawny. Hair abundantly flowing. Eyes blue. Gentle, acute, inventive. Covered with close vestments. Governed by customs.
> African. Black, Phlegmatic, Relaxed. Hair black, frizzled. Skin silky. Nose flat. Lips tumid. Women's bosom a matter of modesty. Breasts give milk abundantly. Crafty, indolent. Negligent. Anoints himself with grease. Governed by caprice.[18]

Linnaeus's use of evaluative terms revealed, at the least, an implicit hierarchy by means of personal preference. It also is important to note that he included some remarks about the African woman, but that he said nothing about the European woman (nor the American and Asiatic woman). It also is significant that in the 1750s when he first acknowledged that hybridization of species occurs, he chose Black people and apes as the probable candidates, while restricting such unions to Black women and male apes.

Georges Louis Leclerc de Buffon accepted hybridization without question in his famous *Natural History of Man* (1778). Although Buffon, like Linnaeus, viewed races as mere chance variations, he held that white was "the real and natural color of man." Black people and other races were variations of this natural color, yet somehow not members of a different species. He remained uncertain about the objective reality of species. Buffon believed that black skin was caused by hot climate and would change if the climate became colder. Although he was a fervent antislavery advocate, he claimed that Black people had "little genius" and then added, "The unfortunate negroes are endowed with excellent hearts, and possess the seeds of every human virtue."[19]

THE EMERGENCE OF MODERN
RACISM: THE SECOND STAGE

In the works of Johann Friedrich Blumenbach, one of the founders of modern anthropology, the aesthetic criteria and cultural ideals of Greece began to come to the forefront. Like Linnaeus and Buffon, Blumenbach held that all human beings belonged to the same species and that races were merely varieties. Yet contrary to the claims by Winthrop Jordan, Ashley Montagu, and Thomas Gossett concerning Blumenbach's opposition to hierarchic racial ranking or irritation at those who use aesthetic standards for such ranking, Blumenbach praised the symmetrical face as the most beautiful of human faces precisely because it approximated the "divine" works of Greek art, and specifically the proper anatomical proportions found in Greek sculpture.[20] Applying the classical ideal of moderation, he claimed that the more moderate the climate, the more beautiful the face. The net result was that since Black people were farthest from the Greek ideal and located in extremely hot climates, they were, by implication, inferior in beauty to Europeans.

The second stage of the emergence of the idea of white supremacy as an object of modern discourse primarily occurred in the rise of phrenology (the reading of skulls) and physiognomy (the reading of faces). These new disciplines—closely connected with anthropology—served as an open platform for the propagation of the idea of white supremacy not principally because they were pseudosciences, but, more important, because these disciplines acknowledged the European value-laden character of their observations. This European value-laden character was based on classical aesthetic and cultural ideals.

Pieter Camper, the Dutch anatomist, made aesthetic criteria the pillar of his chief discovery: the famous "facial angle." Camper claimed that the "facial angle"—a measure of prognathism—permitted a comparison of heads of human bodies by way of cranial and facial measurements. For Camper, the ideal "facial angle" was a 100-degree angle which was achieved only by the ancient Greeks. He openly admitted that this ideal conformed to Winckelmann's classical ideal of beauty. Following Winckelmann, Camper held that Greek proportions and stature exemplified beauty and embodied perfection. Camper further held that a beautiful face, beautiful body, beautiful nature, beautiful character, and beautiful soul were inseparable. He tried to show that the "facial angle" of Europeans measured about 97 degrees and those of Black people between 60 and 70 degrees, closer to the measurements of apes and dogs than to human beings.

Although many anthropologists readily accepted the "facial angle" as a scientific notion,[21] Camper made it clear that his aim was not simply to contribute to the new discipline of anthropology but also to promote the love of classical antiquity to young artists and sculptors. As George Mosse has noted, historians of race theories often overlook the fact that Camper and many subsequent theoreticians of race and racism were trained as artists and writers. Camper was a painter by training and, in fact, won the gold medal of the Amsterdam School of Art two years before he published his work on the "facial angle."[22]

Johann Kaspar Lavater, the father of physiognomy, explicitly acknowledged that the art of painting was the mother of his new discipline. Moreau, an early editor of Lavater's work, clearly noted that the true language of physiognomy was painting, because it spoke through images, equally to the eye and to the spirit.[23] This new discipline linked particular visible characteristics of human bodies, especially those of the face, to the character and capacities of human beings. This discipline openly articulated what many of the early naturalists and anthropologists tacitly assumed: *the classical ideals of beauty, proportion, and moderation regulated the classifying and ranking of groups of human bodies.* In short, physiognomy brought the "normative gaze" into daylight.

Lavater believed that the Greek statues were the models of beauty. His description of the desirable specimen—blue eyes, horizontal forehead, bent back, round chin, and short brown hair—resembled the beautiful person preferred by Camper. The common Greek ideals of beauty, though slightly distorted (to say the least), were the principal source of this "normative gaze." Lavater's new discipline was highly influential among scientists—for example, Jean Baptiste Porta, Christian Meiners—and artists. His close friend, the famous Goethe, aided him in editing and publishing his physiognomic formulations and findings and Sir Walter Scott, among others, popularized them in his novels.

Lavater's promotion of what I call the "normative gaze" consisted no longer of detailed measurements, as was the case with the naturalists, but rather of the visual glance. He wrote: "Trust your first quick impression, for it is worth more than what is usually called observation."[24] Therefore it is not surprising that Lavater put forth an elaborate theory of noses, the most striking member of the face. Neither is it surprising that subsequent classifications of noses, based on Lavater's formulations, associate Roman and Greek noses with conquerors and persons of refinement and taste.

The next and last step we shall consider in this genealogy of racism in late-seventeenth- and eighteenth-century Europe is the advent of phrenology, the new discipline which held that human character could be read through the shape of the human head. Franz Joseph Gall, a highly regarded German physician, argued in 1796 that the inner workings of the brain could be determined by the shape of the skull. For example, he associated an arched forehead with a penchant for metaphysical speculation; a skull arched at the rear with love of fame; and a skull large at the base with a criminal disposition. In the nineteenth century, when racist ideology was systematized, this new discipline took on a life of its own with Johann Kaspar Spurzheim, Anders Retzius, Carl Gustav Carus, and others; it also aided in allying modern racism with nationalism and repressed sexuality in bourgeois morality.

THEORETICAL CONSEQUENCES: RESTRICTIVE POWERS IN MODERN DISCOURSE

A major example of the way in which the restrictive powers of modern discourse delimit theoretical alternatives and strategic options in regard to the idea of white supremacy is seen in writings of radical environmentalists of the period—those one would expect to be open to the idea of Black equality in beauty, culture, and intellectual capacity. Yet even these progressive antislavery advocates remain captive to the "normative gaze."

The major opponent of predominant forms of a hierarchic ranking of races and the outspoken proponent of intermarriage in the United States during this era, Samuel Stanhope Smith, illustrates this captivity. In his day Smith stood at the pinnacle of American academia. He was president of Princeton University and an honorary member of the American Philosophical Society. He was awarded honorary degrees from Harvard and Yale. In his well-known *Essays* of 1787 (and revised in 1810) Smith argued that humankind constituted one species and that human variations could be accounted for in reference to three natural causes: "climate," "state of society," and "habits of living." He believed "that colour may be justly considered as an universal freckle."[25]

The "normative gaze" operative in Smith's viewpoint is located, as in Buffon, in the assumption that physical, especially racial, variations are always degenerate ones from an ideal state. For Smith, this ideal state consisted of highly civilized white people. As Winthrop Jordan notes, "Smith treated the complexion and physiognomy of the white man not merely as indication of superiority but as the hallmark of civilization."[26] Smith justified this ideal standard and legitimized his "normative gaze" by appealing to the classical ideals of beauty. In a patriotic footnote he wrote:

> It may perhaps gratify my countrymen to reflect that the United States occupy those latitudes that have ever been most favourable to the beauty of the human form. When time shall have accommodated the constitution of its new state, and cultivation shall have meliorated the climate, the beauties of Greece and Circasia may be renewed in America; as there are not a few already who rival those of any quarter of the globe.[27]

Smith's radical environmentalism (along with his adherence to Greek aesthetic ideals) led him to adopt the most progressive and sympathetic alternative which promotes the welfare of Black people permissible within the structure of modern discourse: integration which *uplifts* Black people, assimilation which *civilizes* Black people, intermarriage which *ensures less Negroid features* in the next generation. For example, Smith wrote:

> The great difference between the domestic and field slaves gives reason to believe that, if they were perfectly free, enjoyed property, and were admitted to a liberal participation of the society rank and privileges of their masters, they would change their African peculiarities much faster.[28]

This theoretical alternative was taken to its logical consequence by the distinguished American antislavery advocate, publicizer of talented Black writers, and eminent physician, Benjamin Rush. This logical consequence was the elimination of the skin color of Black people. In a paper entitled "Observations Intended to Favour a Supposition that the Black Color (As it is called) of the Negroes is Derived From the Leprosy," Rush denounced the idea of white supremacy, then stated: "Is the color of Negroes a disease? Then let science and humanity combine their efforts and endeavor to discover a remedy for it."[29] In one bold stroke, Rush provided grounds for promoting abolitionism, opposing intermarriage (who wants to marry diseased persons!), and supporting the Christian unity of humankind. In his opinion, his viewpoint also maximized the happiness of Black and white people:

> To encourage attempts to cure this disease of the skin in Negroes, let us recollect that by succeeding in them, we shall produce a large portion of happiness in the world. . . .
>
> Secondly, we shall add greatly to their happiness, for however well they appear to be satisfied with their color, there are many proofs of their preferring that of the white people.[30]

RACISM IN THE ENLIGHTENMENT

The intellectual legitimacy of the idea of white supremacy, though grounded in what we now consider marginal disciplines (especially in its second stage), was pervasive. This legitimacy can be illustrated by the extent to which racism permeated the writings of the major figures of the Enlightenment. It is important to note that the idea of white supremacy not only was accepted by these figures, but, more important, it was accepted by them *without their having to put forward their own arguments to justify it.* Montesquieu and Voltaire of the French Enlightenment, Hume and Jefferson of the Scotch and the American Enlightenment, and Kant of the German Enlightenment not merely held racist views; they also uncritically—during this age of criticism—believed that the *authority* for these views rested in the domain of naturalists, anthropologists, physiognomists, and phrenologists.

Montesquieu's satirical remarks in *Spirit of the Laws* about Black people (and his many revisions of these remarks) may seem to suggest an equivocal disposition toward the idea of white supremacy. Yet his conclusion leaned toward support of the idea:

> It is impossible for us to suppose that these beings should be men; because if we supposed them to be men, one would begin to believe we ourselves were not Christians.[31]

Voltaire's endorsement of the idea of white supremacy was unequivocal. In his essay "The People of America," he claimed that Black people (and Indians) were distinct species from Europeans:

> The Negro race is a species of men as different from ours as the breed of spaniels is from that of greyhounds. The mucous membrane, or network, which nature has spread between the muscles and the skin, is white in us and black or copper-colored in them. . . .
>
> If their understanding is not of a different nature from ours, it is at least greatly inferior. They are not capable of any great application or association of ideas, and seemed formed neither for the advantages nor the abuses of philosophy.[32]

Hume's racism was notorious; it served as a major source of proslavery arguments and anti-Black education propaganda. In his famous footnote to his essay "Of National Characteristics," he stated:

> I am apt to suspect the negroes, and in general all the other species of men (for there are four or five different kinds) to be naturally inferior to the whites. There never was a civilized nation of any other complexion than white, nor even any individual eminent either in action or speculation. No ingenious manufactures amongst them, no arts, no sciences. . . .
>
> In Jamaica indeed they talk of one negroe as a man of parts and learning; but 'tis likely he is admired for very slender accomplishments, like a parrot, who speaks a few words plainly.[33]

Jefferson arrived at mildly similar conclusions in his *Notes on Virginia*. Regarding the intellectual capacities of Black people, he wrote:

> Comparing them by their faculties of memory, reason, and imagination, it appears to me, that in memory they are equal to the whites; in reason much inferior . . . and that in imagination they are dull, tasteless and anomalous. . . . Never yet could I find that a black had uttered a thought above the level of plain narration; never see even an elementary trait of painting or sculpture.[34]

Finally, Kant, whose views were based heavily on Hume's claims, held that "the negroes of Africa have by nature no feeling that rises above the trifling." In his *Observations on the Feeling of the Beautiful and Sublime*, Kant noted:

> Mr. Hume challenges anyone to cite a simple example in which a negro has shown talents, and asserts that among the hundreds of

thousands of blacks who are transported elsewhere from their countries, although many of them have even been set free, still not a single one was ever found who presented anything great in art or science or any other praiseworthy quality, even though among the whites some continually rise aloft from the lowest rabble, and through superior gifts earn respect in the world. So fundamental is the difference between the two races of man, and it appears to be as great in regard to mental capacities as in color.[35]

Kant further revealed his racist views when, in reply to advice that a Black person gave to Father Labat, he wrote,

And it might be that there was something in this which perhaps deserved to be considered; but in short, this fellow was quite black from head to foot, a clear proof that what he said was stupid.[36]

THE EMERGENCE OF MODERN RACISM:
INEVITABLE OR CONTINGENT?

The emergence of the idea of white supremacy as an object of modern discourse seems inevitable in that, besides the practical need to justify nonwhite domination (especially in the early nineteenth century), the only available theoretical alternative for the unhampered search for truth and knowledge in the modern West consisted of detailed observation, measurement, comparison, and ordering of the natural and human kingdom by autonomous subjects in the light of the aesthetic and cultural ideals of classical antiquity. Given the Enlightenment obsession with criticism, especially criticism of the church and religion, the past was divided into four major epochs:

. . . the great river civilizations of the Near East; Ancient Greece and Rome; the Christian millennium; and modern times, beginning with the "revival of letters." These four epochs were rhythmically related to each other: the first and third were paired off as ages of myth, belief and superstition, while the second and fourth were ages of rationality, science and Enlightenment.[37]

The implications of Frank Snowden's thesis in his book *Blacks in Antiquity: Ethiopians in the Greco-Roman Experience* call into question the notion that the Enlightenment recovery of classical antiquity—its aesthetic and cultural ideals—inevitably required, on the discursive level, the emergence of the idea of white supremacy as an object of modern discourse. Snowden's thesis is that racial prejudice did not exist in classical antiquity. He claims that in the first major encounter in European records of Black people in a predominantly white society the idea of Black equality in beauty, culture, and intellectual capacity was seriously entertained. In regard to ideals of beauty, he notes that Herodotus called Ethiopians the most handsome people on earth; Philostratus spoke of charming Ethiopians with their strange color; Pseudo-Callisthenes held the black Queen of Meroë (visited by Alexander the Great) to be of wondrous beauty; and the poet Martial, though pursued by a woman whiter than snow, sought a "super-black" woman.[38] Snowden goes as far as to state: "On the whole . . . the number of expressed preferences for blackness and whiteness in classical literature is approximately equal."[39]

If Snowden's viewpoint is correct, two noteworthy issues arise. First, it permits us to accent the crucial role that the advent of modern science played in *highlighting the physical appearances of people in relation to what it is to be human, beautiful, cultured, and intelligent.* In this regard, the primacy of observation—the "gaze" character of scientific knowledge—may be as important as the classical ideals which are latent in such observations at the inception of modern discourse. Second, Snowden's claims require that I provide an account of why the Enlightenment revival of classical antiquity ignored or excluded Black statues and the proportions and measurements of Black figures as part of classical aesthetic ideals.

Snowden's thesis is highly plausible and extremely provocative, but I find it neither persuasive nor convincing. His claims are too exorbitant, but they do contain kernels of truth. Race indeed mattered much less in classical antiquity than it does in modern times. But race did matter in classical antiquity, as can be seen from the evidence meticulously gathered by Snowden, Sikes, Westermann, and others.[40] The crucial difference seems to be that racial differences were justified on cultural grounds in classical antiquity, whereas at the inception of modern discourse, racial differences are often grounded in nature, that is, ontology and later biology.

And even if race prejudice did not exist in classical antiquity, the minority status of Black people in Greece and Rome still rendered Black statues, proportions, and measurements marginal to cultural life. Hence, the Black presence, though tolerated and at times venerated, was never an integral part of the classical ideals of beauty. The emergence of the idea of white supremacy as an object of modern discourse seems contingent, in that there was no iron necessity at work in the complex configuration of metaphors, notions, categories, and norms that produce and promote this idea. There is an accidental character to the discursive emergence of modern racism, a kind of free play of discursive powers which produce and prohibit, develop and delimit the legitimacy and intelligibility of certain ideas within a discursive space circumscribed by the attractiveness of classical antiquity.

Yet even such claims about the contingency of the emergence of the idea of white supremacy in the modern West warrant suspicion. This is so because, as we noted earlier, this genealogical approach *does not purport to be an explanation of the rise of modern racism, but rather a theoretical inquiry into a particular neglected variable, i.e., the discursive factor, within a larger explanatory model.* This variable is significant because it not only precludes reductionist treatments of modern racism; it also highlights the cultural and aesthetic impact of the idea of white supremacy on Black people. This inquiry accents the fact that the everyday life of Black people is shaped not simply by the exploitative (oligopolistic) capitalist system of production but also by cultural attitudes and sensibilities, including alienating ideals of beauty.

The idea of white supremacy is a major bowel unleashed by the structure of modern discourse, a significant secretion generated from the creative fusion of scientific investigation, Cartesian philosophy, and classical aesthetic and cultural norms. Needless to say, the odor of this bowel and the fumes of this secretion continue to pollute the air of our postmodern times.

But the fact is not that the Negro has no tradition but that there has as yet arrived no sensibility sufficiently profound and tough to make this tradition articulate. For a tradition expresses, after all, nothing more than the long and painful experience of a people; it comes out of the battle waged to maintain their integrity or, to put it more simply, out of their struggle to survive.

James Baldwin
"Many Thousands Gone"

If the ruling and the oppressed elements in a population, if those who wish to maintain the *status quo* and those concerned to make changes, had, when they became articulate, the same philosophy, one might well be skeptical of its intellectual integrity.

John Dewey
"Philosophy and Civilization"

3

The Four Traditions of Response

Modern racist discourse did not go unanswered by Afro-Americans. In this chapter, I shall put forward an interpretation and a description of the Afro-American experience in the light of the Black reactions and responses to the modern justifications of the idea of white supremacy initiated in enlightened Europe and inseminated in the slavery-ridden United States. The interpretation and the description are essentially a reconstruction of the Black counter discourse to modern European racist discourse. They present a hermeneutic of Afro-American history that focuses on the diverse conceptions of self-image and self-determination during the prolonged Afro-American entrance into the corridors of modernity: the long-overdue reaping of the harvest that Afro-Americans helped cultivate, the seizing of opportunities previously closed, and the bruising encounter with the emptiness, sterility, and hypocrisy of postmodernity.

When Afro-Americans are viewed as passive objects of history, Afro-American history is a record of the exclusion of a distinct racial group from the economic benefits and cultural dilemmas of modernity. Politically, this exclusion has meant white ownership of Afro-American persons, possessions, and progeny; severe discrimination reinforced by naked violence within a nascent industrial capitalist order; and urban enclaves of unskilled unemployables and semiskilled workers within a liberal corporate capitalist regime. Culturally, this has meant continual

Afro-American degradation and ceaseless attempts to undermine Afro-American self-esteem.

When Afro-Americans are viewed as active subjects of history, Afro-American history becomes the story of a gallantly persistent struggle, of a disparate racial group fighting to enter modernity on its own terms. Politically, this struggle consists of prudential acquiescence plus courageous revolt against white paternalism; institution-building and violent rebellion within the segregated social relations of industrial capitalism; and cautious reformist strategies within the integrated social relations of "postindustrial" capitalism. Culturally, this has meant the maintenance of self-respect in the face of pervasive denigration.

I will attempt to order and organize some significant aspects of the Afro-American past by delineating four ideal types that embody distinct Afro-American historical traditions of thought and action. These categories incorporate abstract elements of Afro-American historical reality; they are, however, derived from an empirical examination of this reality. Needless to say, they rarely appear empirically in their pure, conceptual form, but may serve as heuristic tools to confer intelligibility on Afro-American history and provide an understanding of this history by revealing its internal rationality.

The four theoretical constructs to be considered are the exceptionalist, assimilationist, marginalist, and humanist traditions in Afro-American history.[1] I shall try to stipulate clear definitions of these traditions so they will not be automatically associated with their previously established meanings within traditional historiography.

The Afro-American exceptionalist tradition lauds the uniqueness of Afro-American culture and personality. It claims a sui generis status for Afro-American life in regard to form and content. It stresses what qualitatively distinguishes Afro-Americans from the rest of humanity, especially what sets them apart from white Americans. This tradition contains two types: strong exceptionalism and weak exceptionalism. Strong exceptionalism makes ontological claims about Afro-American superiority; Afro-Americans stand above other racial groups because of their genetic makeup, divine chosenness, or innate endowments. Weak exceptionalism makes sociological claims about Afro-American superiority; Afro-Americans stand above other racial groups because of certain values, modes of behavior, or gifts acquired from their endurance of political oppression, social degradation, and economic exploitation.

The Afro-American assimilationist tradition considers Afro-American culture and personality to be pathological. It rejects any idea of an independent, self-supportive Afro-American culture. It stresses the inability of Afro-Americans to create adequate coping devices to alleviate the enormous pressures caused by their dire condition. This tradition also contains two types: strong assimilationalism and weak assimilationalism. Strong assimilationalism makes ontological claims about Afro-American inferiority; Afro-Americans stand below other racial groups because of their genetic makeup, divine rejection, or innate deficiency. Weak assimilationalism makes sociological claims about Afro-American inferiority; Afro-Americans stand below other racial groups because of certain values, modes of behavior, or defects acquired from their endurance of political oppression, social degradation, and economic exploitation.

The Afro-American marginalist tradition posits Afro-American culture to be restrictive, constraining, and confining. It emphasizes the suppression of individuality, eccentricity, and nonconformity within Afro-American culture. This tradition is parasitic in that it rests upon either the assimilationalist or humanist tradition.

The Afro-American humanist tradition extolls the distinctiveness of Afro-American culture and personality. It accents the universal human content of Afro-American cultural forms. It makes no ontological or sociological claims about Afro-American superiority or inferiority. Rather, it focuses on the ways in which creative Afro-American cultural modes of expression embody themes and motifs analogous to the vigorous cultural forms of other racial, ethnic, or national groups. This tradition affirms Afro-American membership in the human race, not above it or below it.

My conception of these four traditions in Afro-American thought and action assumes that culture is more fundamental than politics in regard to Afro-American self-understanding. It presupposes that Afro-American cultural perceptions provide a broader and richer framework for understanding the Afro-American experience than political perceptions. As noted earlier, culture and politics are inseparable, but, as I believe Antonio Gramsci has shown, any political consciousness of an oppressed group is shaped and molded by the group's cultural resources and resiliency as perceived by individuals in it.[2] So the extent to which the resources and resiliency are romanticized, rejected, or accepted will deeply influence the kind of political consciousness that individuals possess.

These four traditions of thought and action in Afro-American history can serve as guides for understanding Afro-American culture and politics. They shall represent distinct Afro-American responses to the challenges of self-image and self-determination; they will also be the alternatives from which we choose a desirable response to these challenges.

EXCEPTIONALIST TRADITION

The self-image of Afro-Americans in both types of the exceptionalist tradition is one of pride, self-congratulation, and often heroism. Afro-Americans are considered to be more humane, meek, kind, creative, spontaneous, and nonviolent than members of other racial groups; less malicious, mendacious, belligerent, bellicose, and avaricious. This tradition posits Afro-American superiority, not over all others, but specifically over white Americans.

The strong exceptionalist tradition in Afro-American history does not appear in any substantive manner until the rise of a secular Afro-American intelligentsia. The early religious Afro-American intellectuals, though vehemently opposed to Black oppression and the doctrine of white supremacy, did not subscribe to any form of strong exceptionalism. Despite the fierce fight continually waged for Afro-American enhancement, they refused to make any ontological claims about Afro-American superiority, primarily because of inhibitory, deep Christian roots.

The first major formulation of strong exceptionalism in Afro-American thought appeared in the "germ" theory of New England–born, Harvard-trained W. E. B. Du Bois. Ironically, he borrowed this theory from his teacher at Harvard, Albert Bushnell Hart, who used it to support Teutonic (Anglo-Saxon) superiority. This theory maintained that each race possesses its own "race idea and race spirit" embodying its unique gift to humanity. Du Bois wrote:

> At the same time the spiritual and physical differences of race groups which constituted the nations became deep and decisive. The English nation stood for constitutional liberty and commercial freedom; the German nation for science and philosophy; the romance nations stood for literature and art, and the other race groups are striving, each in his own way, to develop for civilization its particular message, its particular ideal. . . . Manifestly some of the great races today—particularly the Negro race—have not as yet given to civilization the full spiritual message which they are capable of giving.[3]

And what was this message? In *The Souls of Black Folk* (1903) and *The Gift of Black Folk* (1924), he suggested that it was essentially that of meekness, joviality, and humility manifest in the Afro-American gift of spirit. His essay "Of Our Spiritual Strivings," found in the earlier work, rhetorically asked,

> Will America be poorer if she replace her brutal dyspeptic blundering with light-hearted but determined Negro humility? or her coarse and cruel wit with loving jovial good-humor? or her vulgar music with the soul of the Sorrow Songs?[4]

He ended the latter work casting "the sense of meekness and humility" of Afro-Americans against the white man's "contempt, lawlessness and lynching" for domination of the emerging American spirit. The uniqueness of Afro-Americans was even more explicitly endorsed when he wrote: "Negroes differ from whites in their inherent genius and stages of development."[5] Under the influence of Franz Boas and Marxism, Du Bois abandoned the "germ" theory, yet he planted and nurtured its seed long enough for the strong exceptionalist tradition to establish a continued presence in Afro-American thought and action.

James Weldon Johnson gave the strong exceptionalist tradition new life with his notion of the unique creativity of Afro-Americans. In the famous preface to his well-known anthology of Afro-American poetry, he claimed that the true greatness of a civilization should be measured by its creative powers in the arts. He then added,

> The Negro has already proved the possession of these powers by being the creator of the only things artistic that have yet sprung from American soil and been universally acknowledged as distinctive American products.[6]

He attributed these creative powers to the "racial genius" of Afro-Americans,

> . . . us who are warmed by the poetic blood of Africa—old, mysterious Africa, mother of races, rhythmic-beating heart of the world.[7]

And what did this "racial genius" consist of? Like that of Du Bois, it was a God-given (or nature-given) spirit revealed in the pietistic, primitive Christianity of rural Afro-Americans.

The majority of literary works during the Harlem Renaissance mark a shift in the strong exceptionalist tradition. The urban setting and the close interaction with alienated white literary figures groping for the vitality of "noble savages" add new content to Afro-American

uniqueness: the primitivism of Afro-Americans manifest in their unin-
hibited and spontaneous behavior.

In the past decade, the strong exceptionalist tradition has flourished in the religious doctrine of the Black Muslims under the leadership of the late Honorable Elijah Muhammad, the Black theology
of Joseph Washington, and the Black Arts movement promoted by
Imamu Baraka, the late Hoyt Fuller, Addison Gayle, and others. These
groups provided ontological justifications for the inhumanity of white
Americans, hence Afro-American superiority over these whites. The
evidence usually adduced was American history; the conclusion was
to deny American (white) values, defy American (white) society, and
preserve the small dose of (Black) humanity left in America.

The weak exceptionalist tradition began in earnest with the African Methodist Episcopal intelligentsia. The humanity of white people
was not denied, but they were relegated to a lower moral status than
Afro-Americans. For example, R. R. Wright, a leading intellectual of
the African Methodist Episcopal Church at the turn of the century,
wrote: "The white man is selfish and the American white man is the
most grasping breed of humanity ever made."[8] Wright concluded that
whites, because of their materialist greed and moral self-centeredness,
have never understood the Christian message. Only the peaceful, loving, and forgiving Afro-Americans can instill the spirit of Christianity
in the violent, vicious white race: "African Methodism will carry the
Christian message of brotherhood to the white man."[9]

The weak exceptionalist tradition continued with the Garvey movement of the 1920s. Garvey heralded Afro-American pride, beauty,
and strength without claiming innate white inferiority. His program
of racial purity, Black religion (including a Black Christ, Mary, and
God), and Back-to-Africa doctrine was juxtaposed with, for example,
the following judgment on white people:

> We are not preaching a propaganda of hate against anybody. We
> love the white man; we love all humanity, because we feel that we
> cannot live without the other.[10]

Yet Garvey believed that white people behaved in a demonic fashion
within the existing social order:

> I regard the Klan as a better friend of the race than all the groups
> of hypocritical whites put together. You may call me a Klansman,
> if you will, but potentially every white man is a Klansman, as far as

the Negro in competition with whites socially, economically, and politically is concerned, and there is no use lying about it.[11]

The most recent instance of weak exceptionalism is surprisingly the great Martin Luther King's doctrine of nonviolence. This doctrine tends to assume tacitly that Afro-Americans have acquired, as a result of their historical experience, a peculiar capacity to love their enemies, to endure patiently suffering, pain, and hardship and thereby "teach the white man how to love" or "cure the white man of his sickness." King seemed to believe that Afro-Americans possess a unique proclivity for nonviolence, more so than do other racial groups, that they have a certain bent toward humility, meekness, and forbearance, hence are quite naturally disposed toward nonviolent action. In King's broad overview, God is utilizing Afro-Americans—this community of *caritas* (other-directed love)—to bring about "the blessed community." He seemed confident that his nonviolent movement of predominantly Afro-Americans was part of a divine plan. He was the drum major of "this mighty army of love":

> I am sure that the entire world now looks to the Negro in America for leadership in the whole task of building a world without want, without hate, and where all men live together in shared opportunity and brotherhood.[12]

The self-image fostered by both types of the exceptionalist tradition is defensive in character and romantic in content. It is a reaction to the doctrine of white supremacy, an attempt to build Afro-American pride and self-worth upon quixotic myths about the past, exaggerated expectations of the present, and chiliastic hopes for the future.

This self-image reveals the real roots of the Afro-American exceptionalist tradition: the rise of the Afro-American petite bourgeoisie. The exceptionalist claim of Afro-American superiority can be seen as a cloak for the repressed self-doubts, fears, and anxieties of an emerging Afro-American middle class. It resulted from the inevitable questioning of personal identity and the belated quest for wealth, status, and prestige among the Afro-American parvenu petite bourgeoisie caused by interacting with a hostile white (American) society.

In the cultural sphere, Afro-American exceptionalism was begun by talented Afro-Americans extolling the cultural achievements of the West, searching for Afro-American achievements commensurate with those of the West, and ending by conjuring up mythologies that put

Afro-American achievements on a superior footing with those of the West. Personal identity became cushioned by racial myths of superiority; the search for this identity was motivated primarily by the white opposition. Hence, it was extrinsic, containing no enduring sustenance, potency, or authenticity.

In the political sphere, Afro-American exceptionalism started with ambitious Afro-Americans who pursued wealth, status, and prestige in American society, ran up against racist barriers, then returned to the Afro-American world to continue this pursuit, with an acquired hostility toward the society into which they unsuccessfully sought entrance. They amassed wealth, status, and prestige in this world ("big fish in a little pond") and concerned themselves with helping other ambitious socially mobile Afro-Americans, sometimes under the banner of antiwhitism, and often at the expense of the Afro-American masses.

The bourgeois roots of the exceptionalist tradition are most clearly seen in its aims and conceptions of political struggle. Its major form is Afro-American vocation ideology: a calling for Afro-Americans to acknowledge their uniqueness, utilize it to organize and mobilize themselves against the white world, and undermine the inhumanity and hypocrisy of this white world. A cursory examination of the Afro-American exceptionalist approach to political struggle substantiates a revised version of Lenin's famous quip: "Scratch an exceptionalist and underneath is a budding bourgeois."

Du Bois's "germ" theory had its political analogue in his doctrine of the Talented Tenth. He promoted both simultaneously. While the Afro-American masses are busy giving the world its meekness, humility, and joviality, the Talented Tenth are providing leadership and guidance for these spiritual masses, a leadership and guidance that presuppose the sustained wealth, status, and prestige of the Talented Tenth. In other words, the Untalented Ninetieth possess the idealized gift of spirit, while the Talented Tenth acquire the essentials of power, namely, education and skills:[13]

> The Negro race, like all races, is going to be saved by its exceptional men. The problem of education, then, among Negroes must first of all deal with the Talented Tenth; it is the problem of developing the Best of this race that they may guide the Mass away from the contamination and death of the Worst, in their own and other races.[14]

James Weldon Johnson's important role in the National Association for the Advancement of Colored People, that of being its first Black executive secretary, embodied the same relationship, with an integrationist twist: a middle-class approach while idealizing the religious "primitivism" of the Afro-American masses.

The literary artists of the Harlem Renaissance, as well as of the Black Arts movement in the 1960s, represent petit bourgeois fascination with the spontaneity of Afro-American proletarian (and lumpenproletarian) life; the first movement remained much less political than the later one. The Harlem Renaissance writers basically portrayed stereotypical lifestyles with which they were scarcely acquainted; the Black Arts figures promoted so-called "Black" values that rested completely outside the cultural framework of most Afro-Americans. Both movements produced mediocre art, romanticized the Afro-American lower class, and launched lucrative careers for a few middle-class Black artists previously excluded from the white (American) world of art.

R. R. Wright's weak exceptionalist approach culminated in an energetic attempt to organize an Afro-American interest group, an Afro-American political party, and an Afro-American voting bloc: early middle-class attempts to utilize Afro-American cohesion to gain entrance to the political mainstream.

The Garvey movement, after great popular support primarily caused by its powerful reversal of European ideals of beauty and culture, resulted in an aborted trip to Africa. The thousands of dollars that were acquired from Afro-Americans, mainly from small entrepreneurs, who purchased stocks in Garvey's business concerns, were squandered, through ineptitude and graft. The Black Muslims, under the late Honorable Elijah Muhammad, opted for entrepreneurship in urban centers—a gallant yet hapless attempt to secure a notch within a declining entrepreneurial capitalism and an ever-expanding corporate domination of the economy. The same holds for the "Black capitalism" promoted in the past decade by some Black Power advocates.[15]

King's early political viewpoint was more candid than that of others: it literally proclaimed its goal to be American middle-class status. After a harsh political struggle, the federal government was persuaded to legitimize this pursuit. Federal legislation removed certain racist barriers— e.g., disenfranchisement and segregated housing—which increased the possibility of skilled and educated Afro-Americans' acquiring some degree of wealth, status, and prestige in American society. Results for the Afro-American poor have been minimal.[16]

The exceptionalist response to the challenges of self-image and self-determination is this: a romanticization of Afro-American culture that conceals the social mobility of an emerging opportunistic Afro-American petite bourgeoisie. Afro-American exceptionalism offers symbols and rituals to the Afro-American masses which are useful for enhancing the social mobility of Afro-American professional and business groups.[17] It generates cathartic and amorphous feelings of Afro-American pride, self-congratulation, and heroism that contain little substance.

Afro-American philosophy deems the exceptionalist response undesirable. Such a romanticization of Afro-American culture is an escape from reality. It fosters cultural stagnation and leaves Afro-Americans vulnerable to insidious manipulation by Black charismatic figures or socially mobile groups. In other words, it does not enhance the cultural life or ameliorate the socioeconomic conditions of the majority of Afro-Americans.

The hypocrisy of Afro-American exceptionalism is revealed usually ex post facto: when bourgeois nationalists, after acquiring some status, prestige, and wealth, begin to "outgrow their childish past," namely, begin to interact, commune, and even marry the previously "inferior enemy"; and when bourgeois integrationists, after gaining a desired place in American society, remain complacently inert and satisfied in their "promised land," the coveted suburbs. So the Afro-American exceptionalist tradition of both types is a stream of thought and action in Afro-American history which serves principally as a covert strategy for Afro-American entrance into the mainstream of American society.

ASSIMILATIONALIST TRADITION

The self-image of Afro-Americans in both types of the assimilationalist tradition is one of self-hatred, shame, and fear. Afro-Americans are viewed as morbid subhuman monsters. This tradition posits Afro-American inferiority, not against everyone, but specifically to white Americans.

Like the exceptionalist tradition, this stream of thought and action in Afro-American history did not appear in a significant manner until the rise of a secular Afro-American intelligentsia. Aside from occasional remarks by Alexander Crummell and Edward Blyden regarding missionary emigrationism, the early religious Afro-American intelligentsia refused to engage in any talk about Afro-American inferiority, primarily because they headed the institutions (churches) around which Afro-American culture evolved.

The unchallenged theoretician of the weak assimilationalist tradition in Afro-American history is E. Franklin Frazier.[18] The Chicago school of sociology serves as the context in which his brand of weak assimilationalism flourished. Borrowing from the social theory of W. I. Thomas (especially his work on Polish peasants) and Robert Parks (notably his work on urban class and status conflict), Frazier views the history of Afro-American culture as a series of devastating social shocks—the initial act of enslavement from Africa, the cruel voyage across the Atlantic Ocean, the "peculiar institution" of slavery, the vicious postemancipation life, and the disintegration of folk culture in the cities.

In his well-known book, *The Negro Family in the United States* (1939), Frazier suggests that the Afro-American culture basically amounts to superstition, ignorance, self-hatred, and fear. It emanates from political despair and produces a wholly negative self-image. He hopes it will soon disappear.[19]

The weak assimilationalist tradition under the aegis of Frazier has provided the theoretical framework for legal and political argumentation of civil rights during the past two decades. The message was clear: Afro-Americans have been environmentally created less equal and normal than whites, so only assimilation with whites can break the circle of political oppression and pathological behavior.

This message contains the chief aim of political struggle in the Afro-American weak assimilationalist tradition, an ideology of Afro-American uplift: the only hope for Afro-American enhancement is increased interaction with whites, because only assimilation can civilize, refine, and modernize Afro-Americans. In short, it endorses the viewpoints of Samuel Stanhope Smith and Benjamin Rush which we examined in chapter 2. Frazier makes this point crystal clear:

> If the Negro had undertaken to shut himself off from the white culture about him and had sought light from within his experience, he would have remained on the level of barbarism.[20]

Later in life, Frazier began to recognize the belated consequences of his viewpoint. In his scathing critique of the Afro-American middle class, *Black Bourgeoisie* (1962), he castigates their aping of white bourgeois society, their fanciful world of status, wealth, and prestige, and their inability to take each other seriously as professionals. In a later essay, he advised Afro-American intellectuals to provide positive self-images for Black people and to not confuse assimilation with self-effacement.[21] Yet, despite these late attempts that acknowledge the limitations of the weak assimilationist tradition, Frazier almost single-handedly set in motion a stream of Afro-American thought and action which remains highly influential today.

Like the exceptionalist tradition, the assimilationalist one is a petit bourgeois affair; it promotes a self-image that inheres primarily among an insecure, socially mobile Afro-American middle class (and adopted as true by most misguided white social scientists) and posits this largely negative self-image as the only one for all Afro-Americans. Yet, unlike the exceptionalist tradition, it does not romanticize Afro-American culture; instead, it deprecates this culture.

The assimilationalist response to the challenges of self-image and self-determination is this: a rejection of Afro-American culture and total assimilation into American society. It assumes that the universal must wipe clean all particulars, that cosmopolitan society erases all provincialities.

Afro-American critical thought must hold the assimilationalist response to be unacceptable. The wholesale renunciation of Afro-American culture only denigrates Afro-Americans. It deprives them of the autonomous elements of their way of life, the genuine creations of their cultural heritage. The assimilationalist tradition, like the exceptionalist one, is a rash reaction against a hostile white society rather than a responsible response to particular challenges. Both traditions represent the peculiar predicament of the Afro-American middle class. Just as the exceptionalist tradition looks at Afro-American culture and sees no evil, so the assimilationalist tradition looks and sees no good. The major shortcoming of the latter is that it overlooks the possibility of cultural vitality and poverty-ridden living conditions existing simultaneously in Afro-American life.

MARGINALIST TRADITION

The Afro-American marginalist tradition promotes a self-image of both confinement and creativity, restriction and revolt. It encompasses a highly individualistic rebellion of Afro-Americans who are marginal to, or exist on the edges of, Afro-American culture and see little use in assimilating into the American mainstream. It expresses a critical disposition toward Afro-American culture *and* American society.

The early manifestations of Afro-American marginalist thought and action were found in the critical attitudes of religious leaders toward their own church members and American society. But the result was rarely personal rebellion against both, owing to the need for conformity and community under severe oppression.

The marginalist tradition appears more fully in the works of Sutton Griggs and Charles Chesnutt.[22] Central for both of them is the problematic status of the "mulatto" (which derives from the Latin word for mule, *mulus*)—the physically marginal person between Afro-American culture and American society. The authors and their characters maintain a distance and express a denial of Afro-American culture which leaves them uprooted. Their rejection and distrust of American society make them vindictive.

Griggs and Chesnutt were the first archetypes of Afro-American marginalists: individualistic, alienated, searching for a home. Their talent and imagination lifted them above what they conceived to be the uncouth, vulgar, and unrefined Afro-American folk culture, yet this same talent and imagination were denied recognition by whites, hence turned against the white world. In the end, both sought escape from this predicament—Griggs to Africa, Chesnutt ("passing") into the white world he had earlier assailed.

The marginalist tradition blossomed in the works and lives of Nella Larsen and Rudolph Fisher. Both were plagued by the inability to accept themselves and could not find comfort anywhere. Larsen's Helga Crane, the protagonist of *Quicksand* (1928), was an attractive well-bred mulatto who sought to overcome her self-hatred and find herself in a provincial southern Negro college, the urban life of Chicago and Harlem, the cosmopolitan world of Copenhagen, and finally the pietistic Christianity of Afro-American rural life. She—Helga (and Larsen)—was an incessant rebel, unable to come to terms with herself in either world, Black or white.

Rudolph Fisher, the talented physician-writer, fostered early in life a deep hatred of the white world. He also found it hard to appreciate anything in Afro-American urban life. He praised the spirituals, but refused to acknowledge similar artistic richness in the blues and jazz. The latter he considered secular vulgarizations evolved from the former; the cruel urban environment destroyed the pure, religious pathos of Afro-American rural life. Fisher was unable to feel at home in the city. This detachment allowed him to portray Afro-American urban life more honestly than his literary contemporaries did during the Harlem Renaissance. He was more conscious than they of the divisions within Black city life because these divisions affected him more acutely.[23]

The personal revolt of Wallace Thurman may serve as a turning point in the marginalist tradition. It marked the refusal to escape from self-hatred and shame. Prior to Thurman, Afro-American marginalists imagined heroic self-absorbing events, longed for idyllic lifestyles of the rural past, or succumbed to resignation. Thurman candidly confronted his negative view of self, and attempted to see something in it that could help him overcome it. Unfortunately, he discovered little to aid him.

This theme was presented, in embryonic form, in his first novel, *The Blacker the Berry* (1929). The jet-black complexion of Emma Lou, his protagonist, forced her to come to terms with who she was. Only a sincere acceptance of her dark skin color, in contrast to the attitudes of both her own culture and white society, led to personal salvation. In his second novel, *The Infants of the Spring* (1932), Thurman portrayed his own predicament and his efforts to get out of it. He parodied the Harlem Renaissance, its phoniness, self-deception, and barrenness. He depicted how its praise of primitivism concealed self-effacement; how white patrons encouraged literary compromise; how Afro-American pretentiousness hid inferiority complexes. For Thurman, only a Nietzschean Übermensch or a Dostoevskian Underground Man can avoid these traps. Salvation lies in self-definition through art created out of no illusions about the self. Yet his self-acceptance precluded any usage of the positive aspects of Afro-American culture as ingredients for art. He created from a cultural vacuum, from solely personal despair and self-hatred, resulting in an unusually truncated view of life, an extremely limited vision of human experience.

The Afro-American marginalist tradition reached its zenith in the works and life of Richard Wright. The chief motif that pervaded his writings was personal rebellion, against who he was, the culture that nurtured him, the society that rejected him, and the cosmos that seemed indifferent to his plight. Uprooted from the rural life of Mississippi, disgusted with the Black bourgeoisie and the predominantly Jewish Communists in Chicago and New York, alienated within the cosmopolitan world of Paris, and distrustful of emerging African nations, Wright was the marginal man par excellence.

Wright tried to create an Afro-American self-image that rested solely upon personal revolt, whether it was couched in the naturalism of Dreiser or crudely guided by the philosophical existentialism of Sartre or Camus. His revolt was intense, but it never crystallized into any serious talk of concerted action, partly because such talk presupposes a community, a set of common values and goals, at which a marginal man like Wright can only sneer.

Wright's attitude toward Afro-American culture was twofold: a conscious embodiment and rejection of it.[24] In his major novel, *Native Son* (1940), Wright linked himself to the Afro-American community by presenting Bigger Thomas, his main character, as a symbol of this community, of its plight and hopes. Bigger gave visibility and recognition to Afro-Americans. Wright's sometimes subtle, and often overt, derogatory remarks about Afro-American culture were integral elements in the exposure of this culture. His own fear, shame, and self-hatred, he believed, made him intuitively close to the culture he rejected and rebellious against the society partially responsible for his negative self-image. Wright seemed to think he would always be a part of the culture from which he sought escape, and the deeper his repudiation of it, the more tightly he remained tied to it. Why? Because his own negative self-image, he seemed to believe, only mirrored the self-image found in Afro-American culture. Artistic imagination allowed him (only him!) to overcome the deep scars of oppression. These livid scars became, for Wright (who had escaped from the inferno), the chief sources of his art. Hence, the assertions of being in his fiction take the form of violent acts against his culture, society, and world.

The first major critique of Wright's perspective was written by the young James Baldwin. In his influential *Partisan Review* essays (reprinted in *Notes of a Native Son*), he claimed that Wright succumbed to the cold, lifeless, abstract categories of social scientists; in short, Wright endorsed the Afro-American self-image found in the assimilationist tradition. For Baldwin, such a view overlooked the richness and beauty in Afro-American life. Wright adopted a self-image that distorted Afro-American culture, denied Afro-American humanity. Baldwin concluded his remarks stating,

> Our humanity is our burden, our life; we need not battle for it; we need only to do what is infinitely more difficult—that is, accept it.[25]

The greatness of Baldwin as a person and the significance of his work as a writer is his candid portrayal of this burdensome acceptance. In his first, and best, work of fiction, *Go Tell It on the Mountain* (1953), Baldwin discovered that the positive side of Afro-American life was much easier for him to talk about in essays than depict in fiction. When he looked closely into his own life, he saw almost precisely what Wright saw—terror, fear, and self-hatred.[26] These qualities evolved from a rigid, fundamentalist Christian home in the heart of urban America—Harlem.

Baldwin's protagonist, John Grimes, had an immense fear of God, his father (Gabriel), and white society. He was plagued by a cosmic terror. He felt trapped. If he revolted against his Super-egos, he feared perdition; if he submitted, he suffered frustration. The only way out was through a rebellious act of imagination.

Unlike Wright, Baldwin did not rebel for deeper marginality or further isolation. Instead, his was a search for community, a community of love and tolerance denied him by Afro-American culture. Baldwin did not abhor this culture; he simply could not overlook the stifling effects it had on nonconformists. He wanted desperately to identify with Afro-American culture, but he took seriously the Christian, humanist values it espoused and the artistic imagination (the nonverbal or literate expressions) it suppressed. As with Wright, Baldwin was intuitively close to Afro-American culture and simultaneously on the edge of it. But, in contrast to Wright, this marginality was an interim condition, not a permanent state. Baldwin could envisage an escape from the inferno which leads to salvation, whereas Wright's vision landed him in a perennial limbo.

The most recent exponents in the Afro-American marginalist tradition are Gayl Jones and Toni Morrison. They illustrate the restrictive boundaries that confine and stifle Afro-American women. Jones's novels, *Corregidora* (1975) and *Eva's Man* (1976), are essentially indictments of the Afro-American male's sexual exploitation of Afro-American females. Both novels are literally monologues or dialogues about deranged sexual relations within a repressive culture, a culture shaped by white racism and further reinforced by Black machismo. Toni Morrison's first two works of fiction, *The Bluest Eye* (1970) and *Sula* (1974), are lucid portraits of what it is like to be a talented Afro-American woman growing up in a strangling culture which punishes creativity and fears nonconformity. Behavioral patterns for women are rigidly set; violation invariably results in marginality. And marginality for imaginative Afro-American women in a machismo culture and hostile white world often leads to personal rebellion and sometimes self-destruction. Morrison captures this progression in a passage from her second novel:

In a way, her strangeness, her naivete, her craving for the other half of her equation was the consequence of an idle imagination. Had she paints, or clay, or knew the discipline of dance, or strings; had she anything to engage her tremendous curiosity and her gift for metaphor, she might have exchanged the restlessness and preoccupation with whim for an activity that provided her with all she yearned for. And like any artist with no art form, she became dangerous.[27]

It is difficult to discern the conception of political struggle in the marginalist tradition. Given the artistic preoccupation of its members, political matters are secondary. If this tradition contains any conception of political struggle at all, it is a highly moralistic one. For example, the frequently cited last chapter of Wright's *Native Son*, which contains Max's speech, more closely resembles a sermon than a Marxist analysis of society.

Baldwin's masterful essays are grounded in moralism, often echoing the rhythm, syncopation, and appeal of an effective sermon. The salient values are love, mercy, grace, and inner freedom. In his famous work *The Fire Next Time* (1963), he views the racial problem as stemming from truncated personal relationships, from the refusal of Black and white Americans to confront each other as human beings. He sees whites as afraid of being judged by Blacks, scared of being seen as they really are; Blacks as viewing themselves through white eyes, so they know little of who they really are. Even Baldwin's more vitriolic writings about social change have a deep moral fiber which speaks to the heart of individuals rather than to a community planning to undertake concerted political action.

The marginalist response to the challenges of self-image and self-determination is this: a candid acceptance of personal marginality to both Afro-American culture and American society plus moral sermonizing to all Americans. The basic concern of this tradition is to loosen the constraints on individuality in Afro-American life. Thus, it does not provide acute observations on political struggle. The Afro-American marginalist tradition is parasitic in that its members accept the self-image found in the assimilationist and humanist camps.

Despite this dependence on other traditions, the marginalist response is important because it grapples with a personal torment endemic to modernity. This torment is an inevitable alienation and sense of revolt from one's racial group, society, and world, if felt only for a few moments. This tradition endorses a marginality which serves as an impetus to creativity.

HUMANIST TRADITION

The humanist self-image of Afro-Americans is one neither of heroic superhumans untouched by the experience of oppression nor of pathetic subhumans devoid of a supportive culture. Rather, Afro-Americans are viewed as both meek and belligerent, kind and cruel, creative and dull—in short, as human beings. This tradition does not romanticize or reject Afro-American culture; instead, it accepts this culture for what it is, the expression of an oppressed human community imposing its distinctive form of order on an existential chaos, explaining its political predicament, preserving its self-respect, and projecting its own special hopes for the future.

The best example of the Afro-American humanist tradition is its music. The rich pathos of sorrow and joy which are simultaneously present in spirituals, the exuberant exhortations and divine praises of the gospels, the soaring lament and lyrical tragicomedy of the blues, and the improvisational character of jazz affirm Afro-American humanity. These distinct art forms, which stem from the deeply entrenched oral and musical traditions of African culture and evolve out of the Afro-American experience, express what it is like to be human under black skin in America. Afro-American musicians are Afro-American humanists par excellence. They relish their musical heritage and search for ways to develop it. This search proceeds without their having to prove to others that this heritage is worth considering, or that it is superior to any other. Rather, the Afro-American musical heritage develops and flourishes by using both its fertile roots and its elements from other musical traditions—from the first religious hymns and work songs through Scott Joplin, Bessie Smith, Louie Armstrong, Mahalia Jackson, Ella Fitzgerald, Duke Ellington, Coleman Hawkins, Lester Young, Billie Holiday, Charlie Parker, Dizzy Gillespie, Ulysses Kay, Miles Davis, Ornette Coleman, John Coltrane, and contemporary Black music.[28] The heritage remains vibrant, with innovation and originality ensuring continual growth. Indeed, it has become one of the definitive elements in American culture.

The chief literary figures of the Afro-American humanist tradition—the young Jean Toomer, Langston Hughes, Zora Neale Hurston, Sterling Brown, and Ralph Ellison—turn to the culture of the Afro-American masses, to blues, jazz, and folklore, as the ingredients of their art. They feel no need to be either superior to whites or marginal to Afro-American culture. They consider themselves relatively secure with their heritage, as well as with those of other groups or nations.

The first major literary expression of Afro-American humanism is found in Jean Toomer's still insufficiently studied *Cane* (1923). This work is a search for Afro-American humanity in the alluring, beautiful, and burdensome Black folk culture of the South. This unconventional collage of poignant stories and poems—which defies traditional literary genres—is a gem, a relatively untapped treasure that yields deep insights into Afro-American culture.

Toomer describes the myriad of constraining effects resulting from the attitudes and beliefs of Afro-Americans in rural settings. He portrays lives of spirituality and degradation. Women are objects, sex is sterile, human relationships are exploitative and painful. The innocent Karintha is treated as a commodity; Becky is caught in a web of miscegenation, hypocrisy, and sympathy; Fern's otherworldly life melts into nothingness, dissolves into anomie.

When Toomer shifts to the urban setting, despair persists, but possible liberation looms. This liberation lies in the artistic shaping of the past, the discovery of self by understanding the spiritual riches of this past. The central characters, Dan and Kabnis, are archetypes of the Afro-American artist. Dan, whose roots stem from the rural South, comes to the urban North with a messianic mission: to remind the "New Negroes" of their roots. He pursues the socially pretentious and haughty Muriel, who avoids him and ignores his message. Nevertheless, he emerges from the confining Afro-American urban world of self-hatred and shame, aware of the grand challenge of creating an ordered view of life from a fading folk past.

This theme of candid confrontation with the past is further illustrated in "Kabnis," the last and longest story in *Cane*. Kabnis is self-effacing and uncomfortable with southern culture, a culture he knows little of. He confronts his roots in the person of Father John, a former slave. Kabnis, a mulatto, has denied any links with slavery by disavowing any Black ancestors. When Father John utters his long-awaited words of wisdom (Christian quips about the sinfulness and mendaciousness of whites), Kabnis is disappointed and angry. He had expected more than mere small talk about an oppressive past, a past, he believes, filled with Black docility fueled by a slave religion. Kabnis is ashamed of this past and looks into the future with perplexed eye.

Toomer's insight is that any acceptable Afro-American self-image begins with unflinching introspection. For an oppressed people, a mere superficial glance will result in self-gratifying celebration of heroic resistance, or self-pitying lament over the great damage done.

Toomer opts for neither alternative. Instead, he looks into the Afro-American past and sees the small yet cumulative struggles of human beings against overwhelming odds, the creation of both supportive values and stifling mores.

His profound message to Afro-Americans is that in modernity, where alienation is commonplace, it is important to be aware of roots, but even this provides no assurance of ability to achieve a positive self-image in the ever-changing present. The search for personal identity is never a pleasant one if only because the very need for it connotes a misplacement, dislocation, and homelessness of the self. The act of self-definition forever remains open-ended, with no guarantee of triumph. Indeed, the process takes precedence over the result, since any static self-identity soon disintegrates the self.

Only a person highly knowledgeable of, and sensitive to, the Afro-American past, moved by its many struggles, though not blind to its shortcomings, could give such a sympathetic and credibly convincing portrait of an old, God-fearing, Christian Black woman as did Langston Hughes with Aunt Hagar in his only novel, *Not Without Laughter* (1930). Although Hughes unequivocally objects to her orthodox religious beliefs, bourgeois values, and white standards, he admires the perseverance and fortitude of Aunt Hagar. Despite adverse circumstances, she endures, with a joy derived from her Christian faith and its Dionysian rituals. Aunt Hagar triumphs over overwhelming odds in her own dynamic and flexible way, without self-hatred, self-pity, or self-deception. She overcomes by pure, unabated struggle.

This simple but profound message of personal and communal struggles—of persistent negation and transformation of prevailing realities—voices the wisdom of Afro-American folklore, blues, and jazz. It guides the con life of Sterling Brown's Slim Greer in *Southern Road* (1932) and the tenuous and ultimately tragic plight of Zora Neale Hurston's Janie in *Their Eyes Were Watching God* (1937).

The Afro-American humanist tradition reached its literary apex in the writings of Ralph Ellison. He stands out among Afro-American humanists, and all Afro-American artists of the other traditions, not only because of the superb mastery of his craft and the acuteness of his mind but also because he takes the Afro-American art forms of the past with more *intellectual seriousness* than do other Afro-American artists. He understands the spirituals, blues, jazz, and folklore of the Afro-American masses to be, not artifacts for self-congratulation or objects of catharsis, but rather aesthetic modes of expression that represent distinctive perceptions of reality. They serve as media of social communication which express the values for the joint communal existence of Afro-Americans. For Ellison, the task of the Afro-American artist is to locate, articulate, and delineate the universal human core of these Afro-American art forms and transform this discovery into a work of art that portrays the complexity and ambiguity of human existence.

In his early Buster-Riley tales and his more sophisticated short stories—especially "Flying Home" (1944) and "King of the Bingo Game" (1944)—Ellison delves into the depths of the Afro-American predicament. Ellison's masterpieces, *Invisible Man* (1952) and *Shadow and Act* (1964)—notwithstanding their exorbitant American optimism and sometimes repetitious themes—remain the most powerful literary works that capture the complexity and diversity of the Afro-American experience. His penetrating portrayal of and profound pronouncements on the Afro-American struggle for freedom presuppose, preserve, and present the humanity of Black people; he also displays this struggle in its psychological, political, metaphysical, and cosmic dimensions.

Ellison indeed is more subtle when dealing with the matter of cultural self-identity than with political self-determination. This is so primarily because of the European literary tradition he cherishes, the American ideology to which he subscribes, and the Afro-American cultural forms in which he revels. Yet, ironically, this obsession with cultural self-identity is precisely his strength. The perennial questions of "Who am I?" "What is a human being?" "What is an American?" and "What is an Afro-American?" are central to the predicament of Black people. And no one else has grappled more seriously (and productively in the qualitative sense) with these questions than Ralph Ellison.

Ellison's deep yet delightful Hickman stories—which cry out for publication in an accessible edition—further testify to my grandiloquent judgment. These stories exemplify his lifelong dedication and devotion to the demanding and difficult task of making known and making plain what Rev. Hickman means when he eloquently exclaims in the powerful sermonlike story, "Juneteenth":

> We know who we are by the way we walk. We know who we are by the way we talk. We know who we are by the way we sing. We know who we are by the way we dance. We know who we are by the way we praise the Lord on high.[29]

In short, Ralph Ellison is the Afro-American literary humanist par excellence.

The major aim of political struggle in the Afro-American humanist tradition is found in the works of the young A. Philip Randolph and Chandler Owen of *The Messenger,* William Jones of the Baltimore *Afro-American* (all three during the 1920s), the later Du Bois, Paul Robeson, post-Mecca Malcolm X, Huey Newton, Angela Davis, the later Amiri Baraka, and the ministry of Rev. Herbert Daughtry.[30] These thinkers share a certain common value: the necessity for the democratic control over institutions in the productive and political processes. The basic assumption of this Afro-American humanist political viewpoint is that the present economic system and social arrangements cannot adequately alleviate the deplorable socioeconomic conditions of the Afro-American masses. This assumption is linked to a corollary claim, namely, that the circumstances of the Black poor and those of the Black working class (including both blue- and white-collar workers) are qualitatively similar and only quantitatively different. In other words, the Afro-American working class merely (yet significantly, in human terms) have higher-paying jobs than the Afro-American lower class; but neither have any meaningful participation in the decision-making process as to who gets hired or fired, nor any control over the production of goods and services.

The ostensible oppressive circumstances of the Afro-American poor and the less visible ones of the Afro-American working class are both linked to the relative powerlessness of Afro-Americans, not only in the political process *but, more important, in the productive process.* This lack of significant control in the work situation also holds for the white poor and working class. Historically, the white poor and working class have served as formidable obstacles for Afro-American enhancement. Racism has been a source of intraclass conflict. But the future looks different. Expansion of interracial unionization in the South, the radicalization of integrated unions in blue- and white-collar occupations, and the concerted push for federalized policy concerning national problems of unemployment and health care may provide the framework for a new era, an era in which the Black and white poor and working classes unite against corporate domination of the economy and government. The Afro-American humanist political viewpoint eagerly endorses and energetically encourages action to make this era a reality.

The humanist political perspective acknowledges the complex interplay between practicality and ideology, electoral politics and structural social change. It discourages ideological programs that have no reasonable chance of succeeding and practical ones that preclude the possibility of fundamentally transforming the present economic system and social arrangements. This perspective supports the continued participation of Afro-Americans in electoral politics, reformist strategies in the political and productive processes, and reasonable radical agitation on persistent issues of common concern.

The humanist response to the challenges of self-image and self-determination is this: a promotion of an individuality strengthened by an honest encounter with the Afro-American past and the expansion of democratic control over the major institutions that regulate lives in America and abroad. This response contrasts sharply with the exceptionalist and assimilationalist ones. It neither romanticizes nor rejects Afro-American culture; it also avoids the self-serving pursuit of status, wealth, and prestige. Instead, the humanist response provides a cultural springboard useful in facing the ever-present issue of self-identity for Afro-Americans and joins their political struggle to other progressive elements in American society.

Afro-American philosophy deems the norms of the humanist tradition desirable. These norms of individuality and democratic control of the political and productive processes are acceptable because they promote personal development, cultural growth, and human freedom. They foster the fulfillment of the potentialities and capacities of all individuals, encourage innovation and originality in Afro-American culture, and expand people's control over those institutions which deeply affect their lives.

In this way, Afro-American philosophy reconstructs the Afro-American past and critically evaluates Afro-American responses to crucial challenges in the present. It attempts to understand the Afro-American experience in order to enhance and enrich the lives of Afro-Americans; it demands personal integrity and political action.

I read Marx as I read all of the influential historical think-ers—from a dialectical point of view, combining a partial yes and a partial no. In so far as Marx posited a metaphysical materialism, an ethical relativism, and a strangulating total-itarianism, I responded with an unambiguous "no"; but in so far as he pointed to weaknesses of traditional capitalism, contributed to the growth of a definite self-consciousness in the masses, and challenged the social conscience of the Christian churches, I responded with a definite "yes."

Martin Luther King Jr.
Stride toward Freedom

It is impossible for capitalism to survive, primarily because the system of capitalism needs some blood to suck. Capital-ism used to be like an eagle, but now it's more like a vulture. It used to be strong enough to go and suck anybody's blood whether they were strong or not. But now it has become more cowardly, like the vulture, and it can only suck the blood of the helpless. As the nations of the world free them-selves, then capitalism has less victims, less to suck, and it becomes weaker and weaker. It's only a matter of time in my opinion before it will collapse completely.

Malcolm X
"Interview in *Young Socialist*"

4

Prophetic Afro-American Christian Thought and Progressive Marxism

Christianity and Marxism are the most vulgarized, distorted traditions in the modern world, yet I believe the alliance of prophetic Christianity and progressive Marxism provides a last humane hope for humankind. In this chapter, I will present a candid dialogical encounter between prophetic Christianity and progressive Marxism, while highlighting the possible dialogue between Afro-American Christian faith and Marxist social analysis. I shall begin with the Marxist critique of the Christian dialectic of human nature and human history and the Christian critique of the Marxist dialectic of human praxis and human history. I then will note briefly the evolution of prophetic Afro-American Christian thought, examine this intellectual tradition in relation to Marxist social analysis, and suggest that an Afro-American Christian critique of capitalist civilization (and, by implication, "really existing" socialist civilization) is the most appropriate manifestation of this tradition in the postmodern period.

THE MARXIST CRITIQUE OF THE CHRISTIAN DIALECTIC OF HUMAN NATURE AND HUMAN HISTORY

The Marxist critique of the Christian dialectic of human nature and human history is that the Christian negation of what is and the transformation of prevailing realities are impotent, incorrect, and ill-informed.[1] They are impotent because they locate ultimate power in a transcendent God who seems to work most effectively beyond history rather than in history, given the historical evidence so far. They are incorrect in that the very positing of such power and such an almighty Being is intellectually unjustifiable and theoretically indefensible. They are ill-informed because they possess highly limited analytical tools and scientific understanding of power and wealth in the prevailing social realities to be negated and transformed.

The Christian reply to these criticisms is to acknowledge the dimension of impotency of its this-worldly liberation project (and all historical projects), accent the absence of (and lack of need for) intellectual "grounds" to justify its leap of faith in God, and admit the extent to which its project is ill-informed.

The Christian project—even the Marxist-informed Christian project—is impotent in the sense that within the historical process, ultimate triumph eludes it and imperfect products plague it. *Yet, more important, there are varying degrees of imperfection and much historical space for human betterment.* For Christians, the dimension of impotency of all historical projects is not an excuse which justifies the existing status quo, but rather a check on utopian aspirations which often debilitate and demoralize those persons involved in negating and transforming the status quo. Ultimate triumph indeed depends on the almighty power of a transcendent God who proleptically acts in history but who also withholds the final, promised negation and transformation of history until an unknown future. In the interim, imperfect human negations and transformations must persist.

The Christian viewpoint accents the absence of intellectual "grounds"—or the need for philosophical "foundations"—for its leap of faith in God or its description of what it is to be a person, what one should hope for and how one ought to act, because an intellectual search for such "grounds" or a philosophical quest for such "foundations" misconstrues the nature of the leap of faith and the content of the Christian description.[2] The justification, confirmation, or validation of the Christian faith is found neither in a persuasive defense of nontemporal divine causality nor in a convincing account of the relationship of God to the world; such defenses merely enact the pleasures of human intellectual rigor and illustrate the limits of human imaginative constructs. Rather, the justification, confirmation, or validation of the Christian faith rests upon the extent to which it promotes the valuing of certain insights, illuminations, capacities, and abilities in order to confront honestly and cope effectively with the ineluctable vicissitudes and unavoidable limit situations in life.

How, then, do we know that particular Christian descriptions are true, that such leaps of faith are warranted? We are forced to acknowledge that there are no ultimate courts of appeal presently available to us; like ultimate triumph, they rest beyond our finite efforts. Every penultimate court of appeal—every human conception of rationality, objectivity, and scientificity—is surreptitiously linked to a particular description or theory of the self, the world, and God. Therefore the spheres of science, art, and religion do not possess privileged access to ultimate truth and reality.

To believe that truth is a property solely of scientific theories which yield reliable predictions and trustworthy explanations is to fall prey to a narrow positivism. To believe that truth is a characteristic only of art objects which portray the complexity of human existence is to succumb to a self-serving aestheticism. To believe that truth is an attribute attached exclusively to religious descriptions which promote certain insights and capacities for living is to give way to an expedient existentialism. Lastly, to believe that there is a transcendental standard—a theory-neutral, portrayal-independent, description-free criterion—which enables us to choose the true theory, portrayal, and description is to resign to an Archimedean objectivism.

Since we can neither reduce truth to the spheres of science, art, and religion nor view the world *sub species aeternitatis* ("from the standpoint of eternity"), we must acknowledge our finitude and fallenness as human beings. This acknowledgment entails that when we say we "know" that a particular scientific theory, art object, or religious description is true, we are actually identifying ourselves with a specific tradition of social practices, group of persons, or community of believers. There indeed may be good reasons why we identify ourselves with particular traditions, groups, or communities. But there are, ultimately, no reasons with the force of logical necessity or universal obligation that justify, confirm, or validate our preferred theories, art objects, and descriptions. In this sense, there is no one scientific theory, artistic portrayal, or religious description that we all must and should acknowledge as necessarily true, but rather there are specific ever-evolving scientific theories, artistic portrayals, and religious descriptions put forward by particular persons, groups, communities, and traditions.

The Christian tradition has generated numerous Christian descriptions of what it is to be a person, what one should hope for, and how

one ought to act; all these descriptions bear the stamp of their inter-
preters, the social and personal problems they faced, and the particular
Christian-informed solutions they offered. These Christian descriptions are neither true nor false, but rather acceptable or inacceptable,
sufficient or insufficient responses to prevailing problematics generated
by the multidimensional human practices of the period.

The paradox of the Christian tradition is that it precludes its own
descriptions from grasping the truth; that is, the Christian notion of the
fallenness of human creatures does not permit even Christian descriptions to be true. This is so, because, for Christians, Jesus Christ is the
Truth and the reality of Jesus Christ always already rests outside any
particular Christian description.

For Christians, truth is not a property, characteristic, or attribute of
a theory, portrayal, and description, not even a Christian description.
Rather, Jesus Christ is the Truth, a reality which can only be existentially appropriated (not intellectually grasped) by fallen human beings
caught in ever-changing finite descriptions. And the fact that this view
itself is but part of a finite Christian description may be trivially self-
contradictory, but, more important, a self-description of our fallenness
and finitude. In short, we are inscribed within the hermeneutical circle
with a dim hope for awareness of the whole, but with no intellectual
access to it.

If there is any test for the "truth" of particular Christian descriptions, it is their capacity to facilitate the existential appropriation of
Jesus Christ. This means that any "true" Christian description makes
the reality of Jesus Christ available, that it encourages the putting of
oneself on the line in the negation of what is and the transformation of
prevailing realities, of going to the edge of life's abyss and finding out
whether the reality of Jesus Christ—though understood through one's
finite Christian description—yields life sustenance, self-formation, self-
maturation, and societal amelioration. For Christians, "truth talk" precludes disinterest, detachment, and distance because the reality of Jesus
Christ continually performs such tasks; that is, Jesus Christ is literally
the Truth, the Truth which cannot be intellectually reified but rather
existentially appropriated by finite human beings with urgent needs and
pressing problems.

Lastly, the Christian viewpoint—in reply to Marxist criticisms—
admits the degree to which its project may be ill-informed. Given
its conception of truth, even Marxist-informed Christians can never
be assured that their particular analysis of a situation or a society is

necessarily correct or error-proof. No viewpoint, analysis, or tradition is immune to revision. Of course, some social analyses are better than others; some aid in alleviating particular problems and some do not. But no acceptance of a dogmatic viewpoint renders one "informed" and those who differ "ill-informed."

THE CHRISTIAN CRITIQUE OF THE MARXIST DIALECTIC OF HUMAN PRAXIS AND HUMAN HISTORY

The Christian critique of the Marxist dialectic of human praxis and human history is that the Marxist negation of what is and the transformation of prevailing realities are naive, narrow, and nearsighted.[3] They are naive in that they exaggerate the Promethean possibilities of persons and valorize in an uncritical manner the scientific method. They are narrow in that they deal almost exclusively with the socioeconomic and political realities of persons, and virtually ignore the existential and cultural dimensions of human life. They are nearsighted in that they provide profound insights and penetrating illuminations of existing capitalist societies, but are blind to the novel social configurations which may usher forth from such societies.

The Marxist reply to these criticisms is to acknowledge the naive elements in its liberation project, accent the narrowness of its concerns, and admit the nearsightedness of its viewpoint.

The Marxist project—even the Christian-informed Marxist project—is naive in the sense that crypto-Christian pessimism regarding the progressive negation of what is and the radical transformation of prevailing realities permeates and pervades postmodern culture so deeply that naive notions of the Promethean possibilities of persons are necessary in order for the oppressed to take seriously any liberation project or vision.

In fact, postmodern times require an exaggeration of human possibility in order to keep alive the very notions of negation and activity of transformation. The Christian and Marxist views regarding human nature clash—and indeed are irreconcilable—but in one-dimensional societies which render revolutionary praxis a utopian dream and oppositional activity a nostalgic memory, naive overstatements of human possibilities resemble divine revelations.[4]

Unfortunately, the Marxist exaggeration of human possibility is inextricably intertwined with an uncritical valorization of scientific method—more specifically, dialectical method. This Marxist attitude of veneration toward the scientificity of its dialectical method not only reflects the origins of Marxism in the heyday of European modernity when the authority of science flourished; it also reveals the captivity of Marxism to the modern ideology of science initiated by the Enlightenment. The fundamental tenet of this ideology is the desirable creation of a scientific monopoly over a subject matter, a master discourse on particular phenomena. Marxism posits itself as warranting its own scientific monopoly over discerning and explaining power and wealth in modern societies; it prides itself as the master discourse on capitalist societies.[5]

The central Marxist notions of class struggle, social contradictions, historical specificity, and dialectical developments in history indeed are helpful for an understanding of power and wealth in bourgeois capitalist societies—as are Max Weber's ideas of rationalization and status or Georg Simmel's conceptions of abstraction and marginality. But the Marxist clamor for scientific standing discloses the will to power which rests at the center of European modernity: the will to cognition and control, manipulation and mastery.

This Marxist veneration of scientific method not only poisons its otherwise smooth linkage with romantic notions of human possibilities; it also adversely affects its relationships with working-class and poor people. The valorizing of scientific method gives prestige and status to those who have access to the method. The rhetoric of science legitimates the formation of hierarchical organizations which reserves its leadership to "scientific Marxists." Working-class and poor people, already suspicious of rhetorics of science which surreptitiously manipulate and control them, come to see many Marxist organizations as what, in part, they are: anti-democratic hierarchical groupings which merely express the modern European will to power.

The Marxist viewpoint accents its narrowness because its almost exclusive concerns with socioeconomic and political realities are the spheres in which it yields its explanatory power and theoretical richness. The existential and cultural dimensions of human life can be understood within Marxist frameworks, as Georg Lukács, Antonio Gramsci, Lucien Goldmann, Jean-Paul Sartre, Fredric Jameson, Stanley Aronowitz, and Terry Eagleson have shown. But the most persuasive and convincing Marxist insights remain those in the spheres of economics and politics (narrowly construed), and the stressing of such spheres in the writing of history. The Marxist tradition indeed may be in need of more sophisticated cultural critics and existential sages;

but to many Marxists, to give up its narrow concerns is to give up its distinctive identity as a mode of discourse and praxis.

Lastly, the Marxist perspective—in reply to Christian criticisms—admits its nearsightedness regarding postcapitalist developments. The culprit here is Hegel. The Hegelian notion of determinate negation subscribes to the idea that only one genuinely new alternative emerges from the clash of contradictory elements within a specific dialectical configuration.[6] The Marxist conception of historical dialectical development leans heavily upon this Hegelian notion of determinate negation. The new alternative to a particular historical epoch bears the stamp of the old, yet yields something new, and the only alternative to the emerging order is a variation of the old. Hence, the choice between capitalism and socialism, fascism and communism, barbarism and humanism. This choice, though possibly containing a kernel of truth, precludes combinations and amalgamations of the two contending systems, as has occurred in the past few decades. This choice also imposes self-serving alternatives to progressive developing nations that would like to sidestep the imperialist West and East.

Yet, as we observed in chapter 1, regardless of the basic differences and subtle disagreements between the Christian viewpoint and the Marxist viewpoint, their prophetic and progressive wings share one fundamental similarity: *commitment to the negation of what is and the transformation of prevailing realities in the light of the norms of individuality and democracy.*

THE EVOLUTION OF BLACK THEOLOGY

In this section, I shall examine briefly the evolution of the prophetic Christian tradition in the Afro-American experience—which I refer to here as Black theology—and suggest that the present expression of this tradition in postmodern times is Black theology as critique of capitalist civilization.

The first stage can be viewed roughly as "Black Theology of Liberation as Critique of Slavery." This stage, lasting approximately from the middle of the seventeenth century to 1863, consisted of Black prophetic Christian viewpoints and actions that were grounded in the Black slave experience and were critical of the institution of slavery. Many petitions of Black Christians during the first two centuries of slavery expressed this prophetic viewpoint. For example, Black Christian slaves wrote in 1779 to the General Assembly of Connecticut:

> We perceive by our own Reflection, that we are endowed with the same Faculties with our masters, and there is nothing that leads us to a Belief, or Suspicion, that we are any more Obliged to serve them, than they us, and the more we Consider of this matter, the more we are Convinced of our Right (by the laws of Nature and by the whole Tenor of the Christian Religion, so far as we have been taught) to be free.[7]

The prophetic Christian view that the gospel stands unequivocally opposed to slavery led, in some cases, to unsuccessful slave revolts spearheaded by Black Christians. In 1800, a young twenty-five-year-old Black prophetic Christian named Gabriel Prosser appealed to the Samson story in the Old Testament, understood himself as the divinely elected deliverer of Black people, and subsequently engaged in the first thoroughly planned and overtly revolutionary attempt to liberate Black people from slavery. According to conservative estimates, this attempt involved over six thousand Black Christians and non-Christians.[8] Like most other slave insurrectionists, young Gabriel was executed. The famous examples and executions of Denmark Vesey (leader of a slave insurrection in 1822) and Nat Turner (leader of a slave insurrection in 1831) also exemplify the cost that Black prophetic Christians were willing to pay in their Christian-inspired fight for liberation.

The major codified theological expression during this stage is found in David Walker's "Appeal to the Coloured Citizens of the World," which appeared in 1829. Walker's Appeal, as it came to be known, is one of the most powerful theological critiques of slavery to emanate from the Black Christian tradition. Gayraud Wilmore, a noted Black Christian social ethicist and historian, goes as far as to state:

> Walker's Appeal is steeped in Biblical language and prophecy. It is certainly one of the most remarkable religious documents of the Protestant era, rivaling in its righteous indignation and Christian radicalism Luther's "Open Letter to the Christian Nobility of the German Nation," published in Wittenberg in 1520.[9]

In his theological antislavery text, Walker proclaims that slavery

> is ten thousand times more injurious to this country than all the other evils put together; and which will be the final overthrow of its

government, unless something is very speedily done; for their cup is nearly full.—Perhaps they will laugh at or make light of this; but I tell you Americans! that unless you speedily alter your course, you and your Country are gone!!!!!! For God Almighty will tear up the very face of the earth!!![10]

The second stage can be viewed as "Black Theology of Liberation as Critique of Institutional Racism." This stage, which occupied a little over a century (1864–1969), found Black prophetic Christians principally focusing attention on the racist institutional structures in the United States which rendered the vast majority of Black people politically powerless (deprived of the right to vote or participate in governmental affairs), economically exploited (in dependent positions as sharecroppers or in unskilled jobs), and socially degraded (separate, segregated, and unequal eating and recreational facilities, housing, education, transportation, and police protection). This period contains the vicious lynchings of hundreds of Black people alongside the historic refusal of President Woodrow Wilson to sign an antilynching law in 1916; there was also the migration of millions of job-hunting Black people into rat-infested dilapidated ghettos in the urban North, which triggered the historic race riots of 1919, 1943, 1964, 1967, and 1968.

It is no accident that many of the salient Black prophetic Christian leaders—such as Bishop Henry McNeal Turner and Marcus Garvey—favored during this stage a return of Black people to Africa. They were led to this viewpoint from their theological critiques of institutional racism in the United States. They held that this institutional racism so deeply pervaded and permeated US society that only emigration to the Black homeland could rid Black people of their immediate oppression.

The most effective Black prophetic Christian leader during this stage was, of course, Martin Luther King Jr. Upon the strength of the Black prophetic church and liberal white allies, he mobilized and organized Black and white people against blatant institutional racism and waged a successful struggle for Black civil rights—integrated transportation, eating, and recreational facilities, and, most important, the right to vote. The tragic murder of King in 1968 triggered some of the worst race riots the United States had ever witnessed, and included the National Guard protecting the White House for the first time since the Civil War. King's death, along with the Black Power movement led by Stokely Carmichael and H. Rap Brown, also precipitated a great wave of the academic expression of Black theological reflection.

Except for pioneer works by Benjamin Mays, Howard Thurman, George Kelsey, and a few others, Black prophetic Christians had not systematically codified their theological viewpoints.[11] But with the publishing of Albert Cleage's *The Black Messiah* (1968) and James Cone's *Black Theology and Black Power* (1969), a third stage commenced: "Black Theology of Liberation as Critique of White North American Theology." In this stage, which lasted less than a decade (1969–1977), we witnessed the first full-fledged academic expression of liberation theology in general and Black theology of liberation in particular in the United States. James Cone's second book, *A Black Theology of Liberation* (1970), deepened a theological discourse in which many Black theologians played a crucial role, including figures such as Cecil Cone (James Cone's brother), Major Jones, William Jones, Charles Long, J. Deotis Roberts, Joseph Washington, Leon Watts, Preston Williams, and Gayraud Wilmore.[12]

This particular stage was an intellectually creative one—partly in response to the spontaneous rebellion of Black people in the streets, the more disciplined political praxis of Black Power groups, and the paralysis of most white North American theologians. Yet the conception of Black theology was, in retrospect, understandably narrow: it focused principally on the failings of white North American theology, especially its silence on racial justice and the white racism within mainstream establishment churches and religious agencies. In response to this criticism, echoed partially by Cecil Cone, Charles Long, and Gayraud Wilmore, James Cone attempted in his next two books—*The Spirituals and the Blues* (1972) and *God of the Oppressed* (1975)—to broaden his focus by delving into Black cultural sources for theological reflection, such as the spirituals, blues, folktales, sermons, and stories. As Cone notes:

> I have learned much from this discussion on Black religion and Black Theology, because there is a basic truth in the critiques of Long, Cone, and Wilmore. . . . If the struggle of the victims is the only context for the development of a genuine Christian theology, then should not theology itself reflect in its speech the language of the people about whom it claims to speak? This is the critical issue. When this assumption is applied to Black Theology, I think that Black religion or the Black religious experience must become one of the important ingredients in the development of a Black Theology.[13]

The fourth stage—and the stage that Black prophetic theologians are presently transcending—can be viewed as "Black Theology of

Liberation as Critique of U.S. Capitalism." With the presentation of two papers at the Black Theology Conference in Atlanta, Georgia, in 1977, Black theological reflection focused on US capitalism as a major enemy of Black people. The one paper, "Message to the Black Church and Community," was that of the Black Theology Project, which is part of a progressive interethnic, interracial, interdenominational Christian organization called Theology in the Americas; the other, James Cone's essay "Black Theology and the Black Church: Where Do We Go from Here?" In the section entitled "The Roots of the Crisis," the Black Theology Project collectively stated:

> The issue for all of us is survival. The root problem is human sinfulness which nurtures monopolistic capitalism, aided by racism and abetted by sexism.
>
> Our crisis is spiritual, material and moral. Black people seem unable to effectively counter disruptive forces that undermine our quality of life. We seem unable to collectively define our situation, discover the nature of our problems, and develop sustained coalitions that can resolve our dilemmas.
>
> Exploitative, profit-oriented capitalism is a way of ordering life fundamentally alien to human value in general and to black humanity in particular. Racism and capitalism have set the stage for despoliation of natural and human resources all around the world. Yet those who seriously challenge these systems are often effectively silenced. We view racism as criminality and yet we are called criminals. We view racism as a human aberration, yet we are called freaks. The roots of our crisis are in social, economic, media and political power systems that prevent us from managing the reality of our everyday lives.
>
> It is this intolerable, alien order that has driven us to Atlanta seeking a word from the Lord out of the wellsprings of black theological tradition.[14]

And in his essay, Cone explicitly notes:

> There is a little in our theological expressions and church practice that rejects American capitalism or recognizes its oppressive character in Third World countries. The time has come for us to move beyond institutional survival in a capitalistic and racist society and begin to take more seriously our dreams about a new heaven and a new earth. Does this dream include capitalism or is it a radically new way of life more consistent with African socialism as expressed in the Arusha Declaration in Tanzania?[15]

This focus was deepened and sharpened by two of my own essays—
"Black Theology and Marxist Thought" (1979) and "Black Theology
and Socialist Thought" (1980)—which, in a sense, initiated a dialogue
between Black prophetic theologians and progressive Marxist thinkers,
as well as practicing socialists and communists.[16] James Cone's latest
essay, "The Black Church and Marxism: What Do They Have to Say
to Each Other?" pursues this crucial dialogue.[17]

Yet the prevailing conception of Black theology of liberation
remains inadequate. I believe that a new conception of Black theology
of liberation is needed which preserves the positive content of its earlier
historical stages, overcomes its earlier (and inevitable) blindnesses, and
makes explicit its present challenges. The positive content of the earlier
conceptions of Black theology of liberation is as follows:

1. The theological claim (or faith claim) that God sides with the
   oppressed and acts on their behalf.
2. The idea that religion of the oppressed can be either an opiate or
   a source of struggle for liberation.
3. The idea that white racism is a cancer at the core of an exploitative capitalist US society.

The limitations and shortcomings of earlier conceptions of Black theology are:

1. Its absence of a systemic social analysis, which has prevented
   Black theologians from coming to terms with the relationships
   between racism, sexism, class exploitation, and imperialist oppression.
2. Its lack of a social vision, political program, and concrete praxis
   which defines and facilitates socioeconomic and political liberation.
3 Its tendency to downplay existential issues such as death, disease,
   dread, despair, and disappointment which are related to, yet not
   identical with, suffering caused by oppressive structures.

The present challenge to Black theologians is to put forward an
understanding of the Christian gospel in the light of present circumstances that takes into account the complex ways in which racism (especially white racism) and sexism (especially male sexism) are integral
to the class-exploitative capitalist system of production as well as its

repressive imperialist tentacles abroad; and to keep in view the crucial existential issues of death, disease, despair, dread, and disappointment that each and every individual must face within the context of these present circumstances. This theological perspective requires a move into a fifth stage: "Black Theology of Liberation as Critique of Capitalist Civilization." In short, Black theological reflection and action must simultaneously become more familiar with and rooted in the progressive Marxist tradition, with its staunch anticapitalist, anti-imperialist, antiracist, and antisexist stance and its creative socialist outlook; and more anchored in its own proto-Kierkegaardian viewpoint, namely, its proper concern with the existential issues facing individuals.

So Black theologians and Marxist thinkers are strangers. They steer clear of each other, content to express concerns to their respective audiences. Needless to say, their concerns overlap. Both focus on the plight of the exploited, oppressed, and degraded peoples of the world, their relative powerlessness and possible empowerment. I believe this common focus warrants a serious dialogue between Black theologians and Marxist thinkers. This dialogue should not be a mere academic chat that separates religionists and secularists, theists and atheists. Instead, it ought to be an earnest encounter that specifies clearly the different sources of their praxis of faith, yet accents the possibility of mutually arrived-at political action.

The primary aim of this encounter is to change the world, not each other's faith; to put both groups on the offensive for structural social change, not put Black Christians on the defensive; and to enhance the quality of life of the dispossessed, not expose the empty Marxist meaning of death. In short, both Black theologians and Marxist thinkers must preserve their own existential and intellectual integrity and explore the possibility of promoting fundamental social amelioration together.

Black theology and Marxist thought are not monolithic bodies of thought; each contains different perspectives, distinct viewpoints, and diverse conclusions. Therefore it is necessary to identify the particular claims put forward by Black theology and by Marxist thought, those claims which distinguish each as a discernible school of thought. Black theology claims:

1. The historical experience of Black people and the readings of the biblical texts that emerge therefrom are the centers around which reflection about God evolves.

2. This reflection is related, in some way, to the liberation of Black people, to the creation of a more abundant life definable in existential, economic, social, and political terms.

Marxist thought contains two specific elements: a theory of history and an understanding of capitalism. These two elements are inextricably interlinked, but it may be helpful to characterize them separately. The Marxist theory of history claims:

1. The history of human societies is the history of their transitional stages.
2. The transitional stages of human societies are discernible owing to their systems of production, or their organizational arrangements in which people produce goods and services for their survival.
3. Conflict within systems of production of human societies ultimately results in fundamental social change, or transitions from one historical stage to another.
4. Conflict within systems of production of human societies consists of cleavages between social classes (in those systems of production).
5. Social classes are historically transient, rooted in a particular set of socioeconomic conditions.
6. Therefore, the history of all hitherto existing society is the history of class struggles.

The Marxist theory of capitalist society claims: Capitalism is a historically transient system of production which requires human beings to produce commodities for the purpose of maximizing surplus value (profits). This production presupposes a fundamental social relationship between the purchasers and the sellers of a particular commodity, namely, the labor power (time, skill, and expertise) of producers. This crucial commodity is bought by capitalists who own the land, instruments, and capital necessary for production; it is sold by producers, whose labor power is needed for production. The aim of the former is to maximize profits; that of the latter, to ensure their own survival.

I shall claim that Black theology and Marxist thought share three characteristics. First, both adhere to a similar methodology: they have the same way of approaching their respective subject matter and arriving at conclusions. Second, both link some notion of liberation to the future socioeconomic conditions of the downtrodden. Third, and most important, both attempt to put forward trenchant critiques of liberal capitalist America. I will try to show that these three traits provide a springboard for a meaningful dialogue between Black theologians and Marxist thinkers and possibly spearhead a unifying effort for structural social change in liberal capitalist America.

DIALECTICAL METHODOLOGY:
UNMASKING FALSEHOODS

Black theologians have either consciously or unconsciously employed a dialectical methodology in approaching their subject matter. This methodology consists of a three-step procedure of negation, preservation, and transformation; their subject matter, of white interpretations of the Christian gospel and their own circumstances. Dialectical methodology is critical in character and hermeneutic in content.[18] For Black theologians, it is highly critical of dogmatic viewpoints of the gospel, questioning whether certain unjustifiable prejudgments are operative. It is hermeneutic in that it is concerned with unearthing assumptions of particular interpretations and presenting an understanding of the gospel that extends and expands its ever-unfolding truth.

Black theologians have, for the most part, been compelled to adopt a dialectical methodology. They have refused to accept what has been given to them by white theologians; they have claimed that all reflection about God by whites must be digested, decoded, and deciphered. The first theological formulations by Afro-Americans based on biblical texts tried to come to terms with their white owners' viewpoints and their own servitude. Since its inception, Black theology has been forced to reduce white deception and distortion of the gospel and make the Christian story meaningful in the light of their oppressive conditions.

The reflection by Black theologians begins by negating white interpretations of the gospel, continues by preserving their own perceived truths of the biblical texts, and ends by transforming past understandings of the gospel into new ones. These three steps embody an awareness of the social context of theologizing, the need to accent the historical experience of Black people and the insights of the Bible, and the ever-evolving task of recovering, regaining, and repeating the gospel.

Black theologians underscore the importance of the social context of theological reflection.[19] Their dialectical methodology makes them sensitive to the hidden agendas of the theological formulations they negate, agendas often guided by social interests. Their penchant for revealing distortions leads them to adopt a sociology of knowledge approach that stresses the way in which particular viewpoints endorse and encourage ulterior aims.

An interpretation of the Black historical experience and the readings of the biblical texts that emerge out of this experience constitute the raw ingredients for the second step of Black theological reflection. By trying to understand the plight of Black people in the light of the Bible, Black theologians claim to preserve the biblical truth that God sides with the oppressed and acts on their behalf.[20] Subsequently, the Black historical experience and the biblical texts form a symbiotic relationship, each illuminating the other.

Since Black theologians believe in the living presence of God and the work of the Holy Spirit, they acknowledge the constant unfolding process of the gospel. Paradoxically, the gospel is unchanging, yet it is deepened by embracing and encompassing new human realities and experiences. The gospel must speak to every age. Therefore it must be recovered and repeated, often sounding different, but in substance remaining the same. For Black theologians, it sounds different because it addresses various contexts of oppression; it remains the same because it is essentially a gospel of liberation.

Marxist thinkers, like Black theologians, employ a dialectical methodology in approaching their subject matter. But they do so consciously and their subject matter is bourgeois theories about capitalist society. The primary theoretical task of Marxist thinkers is to uncover the systematic misunderstanding of capitalist society by bourgeois thinkers; to show how this misunderstanding, whether deliberate or not, supports and sanctions exploitation and oppression in this society; and to put forward the correct understanding of this society in order to change it.

Marxist social theory is first and foremost a critique of inadequate theories of capitalist society and subsequently a critique of capitalist society itself. The subtitle of Marx's magnum opus, *Capital*, is "A Critique of Political Economy," not "A Critique of Capitalism." This work takes bourgeois economists to task for perpetuating falsehoods, which then results in revealing the internal dynamics of capitalism and the inhumane consequences. For Marx, a correct understanding of capitalist society is possible only by overcoming present mystifications of it; and this correct understanding is requisite for a propitious political praxis.

Marxist thought stresses the conflict-laden unfolding of history, the conflict-producing nature of social processes. Therefore it is not surprising that Marxist thinkers employ a dialectical methodology, a methodology deeply suspicious of stasis and stability, and highly skeptical of equilibrium and equipoise. This methodology, like that of Black theologians, is critical in character and hermeneutic in content. It is critical of perspectives presented by bourgeois social scientists, questioning whether certain ideological biases are operative. It is hermeneutic in that it is obsessed with discovering the correct understanding underneath wrong interpretations, disclosing latent truths behind manifest distortions. For Marx, to be scientific is to be dialectical and to be dialectical is to unmask, unearth, to bring to light.[21]

This conception of science, derived from Hegel, attempts to discern the hidden kernel of an evolving truth becoming manifest by bursting through a visible husk. The husk, once a hidden kernel, dissolves, leaving its indelible imprint upon the new, emerging kernel. This idea of inquiry highlights the moments of negation, preservation, and transformation. By presenting his theory of history and society from this perspective, Marx provided the most powerful and penetrating social criticism in modern times. Dialectical methodology enabled him to create a whole mode of inquiry distinctively his own, though often appearing hermetic and rigid to the untutored and the fanatic.

Despite the similar procedure that Black theologians and Marxist thinkers share, there has been little discussion about it between them. This is so, primarily because a dialectical methodology is implicit, hence undeveloped and often unnoticed, in Black theology. This failure to examine the methodological stance embodied in Black theological reflection obscures its similarity with that of Marxist thought.

LIBERATION: ITS CONSTITUTIVE ELEMENTS

Black theologians all agree that Black liberation has something to do with ameliorating the socioeconomic conditions of Black people. But it is not clear what this amelioration amounts to. There is little discussion in their writings about what the liberating society will be like. The notion and the process of liberation are often mentioned, but, surprisingly, one is hard put to find a sketch of what liberation would actually mean in the everyday lives of Black people, what power they would possess, and what resources they would have access to.

There are two main reasons for this neglect among Black theologians. First, a dialectical methodology discourages discussions about the ideal society and simply what ought to be. Instead, it encourages criticizing and overcoming existing society, negating and opposing what is.

The second reason, the one we shall be concerned with in this section, is the failure of Black theologians to talk specifically about the way in which the existing system of production and the social structure relate to Black oppression and exploitation. Without a focus on this relationship, it becomes extremely difficult to present an idea of liberation with socioeconomic content. In short, the lack of a clear-cut social theory prevents the emergence of any substantive political program or social vision.

Aside from James Cone in his latest writings, Black theologians remain uncritical of America's imperialist presence in Third World countries, its capitalist system of production, and its grossly unequal distribution of wealth. Therefore we may assume they find this acceptable. If this is so, then the political and socioeconomic components of Black liberation amount to racial equality before the law, equal opportunities in employment, education, and business, and economic parity with whites in median income.

Surely, this situation would be better than the current dismal one, but it hardly can be viewed as Black liberation. It roughly equates liberation with American middle-class status, leaving the unequal distribution of wealth relatively untouched and the capitalist system of production, along with its imperialist ventures, intact. Liberation would consist of including Black people within the mainstream of liberal capitalist America. If this is the social vision of Black theologians, they should drop the meretricious and flamboyant term "liberation" and adopt the more accurate and sober word "inclusion."

Marxist thought, like Black theology, does not elaborate on the ideal society. As we noted earlier, a dialectical methodology does not permit this elaboration. But the brief sketch that progressive Marxist thinkers provide requires a particular system of production and political arrangement—namely, participatory democracy in each. Human liberation occurs only when people participate substantively in the decision-making processes in the major institutions that regulate their lives. Democratic control over the institutions in the productive and political processes in order for them to satisfy human needs and protect personal liberties of the populace constitutes human liberation.

Progressive Marxist thinkers are able to present this sketch of human liberation primarily because they stress what people must liberate themselves from. They suggest what liberation is for only after understanding the internal dynamics of the society from which people must be liberated. Without this clear-cut social theory about what is, it is difficult to say anything significant about what can be. The possibility of liberation is found only within the depths of the actuality of oppression. Without an adequate social theory, this possibility is precluded.

SOCIAL CRITICISM: CLASS, RACE, AND CULTURE

Black theology puts forward a vehement, often vociferous, critique of liberal capitalist America. One of its most attractive and alluring characteristics is its theological indictment of racist American society. An undisputable claim of Black theology is America's unfair treatment of Black people. What is less apparent is the way in which Black theologians understand the internal dynamics of liberal capitalist America, how it functions, why it operates the way it does, who possesses substantive power, and where it is headed. As noted earlier, Black theologians do not utilize a social theory that relates the oppression of Black people to the overall makeup of America's system of production, foreign policy, political arrangement, and cultural practices.

Black theologians hardly mention the wealth, power, and influence of multinational corporations that monopolize production in the marketplace and prosper partially because of their dependence on public support in the form of government subsidies, free technological equipment, lucrative contracts, and sometimes even direct transfer payments. Black theologians do not stress the way in which corporate interests and the government intermesh, usually resulting in policies favorable to the former. Black theologians fail to highlight the fact that in liberal capitalist America one half of 1 percent own 22 percent of the wealth, 1 percent own 33 percent of the wealth, the lower 61 percent own only 7 percent of the wealth, and the bottom 45 percent own only 2 percent of the wealth.[22] Lastly, Black theologians do not emphasize sufficiently the way in which the racist interpretations of the gospel they reject encourage and support the capitalist system of production, its grossly unequal distribution of wealth, and its closely connected political arrangements.

Instead of focusing on these matters, Black theologians draw attention to the racist practices in American society. Since these practices constitute the most visible and vicious form of oppression in America, Black theologians justifiably do so. Like the Black Power proponents of the 1960s, they call for the empowerment of Black people, the need for Black people to gain significant control over their lives. But neither Black Power proponents nor Black theologians have made it sufficiently clear as to what constitutes this Black control, the real power to direct institutions such that Black people can live free of excessive exploitation and oppression. The tendency is to assume that middle-class status is equivalent to such control, that a well-paying job amounts to such power. Surely, this assumption is fallacious.

The important point here is not that racist practices should be stressed less by Black theologians, for such practices deeply affect Black people and shape their perceptions of American society. What is crucial is that these practices be linked to the role they play in buttressing the current mode of production, concealing the unequal distribution of wealth, and portraying the lethargy of the political system. Black theologians are correct in relating racist practices to degrees of Black powerlessness, but they obscure this relation by failing to provide a lucid definition of what power is in American society. Subsequently, they often fall into the trap of assuming power in American society to be synonymous with receiving high wages.

Marxist social criticism can be quite helpful at this point. For Marx, power in modern industrial society consists of a group's participation in the decision-making processes of the major institutions that affect their destinies. Since institutions of production, such as multinational corporations, play an important role in people's lives, these institutions should be significantly accountable to the populace. In short, they should be democratically controlled by the citizenry; people should participate in their decision-making processes. Only collective control over the major institutions of society constitutes genuine power on behalf of the people.

For Marx, power in modern industrial society is closely related to a group's say over what happens to products produced in the work situation, to a group's input into decisions that direct the production flow of goods and services. The most powerful group in society has the most say and input into decisions over this production flow; the least powerful group does not participate at all in such decisions. In liberal capitalist America, the former consist of multiple corporate owners who dictate policies concerning the mass production of a variety of products produced by white- and blue-collar workers who receive wages in return. The latter consist of the so-called underclass, the perennially unemployed who are totally removed from the work situation, precluded from any kind of input affecting the production flow, including negotiation and strikes available to white- and blue-collar workers.

Racist practices intensify the degree of powerlessness among Black people. This is illustrated by the high rate of Black unemployment, the heavy Black concentration in low-paying jobs, and inferior housing, education, police protection, and health care. But it is important to note that this powerlessness differs from that of white- and blue-collar workers in degree, not in kind. In human terms, this difference is immense, incalculable; in structural terms, this difference is negligible, trifling. In other words, most Americans are, to a significant degree, powerless. They have no substantive control over their lives, little participation in the decision-making process of the major institutions that regulate their lives. Among Afro-Americans, this powerlessness is exacerbated, creating an apparent qualitative difference in oppression.

This contrast of the social criticism of Black theologians and Marxist thinkers raises the age-old question as to whether class position or racial status is the major determinant of Black oppression in America. This question should be formulated in the following way: whether class position or racial status contributes most to the fundamental form of powerlessness in America.

Racial status contributes greatly to Black oppression. But middle-class Black people are essentially well-paid white- or blue-collar workers who have little control over their lives primarily because of their class position, not their racial status. This is so because the same limited control is held by white middle-class people, despite the fact that a higher percentage of whites are well-paid white- and blue-collar workers than Blacks. Significant degrees of powerlessness pertain to most Americans and this could be so only if class position determines such powerlessness. Therefore, class position contributes more than racial status to the basic form of powerlessness in America.

I am suggesting that the more Black theologians discard or overlook Marxist social criticism, the farther they distance themselves from the fundamental determinant of Black oppression and any effective strategy to alleviate it. This distancing also obscures the direct relationship of Black oppression in America to Black and Brown oppression in Third World countries. The most powerful group in America, those multiple corporate owners who dictate crucial corporate policies over a variety of production flows, are intimately and inextricably linked (through their highly paid American and Third World white-collar workers and grossly underpaid Third World blue-collar workers) to the economies and governments of Third World countries, including the most repressive ones. Marxist social criticism permits this relationship to come to light in an extremely clear and convincing way.

The social criticism of Black theologians reflects the peculiar phenomenon of American liberal and radical criticism. This criticism rarely has viewed class position as a major determinant of oppression primarily because of America's lack of a feudal past, the heterogeneity of its population, the many and disparate regions of its geography, and the ever-increasing levels of productivity and growth. These facts make it difficult to see class divisions, and, along with other forms of oppression, make it almost impossible. But, like protons leaving vapor trails in a cloud chamber, one is forced to posit them in the light of the overwhelming evidence for their existence. Only class divisions can explain the gross disparity between rich and poor, the immense benefits accruing to the former and the depravity of the latter.

Region, sex, age, ethnicity, and race often have been considered the only worthy candidates as determinants of oppression. This has been so primarily because American liberal and radical criticism usually has presupposed the existing system of production, assumed class divisions, and attempted only to include marginal groups in the mainstream of liberal capitalist America. This criticism has fostered a petit bourgeois viewpoint that clamors for a bigger piece of the ever-growing American pie, rarely asking fundamental questions such as why it never gets recut more equally or how it gets baked in the first place. In short, this criticism remains silent about class divisions, the crucial role they play in maintaining the unequal distribution of goods and services, and how they undergird discrimination against regions, impose ceilings on upward social mobility, and foster racism, sexism, and ageism. As has been stated above, with the exception of James Cone in his most recent writings contemporary Black theologians suffer from this general myopia of American liberal and radical criticism.

Despite this shortsightedness, Black theologians have performed an important service for Marxist thinkers, namely, emphasizing the ways in which culture and religion resist oppression. They have been admirably sensitive to the Black cultural buffers against oppression, especially the Black religious sources of struggle and strength, vitality and vigor. They also have stressed the indispensable contribution the

Black churches have made toward the survival, dignity, and self-worth of Black people.

Contrary to Marxist thinkers, Black theologians recognize that cultural and religious attitudes, values, and sensibilities have a life and logic of their own, not fully accountable in terms of a class analysis. Subsequently, racist practices are not reducible to a mere clever and successful strategy of divide and conquer promoted by the ruling class to prevent proletarian unity. Rather, racism is an integral element within the very fabric of American culture and society. It is embedded in the country's first collective definition, enunciated in its subsequent laws, and imbued in its dominant way of life.

The orthodox Marxist analysis of culture and religion that simply relates racist practices to misconceived material interests is only partially true, hence deceptive and misleading. These practices are fully comprehensible only if one conceives of culture, not as a mere hoax played by the ruling class on workers, but as the tradition that informs one's conception of tradition, as social practices that shape one's idea of social practice.

The major objection to the orthodox Marxist analysis of culture and religion is not that it is wrong, but that it is too narrow, rigid, and dogmatic. It views popular culture and religion only as instruments of domination, vehicles of pacification. It sees only their negative and repressive elements. On this view, only enlightenment, reason, or clarity imposed from the outside can break through the cultural layers of popular false consciousness.[23] Therefore, the orthodox Marxist analysis refuses to acknowledge the positive, liberating aspects of popular culture and religion, and their potential for fostering structural social change.

This issue is at the heart of the early stages of the debate over the adequacy of a Marxist analysis between Black theologians and Latin American liberation theologians. The latter tended to adopt the orthodox Marxist view, paying little attention to the positive, liberating aspects of popular culture and religion.[24] They displayed a contempt for popular culture and religion, a kind of tacit condescension that reeks of paternalism and elitism. They often spoke of the poor possessing a privileged access to truth and reality, but rarely did they take seriously the prevailing beliefs, values, or outlooks of the poor. Instead, Latin American liberation theologians stressed the discontinuity and radical rupture of progressive consciousness with popular culture and religion, suggesting a desire to wipe the cultural slate clean and begin anew.

To the contrary, Black theologians recognize the positive and negative elements, the liberating and repressive possibilities, of popular culture and religion. To no surprise, they devote much attention to the armors of survival, forms of reaction, and products of response created by Black people in order to preserve their dignity and self-respect.[25] Black theologians view themselves as working within a tradition of political struggle and cultural and religious resistance to oppression. They emphasize their continuity with this tradition.

It is possible to account for this important early difference between Black theologians and Latin American liberation theologians by appealing to the different histories of the particular countries about which they theorize. But there is possibly a deeper reason for this disagreement. It relates directly to the composition of the two groups of theologians.

For the most part, Latin American liberation theologians belong to the dominant cultural group in their respective countries. As intellectuals educated in either European schools or Europeanized Latin American universities and seminaries, they adopt cosmopolitan habits and outlooks.[26] Like their theoretical master Karl Marx, a true cosmopolitan far removed from his indigenous Jewish culture, they tend to see popular culture and religion as provincial and parochial. It is something to be shed and ultimately discarded, replaced by something qualitatively different and better. They do not seem to have encountered frequently situations in which they were forced to rely on their own indigenous cultural and religious resources in an alien and hostile environment. So their own experiences often limit their capacity to see the existential richness and radical potential of popular culture and religion.

In contrast to this, Black theologians belong to the degraded cultural group in the United States. As intellectuals trained in American colleges, universities, and seminaries, they have firsthand experience of cultural condescension, arrogance, and haughtiness. They know what it is like to be a part of a culture considered to be provincial and parochial. Hence, they view Black culture and religion as something to be preserved and promoted, improved and enhanced, not erased and replaced. In short, Black theologians acknowledge their personal debts to Black culture and religion, and incorporate its fecundity and fertility in their understanding of American society.

Latin American liberation theologians and Black theologians can learn from each other on this matter. The former must be more sensitive to the complexities and ambiguities of popular culture and religion; the latter should relate more closely their view of Black culture and religion to a sophisticated notion of power in liberal capitalist America. And both can learn from the most penetrating Marxist theorist of culture in this century, Antonio Gramsci.[27]

Gramsci provides a valuable framework in which to understand culture, its autonomous activity and status, while preserving its indirect yet crucial link with power in society. Unlike the Latin American liberation theologians, he does not downplay the importance of popular culture; unlike the Black theologians, he does not minimize the significance of class. Instead, he views the system of production and culture in a symbiotic relationship, each containing intense tension, struggle, and even warfare. Class struggle is not simply the battle between capitalists and the proletariat, owners and producers in the work situation. It also takes the form of cultural and religious conflict over which attitudes, values, and beliefs will dominate the thought and behavior of people. For Gramsci, this incessant conflict is crucial. It contains the key to structural social change; it is the springboard for a revolutionary political praxis.

According to Gramsci, no state or society can be sustained by force alone. It must put forward convincing and persuasive reasons, arguments, ideologies, or propaganda for its continued existence. A state or society requires not only military protection but also principled legitimation. This legitimation takes place in the cultural and religious spheres, in those arenas where the immediacy of everyday life is felt, outlooks formed, and self-images adopted.

Gramsci deepens Marx's understanding of the legitimation process by replacing the notion of ideology with his central concept of hegemony. For Marx, ideology is the set of formal ideas and beliefs promoted by the ruling class for the purpose of preserving its privileged position in society; for Gramsci, hegemony is the set of formal ideas and beliefs and informal modes of behavior, habits, manners, sensibilities, and outlooks that support and sanction the existing order.

In Gramsci's view, culture is both tradition and current practices. Tradition is understood, not as the mere remnants of the past or the lingering, inert elements in the present, but rather as active formative and transformative modalities of a society. Current practices are viewed as actualizations of particular modalities, creating new habits, sensibilities, and worldviews against the pressures and limits of the dominant ones.

A hegemonic culture subtly and effectively encourages people to identify themselves with the habits, sensibilities, and worldviews supportive of the status quo and the class interests that dominate it. It is a culture successful in persuading people to "consent" to their oppression and exploitation. A hegemonic culture survives and thrives as long as it convinces people to adopt its preferred formative modality, its favored socialization process. It begins to crumble when people start to opt for a transformative modality, a socialization process that opposes the dominant one. The latter constitutes a counterhegemonic culture, the deeply embedded oppositional elements within a society. It is these elements the hegemonic culture seeks to contain and control.

Basing my study on the insights of Gramsci, along with those of the distinguished English cultural critic Raymond Williams, I shall present a theoretical framework that may be quite serviceable to Black theologians, Latin American liberation theologians, and Marxist thinkers.[28] Cultural processes can be understood in the light of four categories: hegemonic, prehegemonic, neohegemonic, and counterhegemonic.

Hegemonic culture is to be viewed as the effectively operative dominant worldviews, sensibilities, and habits that sanction the established order. Prehegemonic culture consists of those residual elements of the past which continue to shape and mold thought and behavior in the present; it often criticizes hegemonic culture, harking back to a golden age in the pristine past. Neohegemonic culture constitutes a new phase of hegemonic culture; it postures as an oppositional force, but, in substance, is a new manifestation of people's allegiance and loyalty to the status quo. Counterhegemonic culture represents genuine opposition to hegemonic culture; it fosters an alternative set of habits, sensibilities, and worldviews that cannot possibly be realized within the perimeters of the established order.

This framework presupposes three major points. First, it accents the equivocal character of culture and religion, their capacity to be instruments of freedom or domination, vehicles of liberation or pacification. Second, it focuses on the ideological function of culture and religion, the necessity of their being either forces for freedom or domination, liberation or pacification. Third, it views the struggle between these two forces as open-ended. The only guarantee of freedom rests upon the contingencies of human practice; the only assurance of liberation relies on the transformative modalities of a society. No matter how wide the scope of hegemonic culture may be, it never encompasses or exhausts all human practice or every transformative modality in a society. Human struggle is always a possibility in any society and culture.

In order to clarify further my four categories, I shall identify them crudely with particular elements in contemporary American society. Hegemonic culture can be seen as the prevailing Horatio Alger mystique, the widespread hopes and dreams for social upward mobility among Americans. This mystique nourishes the values, outlooks, and lifestyles of achievement, careerism, leisurism, and consumerism that pervade American culture. Prehegemonic culture is negligible, owing to the country's peculiar inception, namely, that it was "born liberal." Subsequently, American conservatives and reactionaries find themselves in the ironic position of quarreling with liberals by defending early versions of liberalism. Neohegemonic culture is best illustrated by the countercultural movement of the 1960s, specifically the protests of white middle-class youth (principally spin-offs of the Black political struggles), which with few exceptions was effectively absorbed by the mainstream of liberal capitalist America. The continuous creation of a counterhegemonic culture is manifest in the multifarious, though disparate, radical grass-roots organizations; elements of the socialist feminist groups; and aspects of Afro-American culture and religion.

A present challenge confronting Black theologians is to discover and discern what aspects of Afro-American culture and religion can contribute to a counterhegemonic culture in American society. They may find Gramsci's conception of organic intellectuals helpful on this matter.[29] Gramsci views organic intellectuals as leaders and thinkers directly tied into a particular cultural group primarily by means of institutional affiliations. Organic intellectuals combine theory and action, and relate popular culture and religion to structural social change.

Black religious leadership can make an enormous contribution to a counterhegemonic culture and structural social change in American society. Black preachers and pastors are in charge of the most numerous and continuous gatherings of Black people, those who are the worst victims of liberal capitalist America and whose churches are financially, culturally, and politically free of corporate influence.[30] This freedom of Black preachers and pastors, unlike that of most Black professionals, is immense. They are the leaders of the only major institutions in the Black community that are not accountable to the status quo. Needless to say, many abuse this freedom. But what is important to note is that the contribution of Black religious leaders can be prodigious, as exemplified by the great luminaries of the past, including Nat Turner, Martin Delaney, Martin Luther King Jr., and Malcolm X.

BLACK THEOLOGY AS CRITIQUE
OF CAPITALIST CIVILIZATION

I will try to explain what I mean by the vague word "critique." First, I understand this term in a Marxian way; that is, critique is not simply moral criticism of a state of affairs. Rather, critique is a theoretical praxis which

1. Presupposes a sophisticated understanding of the internal dynamics or power relations of a society or civilization. This understanding requires a social theory whose aim is to demystify present ideological distortions or misreadings of society, to bring to light who possess power and wealth, why they do, how they acquired it, how they sustain and enlarge it, and why the poor have little or nothing.
2. Is integrally linked with a praxis of faith or political movement which is capable in the near future of fundamentally transforming the present order.
3. Is capable of ushering forth a new order, of organizing, administering, and governing a more humane social order.

Therefore the crucial characteristics of an acceptable and appropriate critique are moral sensitivity to the plight of the exploited and oppressed; high-level social analysis of the sources of exploitation and oppression; objective possibility of weakening the present order; and praxis of faith or political movement with organization, power, and social vision, with leaders of impeccable integrity.

Let us look briefly at the capitalist system of production which undergirds what I call "capitalist civilization." Capitalism is an *antidemocratic* mode of socioeconomic organization in that it requires the removal of control of production from those engaged in production. Capitalism is a particular system of production in which capital accumulation for profit maximization is achieved at the expense of excluding democratic participation (of those principally responsible for production) in investment decisions. At present, capitalism is inseparable from imperialism in that the latter is an extension of capitalism across national borders and political boundaries. Imperialism is a system of capital accumulation for profit maximization based on a developed country's acquisition of control over the land and means of production in less developed countries. This control is preserved and protected by the military and political resources of developed countries. Multinational corporations—the "materializations" of international capital—are the principal controllers of the land and the means of production in less developed countries.

The antidemocratic character of capitalism can be seen most clearly in its present imperialist manifestation. On the one hand, capital accumulation for profit maximization requires that multinational corporations promote its products no matter how appropriate these products may be for the less developed countries; and the effect of the multinationals' stronghold on the local economy is to restrict local entrepreneurs to low-return routine kinds of production. On the other hand, the products promoted by multinationals (principally luxury consumer goods) find their market primarily among the elite groups in less developed countries.

This mode of capital accumulation contributes to antidemocratic conditions in two basic ways. First, it encourages the exclusion of producers—and casts the organizing efforts of workers in a negative light—since an increase in wages would threaten the attractiveness of a less developed country as a site for multinational corporate investment. Second, this mode of capital accumulation contributes to gross economic and class inequality, since it ensures a market for multinational products geared principally to the affluent. This dialectic of capital accumulation and political exclusion often leads to military rule and abominable repression—under the guise of "development" or "democratic openings."[31]

Let us look briefly at what I mean by "civilization." Civilization is often understood as an achieved condition or way of life characterized by refinement and order.[32] I understand "civilization" in my phrase "capitalist civilization" as those self-images and self-identities, values and sensibilities, institutions and associations, ways of life and ways of struggle which are shaped and molded by the four major kinds of oppression in our time: imperialist oppression, class exploitation, racial oppression, and sexual oppression. The concrete consequences of these forms of oppression are not only poverty, disease, lack of self-esteem, and despair but also the suppression of individuality (or self-realization within community). Ironically, the ethos of rapacious individualism in capitalist civilization prohibits the flowering of individuality.

Capitalist civilization is circumscribed primarily by the two major modern historical events and processes: the Industrial Revolution and bourgeois political revolutions. These two epoch-making historical processes reinforced the four major types of oppression—and these kinds of oppression persist in so-called "postindustrial" capitalist societies.

Let us look briefly at both the Industrial Revolution and the American bourgeois political "revolution" to see why this is so.

The Industrial Revolution can be defined as "the triumph of capitalist industry which results in the creation of a mechanized production unit which yields such vast quantities of goods and products and at such rapidly diminishing cost as to be no longer dependent on existing demand, but to create its own market."[33] The Industrial Revolution, as is well known, emerged and escalated in the late eighteenth century in Britain. Britain was the fertile soil for this flowering, not because of its scientific advancement or technological superiority—France and Germany were far ahead in these areas—but rather because of its rapid and propitious dissolution of the feudal British peasantry and the strong commitment of its government to economic development. Britain had, by various means (Enclosure Acts, etc.), transformed its old collective economy of the feudal village into a capitalist mode of agricultural production, that is, into a few profit-oriented landlords and a moderate number of tenant farmers who employed a large number of landless, hired laborers. This capitalist mode of agricultural production was geared primarily to feed a rising nonagricultural, urbanized population and to yield a surplus for the accumulation of capital to be used for further industrialized differentiation in the economy.

Primarily because of overseas colonial trade and the cheapest labor available—namely, African slaves in the diaspora—the cotton industry was the first major industry to be revolutionized. The cotton industry, whose raw materials were literally picked by the hands of African slaves, was the first to secure a large export market and thereby ensure rapid expansion. It also was the first major industry to establish mass production, as witnessed in the famous Lancashire mills, the very symbols of the first stages of the Industrial Revolution. In short, the cotton industry was the modus operandi of the early stages of the Industrial Revolution, the heart of Britain's economy. As Eric Hobsbawm has noted:

> Cotton manufacturers formed between 40 and 50 per cent of the annual declared value of *all* British exports between 1816 and 1848. If cotton flourished, the economy flourished, if it slumped, so did the economy.[34]

This brief yet important illustration of the first major industry to be revolutionized displays the central presence of the four types of oppressions mentioned earlier. Forms of class exploitation occurred in both the cotton plantations in the Americas and in the mills in

Britain; imperialist oppression took place in Britain's control of territory, resources, and people in the Americas; racism provided the chief ideological justification for the use of Africans as slaves in the Americas; and sexism was employed to defend the abuse of women both on the plantations in the Americas and within the mills in Britain.

This crude example can serve as a microcosm of the kind of self-images and self-identities, values and sensibilities, institutions and associations, ways of life and ways of struggle required and reinforced by the capitalist system of production. Already we can see the contours that partially shape and mold capitalist civilization: how the profit-maximizing activity of a few is integrally linked to the dehumanization of the many; the collapse of organic communities and the growth of impersonal bureaucratic control; the prohibition of individuality owing to prevailing norms of possessive individualism; the richness and plurality of cultures discouraged in lieu of a shoddy, homogenizing cosmopolitanism. And, most important, the early stages of the Industrial Revolution embody and prefigure, promote and encourage the idea of white supremacy and male supremacy. In short, from its emergence through its duration to its decline, capitalist civilization remains racist and sexist at its core and based upon class exploitation and imperialist oppression.

The four major types of oppression also set the framework for our view of the American bourgeois political "revolution." This event, along with the crucial French Revolution, provided the emerging capitalist civilization with its liberal political language, its rhetorical self-understanding. The grand ideals of liberty and equality, the principles of procedural justice, and the notion of participatory democracy were—and remain—restricted and restrained by the cancers of class exploitation, imperialist oppression, racism, and sexism. Even the most cherished idea of bourgeois political revolutions—namely, that of the nation-state or nationalism—is opposed by the profit-making activity of firms (and later corporations) of capitalist civilization which have more loyalty to self-aggrandizement than allegiance to their native territories. And, of course, at its inception, the United States government in its Constitution excluded Africans (or fifth-generation Black Americans) from the human race and all women from participation in government (as well as propertyless men), and had its eyes on further territorial expansion and imperialist dominion over indigenous and Mexican peoples.

It is noteworthy that this rhetorical self-understanding employed in and after the American and French Revolutions did contain allusions to the norms of individuality and democracy. This self-understanding constitutes the liberal vision within capitalist civilization. This vision was—and remains—the grandest vision capitalist civilization has to offer. But it is, for the most part, limited to the sphere of governmental affairs, corrupted by the institutionalization and legitimation of white and male supremacy, and rendered nearly obsolete by unaccountable economic power principally in the form of private multinational corporations.

AN ALLIANCE OF BLACK THEOLOGY AND MARXIST THOUGHT: THE CASE OF REV. GEORGE WASHINGTON WOODBEY

The best historical example of a Black religious thinker and leader who combined the insights of Black theological reflection and Marxist social theory was Reverend George Washington Woodbey.[35] He devoted his life to promoting structural social change and creating a counterhegemonic culture in liberal capitalist America.

Rev. Woodbey was a Baptist preacher, for many years pastor of Mt. Zion Baptist Church in San Diego, California, and a major socialist leader in the first few decades of this century. He was uncompromising in his religious faith, unyielding in his confidence in the radical potential of Black culture and religion, and unrelenting in his devotion to fundamental social change. Widely known in California during his day as "The Great Negro Socialist Orator," Woodbey delivered poignant yet incisive lectures across the country, including his famous reply to Booker T. Washington's "Capitalist Argument for the Negro." Woodbey also wrote books such as *The Bible and Socialism: A Conversation between Two Preachers* (1904) and *The Distribution of Wealth* (1910), and such essays as "Why the Negro Should Vote the Socialist Ticket" (1908) and "Why the Socialists Must Reach the Churches with Their Message" (1915).[36]

Woodbey's most influential work, *What to Do and How to Do It, or Socialism vs. Capitalism* (1903), was translated into three languages. It was often compared to Robert Blatchford's *Merrie England,* the most widely read socialist educational publication at the turn of the century.

Woodbey's important work consists of a conversation between himself and his mother after a long separation. She begins with the question, "Have you given up the Bible and the ministry and gone into politics?" He replies that he became a Socialist precisely because of his strict adherence to principles put forward in the Bible. She then points out that many of his comrades do not believe in God or in biblical truths.

He reminds her that other political parties, such as the Republican and Democratic parties, have their equal portion of nonbelievers. He assures her that he does not fully agree with some of his comrades on religious matters, but since socialism is "a scheme for bettering things here first," he can be a Socialist without giving up his religious beliefs. He then states that under socialism, religious freedom will be guaranteed.

Later on, his mother asks, "Like all other women, I want to know where we are to come in?" He answers that it is in the interest of "the women, more than the men, if possible, to be Socialists because they suffer more from capitalism than anyone else." Under socialism, each woman will receive her own income and be an equal shareholder in the industries of the country. Under these conditions, there will be no need for a woman to "sell herself through a so-called marriage to someone she did not love, in order to get a living"; instead, she could marry for genuine love. In capitalist society, a workingman is a slave, "and his wife is the slave of a slave."[37] Therefore liberation of both would enhance the position of women more than that of men. This conversation ends with the mother's conversion to socialism and commenting,

> Well, you have convinced me that I am about as much a slave now as I was in the south, and I am ready to accept any way out of this drudgery.[38]

Reverend Woodbey was the only Black delegate to the Socialist Party conventions of 1904 and 1908. In the latter convention, he was nominated as Eugene Debs's running mate in the presidential election of 1908. He was once described as "the greatest living negro in America. . . . His style is simple and his logic invincible. He knows the race question, and one of his most popular lectures relates to the settlement of this vexed question under Socialism."[39]

Jailed frequently, hospitalized more than once owing to police brutality, barely escaping murder during the famous 1912 free speech fight in San Diego, Reverend Woodbey was a devoted Christian who sacrificed greatly for fostering a counterhegemonic culture and promoting structural social change in liberal capitalist America. He was a man of inexorable Christian faith, anchored deep in the best of Black culture and religion, and of intransigent socialist conviction. His life and writings best exemplify the point at which Black theologians and Marxist thinkers are no longer strangers.

Yet, most strangely, and from deeps not before discovered, his faith looked up; before the wickedness that he saw, the wickedness from which he fled, he yet beheld like a flaming standard in the middle of the air, that power of redemption to which he must, till death, bear witness; which, though it crush him utterly, he could not deny; though none among the living might ever behold it, *he* had beheld it, and must keep the faith. He would not go back into Egypt for friend, or lover, or bastard son: he would not turn his face from God, no matter how deep might grow the darkness in which God hid His face from him. One day God would give him a sign, and the darkness would all be finished—one day God would raise him, who had suffered him to fall so low.

James Baldwin
Go Tell It on the Mountain

I am a Socialist-of-the-Path. I do not believe in the complete socialization of the means of production—the entire abolition of private property in capital—but the Path of Progress and common sense certainly leads to a far greater ownership of the public wealth for the public good than is now the case. . . . In the socialistic trend thus indicated lies the one great hope of the Negro American. We have been thrown by strange historic reasons into the hands of the capitalists hitherto. We have been objects of dole and charity, and despised accordingly. We have been made tools of oppression against the workingman's cause—the puppets and playthings of the idle rich. Fools! We must awake! . . . Watch the Socialists. We may not follow them and agree with them in all things. I certainly do not. But in trend and ideal they are the salt of this present earth.

W. E. B. Du Bois
"Negro and Socialism"

5

Afro-American Revolutionary Christianity

Revolutionary Christian perspective and praxis enact the Afro-American humanist tradition in the postmodern period. These are guided by the norms of individuality and democracy as proposed by the prophetic Christian viewpoint, promoted by the progressive Marxist orientation, and promulgated by revolutionary activity. A Black Christian position contains four central elements: the philosophical methodology of dialectical historicism, the theological worldview of prophetic Christianity, the cultural outlook of Afro-American humanism, and the social theory and political praxis of progressive Marxism. An ambitious systematic treatment of these four elements must await another occasion. My aim in this final chapter is to put forward the practical and programmatic dimensions of revolutionary Christian perspective and praxis.

THE MARGINALITY OF MARXISM IN AMERICAN LIFE

To be a progressive Marxist in the United States is to be marginal; to be a revolutionary Christian in the United States is to be even more marginal. Marxism is marginal in American life primarily because of the failure of class politics in American society—that is, because a socialist movement has never become a major force in this country. I shall attempt to account for this failure of class consciousness, class organization, and class formation by appealing to ideological, political, and economic factors which characterize the emergence, growth, and development of the United States.[1]

On the ideological front, the United States is the first and only country in the world to be born modern, born liberal, and born bourgeois.[2] In the northern states, the relative absence of a feudal past gave way to an agrarian utopia of free independent farmers on "free" land.[3] This dominance of small capitalist farmers—yeoman farmers—generated the ideological hegemony of the classical liberal, Lockean outlook which permeated and pervaded American life. In the southern states, the thriving economy of slavery underscored an aristocratic ethos and an entrepreneurial ethic. Hence, both North and South became deeply committed to the "political unconscious" of American society: the sanctity of private property and the virtue of capital accumulation.

This political unconscious crystallized into an articulate ideology of Americanism which extolled the freedom to own property and to accumulate capital without public interference, and the right to be treated equal under the law. This ideology entailed an abiding distrust of institutional power, bureaucracy, and especially the state; it also placed unprecedented emphasis on the welfare of people as isolated individuals (rather than as community dwellers or civic citizens). As Alexis de Tocqueville observed, voluntary associations flourished, but they were organized primarily to secure personal benefits rather than promote issues concerning the common good or principles regarding the public interest.[4] The ideology of Americanism promoted the ideals of bourgeois freedom and formal equality which reinforced the already rapacious individualism that accompanied the profiteering proclivities of the yeoman farmer and slaveholder.

Ironically, this ideology of Americanism became a beacon to oppressed social classes and ethnic groups around the world. Widespread immigration to the United States contributed to the first ecumenical, multiethnic, and multiracial working class in the world and the most complex heterogeneous population in modernity.[5] In addition, the boomtown character of American industrialization—urban centers which appeared virtually overnight—set the context for the flowering of nativism, jingoism, anti-Semitism, sexism, and, above all, racism.

On the political front, the American working class was the only modern proletariat to receive the right to vote without an organized struggle.[6] This "gift of suffrage" occurred prior to widespread industrialization, hence substantive class formation. When class formation intensified, coalitional politics and urban political machines within the framework of the two-party system reinforced deep splits in the working class in the form of religious, ethnic, sexual, and racial divisions.[7] And outright legal and illegal state repression of Leftist and Marxist movements deterred already anxiety-ridden would-be radicals.[8]

On the economic front, extraordinary productivity, technological innovation, and abundant natural resources facilitated social upward mobility unknown in the modern world.[9] The distribution of goods, luxuries, and conveniences among large segments of the population projected a fluid social structure which fueled a Horatio Alger ideology, subscribed to even by those in the lower classes. The hierarchical organization of the workplace produced professionalization and specialization which resulted in deeper class fragmentation.[10] For example, skilled white-collar employees set themselves apart from unskilled blue-collar workers. In short, another element of intraclass conflict was accented.

The uneven regional economic development in the United States, with varying sectional rates of industrialization and proletarianization, generated different (often opposing) strategies and tactics for class mobilization and organization. Lastly, the fundamental American commitment to economic growth welded together the state, banks, and large corporations into a close partnership which sustained a rising standard of living and a relatively stable economy.[11]

The ideological factors prevented the rise of widespread class consciousness in that the relative absence of a feudal past deeply ingrained bourgeois values of private property and unrestrained capital accumulation into American life; the ideology of Americanism deceptively paraded as an ideology of genuine freedom and substantive equality; and the religious, ethnic, and racial mixture of the proletariat provided the ingredients for intraclass xenophobia.

The political factors undermined the possibility of successful class organization in that the gift of suffrage robbed the American working class of the experience of collective struggle to enter bourgeois politics; coalitional compromises and urban machines in the two-party system channeled idealistic class organizational sentiments into practical interest group sensibilities and relegated radical movements to ill-fated third parties; and harsh state repression of Leftist and Marxist movements discouraged the sensible and encouraged the adventurous.

The economic factors precluded national class formation in that prolonged periods of prodigious productivity and technological innovation permitted the bourgeois ideal of personal achievement to flourish rather than the Marxist ideal of class enhancement; the hierarchical organization of the workplace fueled craft consciousness (not class consciousness), strengthened conservative leadership in the reformist trade-union movement, and disguised redistribution of income within the working class as redistribution of wealth in the country; the uneven regional economic development often pitted workers from one region against those from another owing to different levels of unionization, organization, and politicalization; and the American commitment to economic growth deepened class collaboration by proletarian groupings because such growth seemed to presuppose the partnership of the state, banks, and corporations.

This brief scenario seems to justify a far from sanguine view of Marxism's ever becoming a major force in American life. And it indeed may be that the United States lacks the cultural resources and political wherewithal—the potential as a nation—to undergo structural social change or fundamental transformation. If this is so, commitment to revolutionary Christian perspective and praxis becomes purely a matter of principle and right—with no possibility of effective transformative praxis or realizable principled might. Yet such speculation is academic—and ultimately paralyzing—for those whose backs are against the wall or for those who believe in a God who sides with the oppressed, sits high, looks low, and works in strange and mysterious ways. For Americans, especially Afro-Americans, adopting a particular Marxist perspective and praxis is an act of desperation, yet we live in desperate times; it proceeds from a persistent pessimism regarding the American way of life, yet such pessimism is, for the most part, warranted.

THE PROGRESSIVE STREAM IN
THE MARXIST TRADITION

If one is to take seriously the Marxist tradition, it is necessary to have some knowledge of and an attitude toward the particular streams within this tradition. I will examine the major streams in the Marxist tradition, highlighting the progressive stream. Given the focus on the United States, this examination will be limited to the Marxist tradition in the advanced industrial capitalist world.

There are six major streams in the Marxist tradition: the Bernsteinian, Leninist, Stalinist, Trotskyist, Councilist, and Gramscian streams. These diverse streams all adhere to the broad tenets of

Marxism: commitment to the dialectical method for understanding social reality, viewing class struggle as a central dynamic of the historical process, and affirming socialism as a desirable social arrangement. To employ a Marxist analysis—despite the stream one opts for—is first and foremost to understand the present capitalist order as a concrete totality and momentary stage in a historical process, a totality and stage wrought with various levels of overdetermined contradictions, cleavages, and conflicts within which a new order is immanent and, by means of collective praxis, a socialist society is realizable.

The Bernsteinian stream, often coined revisionist Marxism, follows the position put forward in Eduard Bernstein's *Evolutionary Socialism* (1899).[12] This view holds that socialism can arise through legislation and bourgeois electoral politics. Therefore it claims that Marxists should invest their time and energy in parliamentary political parties, either those of the bourgeoisie or their own parties. Based initially on an emasculated version of Friedrich Engels's introduction to Marx's *Class Struggles in France* (1895) in which Engels seems to endorse an anti-insurrectionist, pro-legalist road to political power, the Bernsteinian stream promotes reformist and peaceful means to socialism.

The Leninist stream, usually viewed as orthodox Marxism, proceeds from Vladimir Lenin's *What Is to Be Done?* (1902) and *One Step Forward, Two Steps Back* (1903).[13] In these influential texts, Lenin argues for the need of a vanguard party composed of professional revolutionaries which leads and guides the working-class movement. He advocates the principle of democratic centralism in the vanguard party which permits and encourages disagreement and debate on crucial issues, yet reserves decisions to be made by a central committee which reflects the different viewpoints in the party. Discipline requires that all members abide by such decisions. Violent means of transforming the prevailing order is neither valorized nor venerated; but avoiding it is believed to be nearly impossible.

The Stalinist stream flows from Joseph Stalin's *The Foundations of Leninism* (1924) and *On Lenin and Leninism* (1924).[14] Stalin vulgarizes Lenin's position by precluding disagreement and debate on major issues, trivializes the diverse makeup of the central committee by requiring a uniform outlook, and gives decision-making powers to one dictatorial figure.

The Trotskyist stream is based on Leon Trotsky's *The New Course* (1924).[15] Trotsky presents essentially a Leninist position which is adamantly anti-Stalinist. He rejects the Stalinist conception of Leninism as a body of authoritative party doctrine and instead views Leninism as a tentative yet acceptable program of revolutionary praxis. Trotskyism attempts to revive Leninism after the Stalinist-distorted appropriation of Leninism.

The Councilist stream, often labeled left-wing Marxism, derives from Rosa Luxemburg's *Social Reform or Revolution* (1899) and "Organizational Questions in Russian Social Democracy" (1904), Anton Pannekoek's "Marxist Theory and Revolutionary Tactics" (1912), and Karl Korsch's "Fundamentals of Socialization" (1919).[16] This viewpoint eschews Bernstein's reformism and Lenin's elitism. Instead, it favors the self-organization and self-guidance of the working-class movement. It criticizes Bernsteinian reformism and trade unionism for its procapitalist outlook, for viewing workers primarily as mere wage earners, voters, and consumers, thereby promoting class collaborationist ideology. It castigates Leninist elitism for its managerial orientation, for viewing workers principally as mere raw material for party (bourgeois intellectual) manipulation, hence encouraging authoritarian ideological leadership.

The Councilist position endorses the doctrine of prefigurativism: the notion that the revolutionary organization of workers which seizes power should prefigure the kind of socialist society to be created. It views workers as producers who educate and cultivate themselves—on the technical, cultural, and ideological levels—for the coming (peaceful or violent) takeover of society.

Lastly, the Gramscian stream emanates from Antonio Gramsci's "Workers Democracy" (1919) and "The Modern Prince" (1933–34).[17] Gramsci combines the Leninist and Councilist viewpoints in a unique manner. He holds roughly that under prerevolutionary conditions or during the "war of position" the Councilist stance should be adopted; and in revolutionary circumstances or during the "war of movement" a Leninist-like vanguard party should emerge and lead, though he conceives of the vanguard party in a more democratic and fluid way than did Lenin.

The progressive stream in the Marxist tradition is that viewpoint which most closely embodies and encourages the norms of individuality and democracy as delineated in the previous two chapters. The Stalinist stream is the least progressive one owing to its disregard of individuality and its disparagement of democracy. *Stalinism is to Marxism what the Ku Klux Klan is to Christianity: a manipulation of the chief symbols yet diametrically opposed to the central values.*

The Leninist and Trotskyist streams are much more progressive than the Stalinist one, but still remain a part of what I call regressive, or right-wing, Marxism. Both streams reek of the rigidity, dogmatism, and elitism characteristic of the very ruling class they oppose. The norms of individuality and democracy are upheld in rhetoric (unlike Stalinism), but perennially sacrificed for expediency. *Leninism and Trotskyism are to Marxism what conservative evangelicalism is to Christianity: orthodox and fundamentalist outlooks which give self-serving lip service to truncated versions of the major norms.*

The Gramscian and Bernsteinian streams constitute what I call the center right and center left of the Marxist tradition. The Gramscian stream is Leninist in spirit, though open to taking seriously the values of individuality and democracy. Yet this openness is primarily strategic, not principled. Therefore the Gramscian stream leans toward progressive or left-wing Marxism, but remains tied to regressive or right-wing Marxism owing to its avowed neo-Leninism. *Gramscianism is to Marxism what neo-orthodoxy is to Christianity: an innovative revision of dogmas for dogmatic purposes.*

The Bernsteinian stream completely breaks with right-wing Marxism. In fact, its rhetoric, though socialist, is as adamantly anticommunist as that of the very ruling class with which it usually collaborates. The Bernsteinian criticisms of the shortcomings of right-wing Marxism—made in the name of individuality and democracy—constitute in part the line of demarcation between regressive Marxism and progressive Marxism.

The major problem of the Bernsteinian stream is that its criticisms of Stalinism, Leninism, and Trotskyism are progressive within Marxism, yet its projects of reformism and trade-unionism are regressive within the capitalist order from a Marxist perspective. The Bernsteinian stream sets the stage for progressive Marxism, but symbolizes regressive Marxist praxis in capitalist society. *Bernsteinianism is to Marxism what the social gospel is to Christianity: powerful critiques tied to abortive praxis.*

The Councilist stream constitutes the progressive stream in the Marxist tradition. Councilism is left-wing Marxism. It incorporates the Bernsteinian critiques of right-wing Marxism and the right-wing Marxist critiques of Bernsteinian praxis. Councilism is committed first and foremost to the norms of individuality and democracy within the workers (and other progressive) movements—and within the future socialist society. This normative commitment to prefigurativism, along with an adamant anticapitalist and anti-imperialist stance, is the distinctive feature of the Councilist stream in the Marxist tradition. *Councilism is to Marxism what liberation theology is to Christianity: a promotion and practice of the moral core of the perspective against overwhelming odds for success.*

THE MARXIST TRADITION IN
THE AFRO-AMERICAN EXPERIENCE

Similar to the American experience, the Marxist tradition in the Afro-American experience has been dominated by the Leninist stream. Yet the first generation of Afro-American Marxists were primarily Bernsteinians, all members of the Socialist Party: Peter Clark, William Costley, Edward D. McKay, M. R. Smith, Charles G. Baylor, Rev. J. M. Moore, Rev. George Frazier Miller, and Rev. George Washington Woodbey. The notable exceptions of Ben Fletcher and Hubert Harrison—both avid supporters of the Industrial Workers of the World—signify the tension between the Bernsteinian Socialist Party and the proto-Councilist (syndicalist) Industrial Workers of the World.[18]

In the next generation of Afro-American Marxists, this tension crystallized into a major ideological division which existed between the New Negro Harlem Radicals (led by Chandler Owen and A. Philip Randolph) and the African Blood Brotherhood (headed by Cyril Briggs, Richard B. Moore, and Otto Huiswood). Owen and Randolph, both young, energetic radicals from the South, started their new magazine, *The Messenger,* in the fall of 1917 which soon became the first national socialist magazine edited by and for Black people in the United States.[19] With a brilliant staff, which included George Schuyler (before he turned conservative), W. A. Domingo, and Rev. George Frazier Miller, the magazine reached over thirty-three thousand readers at its peak. The magazine was closely affiliated with the Bernsteinian Socialist Party: strongly antiwar, surprisingly pro-Bolshevik, and staunchly anti–Black nationalist (anti-Garvey). Its support of the 1917 mayoralty candidacy in New York City of the Socialist Party leader Morris Hillquit clearly illustrated these positions.

Cyril Briggs, Richard B. Moore, and Otto Huiswood, highly committed young West Indians, established the African Blood Brotherhood in the fall of 1917.[20] Similar to Hubert Harrison's Afro-American Liberty League which evolved from the Colored Socialist Club within Branch 5 of the Socialist Party and blended Black nationalism with socialism, the African Blood Brotherhood began as a left-wing breakaway from the Socialist Party. The African Blood Brotherhood combined Black nationalism (as opposed to Garvey's Black Zionism), socialism, and, most important, anti-imperialism; it was the first Afro-American Pan-Africanist socialist organization in the United States. Its periodical, *The Crusader*, also aided by the skills of W. A. Domingo (who earlier had worked on Garvey's *Negro World!*), stressed the theme of Black self-determination in the United States and anticolonial movements in Africa. More a secret fraternal order than a public political organization, the African Blood Brotherhood enlisted over twenty-five hundred members, including large numbers of militant Black coal miners in West Virginia.

The Leninist domination of the Marxist tradition in the Afro-American experience began when Cyril Briggs and Richard B. Moore joined the Communist Party U.S.A. in 1921. The only other Afro-American in the party at this time was their old friend Otto Huiswood. In a few years more Afro-American recruits enlisted in the Leninist Communist Party U.S.A.: Grace Campbell, schoolteacher; George Padmore, journalist; Solomon Harper, engineer; William Patterson, lawyer; Lovett Fort-Whiteman, former drama critic of *The Messenger* and *The Crusader;* Harry Haywood, the father of right-wing Marxism in Afro-America; and Otto Hall, Harry's elder brother.

From this time to the present, Afro-American Marxists remained, for the most part, in Leninist captivity.[21] Right-wing Marxism was embraced by James Ford, Benjamin Davis, Merrill Work, James Ashford, Manning Johnson, Abner Bracey, Bonita Williams, Claudia Jones, Eloise Moore, Audley Moore, Henry Winston, Paul Robeson, W. E. B. Du Bois, Claude Lightfoot, and Angela Davis. Principally because of the Depression and the famous 1928 and 1930 Third Communist International Resolutions supporting the right of self-determination for the oppressed Negro Nation in the Southern U.S.A., by the mid-1930s more than fifteen thousand Afro-Americans were members of the Communist Party U.S.A. (over 30 percent of the Party).[22] There also were many Black members (up to 20 percent at one time) of the Socialist Workers Party (SWP) founded in 1938, the second largest Marxist party in the United States. It is a Trotskyist party, hence also Leninist to the core.[23]

This Leninist dominance of the Marxist tradition in the Afro-American experience is attributable primarily to the relative absence of progressive Marxism in American life. Left-wing Marxism has been nearly nonexistent in American society. Therefore the only Marxism that most Americans—educated or uneducated, Black or white—are ever exposed to or hear of is right-wing Marxism, and especially Leninism. It is no accident that in American lingo Marxism is synonymous with Sovietism. It is as if the only Christianity that Americans were ever exposed to or heard of was that of Jerry Falwell's Moral Majority. Yet this malady persists, American Marxism suffers, and progressive Marxism suffocates.

The few flickerings of progressive Marxism in the United States have been the brief presence of the Industrial Workers of the World, the momentary life of A. J. Muste's American Workers Party, and Paul Mattick's *Living Marxism* in the 1930s, the few years of the National Negro Labor Council in the early 1950s, the Root and Branch movement in the 1960s, and the League of Revolutionary Black Workers in Detroit in the late 1960s and early 1970s.[24]

This relative absence of progressive Marxism in American society is exacerbated by the reluctance of American Marxism as a whole to take seriously indigenous American radicalism. American Marxism has virtually coopted Afro-American nationalism, shunned American populism, and ignored American feminism.[25] A distinctive virtue of progressive Marxism linked to prophetic Christianity is the ease with which it can cooperate with non-Marxist progressive movements; for any radical movement without a Christian counterpart in American society is doomed. In fact, the hope for progressive Marxism in the United States indeed may rest with counterhegemonic micropolitical (non-class-based) movements, with feminists, Black nationalists, anti-imperialists (including indigenous peoples in the United States), ecologists, the elderly, and marginal rank-and-file labor caucuses who share a socialist vision of a free and democratic society.

REVOLUTIONARY CHRISTIAN PRAXIS AND THE AFRO-AMERICAN LIBERATION STRUGGLE

Revolutionary Christian perspective and praxis bear directly on the Afro-American liberation struggle. The central political concern is twofold: *to weaken the hegemony of liberalism over the Afro-American community (especially its leadership) and to break the stronghold of Leninism over Afro-American Marxists.* Both concerns enable Black prophetic Christians and Black progressive Marxists to take each other seriously, and hence more effectively to intervene in Afro-American public discourse.

I will begin with a brief historical overview of the Afro-American liberation movement in this century.[26] As we observed in chapter 1, the famous debate between W. E. B. Du Bois and Booker T. Washington set the framework for the Afro-American liberation movement in the early years of this century. This crucial debate signified the internal struggles of the Afro-American petite bourgeoisie—a group supported by the liberal elements of the American bourgeoisie, denigrated by the American working-class movement, and venerated by the Afro-American masses.

Du Bois's program of liberal education, social reform, and political agitation became the outlook of the National Association for the Advancement of Colored People (NAACP). Washington's project of economic self-help, entrepreneurial initiative, and relative political complacency shaped the perspective of the National Urban League (NUL). Despite the strategic differences and tactical tensions between these two groups, both shared three fundamental commitments: *relative silence regarding the cultural component of the Afro-American liberation movement, political and economic integration into the mainstream of American life, and affirmation of the liberal capitalist vision of society.* The first major framework for the Afro-American liberation movement in this century was circumscribed by *cultural ambiguity, political liberalism,* and *entrepreneurial capitalism.*

The two minor interventions into this debate by the New Negro Harlem Radicals and the African Blood Brotherhood called into question these three fundamental commitments. Yet both positions were inevitably utopian. The urgent needs and pressing problems of the oppressed Afro-American masses remained far removed from such far-fetched socialist visions.

The major intervention into the evolving Du Bois–Washington debate occurred on the cultural front: Marcus Garvey's Black nationalist movement.[27] Garveyism seized the moment primarily because of the cultural ambiguity contained in the two leading programs of the Afro-American petite bourgeoisie. Uprooted Black rural folk in the hostile urban environment yearned for a new cultural self-identity and self-image. The NAACP and the NUL lacked the imagination and resources to respond to such yearning; the so-called Harlem Renaissance certainly could not fulfill such existential longing. The Garvey movement filled this cultural vacuum, and it became the first mass movement among Afro-Americans. Despite its cultural militancy, Garveyism endorsed political liberalism and entrepreneurial capitalism (as interim strategies prior to migration to Africa). Yet Garvey's bourgeois Black nationalism altered the framework initiated by the Du Bois–Washington debate: *The cultural component of the Afro-American liberation movement could no longer be overlooked.*

The first inclusion of Afro-Americans in a major political machine by the Chicago Republican Bill Thompson in the mayoralty election of 1919 represented both the end of an era in Black politics and the portent of what was to come: the end of Republican dominance of Afro-American voters and Black inclusion within mainstream electoral politics in American society.[28] By the election of Franklin Delano Roosevelt in 1936, the Black shift to the Democratic Party was complete. The hegemony of political liberalism over the Afro-American community was not only deepened, but, more important, it began to produce some payoffs. In Chicago, political Black elites and white-collar jobs for Afro-Americans increased and the first Black congressman since the Radical Reconstruction was elected: Republican Oscar DePriest in 1928. Thereafter, starting with Arthur Mitchell (a Republican turned Democrat) in 1934, Black Democrats would hold this congressional seat from Chicago. In New York City, the most effective and colorful Black congressman was elected: Harlem's Rev. Adam Clayton Powell Jr. As Black migration, urbanization, and proletarianization escalated, patronage relations with white Democratic political bosses and economic elites facilitated slow and selective Afro-American upward social mobility.

Alongside this bourgeois electoral activity was the rampant organizing and mobilizing of Black people into local, regional, and national groups for civil rights as well as job and educational opportunities. With the aid of progressive white groups—from the Communist Party U.S.A. and Leftist trade unions to liberal Democrats—Black organizations, most notably A. Philip Randolph's National Negro Congress and the National Negro Labor Council (led by William Hood, Ernest Thompson, Coleman Young, and Victoria Garvin), broadened the scope of Afro-American advancement.

This advancement was best signified by the 1954 *Brown v. Board of Education* Supreme Court decision on school integration. This decision was not simply a hard-won victory for the NAACP, but, more important, it ensured the triumph of political liberalism in the Afro-American community. This triumph—along with McCarthyism—effectively marginalized the Black Left in the Afro-American community; contributed to the organizational breakdown and reformist orientation of the only Marxist Party with noteworthy inroads in the Afro-American community, the Communist Party U.S.A.; and set the stage for the most important Black bourgeois liberal movement in this century, the civil rights movement led by Rev. Martin Luther King Jr.[29]

The genius of King's civil rights movement was that it seized upon the newly felt sense of Black triumph of political liberalism within the belly of the segregated South, thereby sending progressive ripples throughout the country which culminated in the unleashing of the multifarious possibilities immanent in political liberalism for all Americans. The civil rights movement succeeded primarily because of the talent, skill, and courage of the civil rights activists, its pronounced Black cultural potency (rooted in Black southern churches), and the rising tide of political liberalism facilitated by an expanding American economy (at home and abroad). In dialectical fashion, this success both rested upon its initial liberal impetus and dealt the deathblow to political liberalism.

The ineluctable shortsightedness of the civil rights movement was that its leaders could not transcend political liberalism. The more the movement achieved its aims, the more convinced they became of the virtues of liberalism. Yet, as the successes of the movement unfolded, the impotency of liberalism in the face of structural unemployment and class inequality became more apparent. Nevertheless, post–civil rights leaders clung to the rhetoric of liberalism. This was seen most clearly in their support of the last pillar of the first major framework of the Afro-American liberation movement—the affirmation of the liberal capitalist vision of society—which remained a tacit presupposition of their perspective. Even the early years of the Student Nonviolent Coordinating Committee (SNCC), a radical breakaway from King's Southern Christian Leadership Conference (SCLC)—as well as its religious counterpart, the National Committee of Black Churchmen (NCBC), did not reject this presupposition.

The genius of Malcolm X was that he understood that political liberalism could not deliver what it promised (namely, Afro-American freedom), that he articulated his wholesale rejection of liberalism in language intelligible to the Afro-American masses, and that he acknowledged that the new Black vision of society had to be informed by the anticolonial struggles occurring around the world.[30] The tragedy of Malcolm X (similar to that of King) was that he did not live long enough to project this new Black vision of society. Unlike King, he precluded capitalism (and any version thereof) as a possibility, but he never unequivocally affirmed the socialist vision that was later put forward by his most notable legatees, the Black Panther Party and the League of Revolutionary Black Workers. Malcolm X is the transitional figure who stands between King and the Black Marxists, between Black liberalism and Black socialist nationalism. My hunch is that his religious sensibilities (absent in his major legatees), Black cultural sentiments, moral convictions, political consciousness, and personal engagement would have evolved into revolutionary Islamic perspective and praxis closely similar to the viewpoint put forward in this book.

The turning point of the Afro-American liberation movement in this century occurred with the appearance of the Black Panther Party (BPP) in Oakland, California (1966), and the League of Revolutionary Black Workers (LRBW) in Detroit, Michigan (1969). These two indigenous Black Marxist groups, notwithstanding their naivete, inexperience, and misguidance, symbolize the most significant and salient Afro-American rejection of the three fundamental commitments of the initial framework of the Afro-American liberation movement in this century. These Black Marxist organizations radically called into question cultural ambiguity, political liberalism, and entrepreneurial capitalism—the three pillars upon which rests the old framework. *For the first time in this century, the obsolescence of this framework became a major issue in Afro-American public discourse.*

Both the BPP and the LRBW combined Black nationalist sentiments and revolutionary socialist ideology. Of course, Hubert Harrison's Afro-American Liberty League and Cyril Briggs's African Blood Brotherhood prefigure this position, but the *historical timing* of the BPP and the LRBW warrants their distinctive importance: they project a Black postliberal socialist vision of society just as the immanent possibilities of political liberalism approach the point of exhaustion.

The major effect of the BPP and the LRBW has been the dissemination of the Marxist tradition among a significant segment of Afro-Americans, especially young adults. These seeds are sprouting in a variety of ways, but principally in the form of an increasing influx of Afro-Americans into old Marxist parties such as the Communist Party U.S.A. and SWP and into new heavily Black-populated Marxist parties which include the Communist Labor Party (CLP), Communist Workers Party (CWP), and the U.S. League of Revolutionary Struggle.

But political liberalism in the Afro-American community is far from dead; though frail and beleaguered, it limps on. Elected political officials, the NAACP, and the Urban League persist as the hallmarks of Black leadership—and chief carriers of Black liberalism. The other three major Black organizations, People United to Save Humanity

(PUSH), Southern Christian Leadership Conference (SCLC), and the Coalition of Black Trade Unionists (CBTU), do not rival the NAACP and the Urban League in respect, reverence, and revenue, yet all three also are bastions of Black liberalism.

Political liberalism is alive in the Afro-American community not simply because it undergirds the role and function of the Black elites who articulate it but also because as long as the only alternatives presented to Afro-Americans are liberalism and right-wing Marxism, liberalism will prevail. Black conservatives (who are what and where they are owing to the victories of political liberalism) are presently discrediting liberalism and offering an old-style procapitalist viewpoint, but it is attractive primarily to a small section of the Afro-American petite bourgeoisie.[31] *The present dilemma of the Afro-American liberation movement is to find its way between the Scylla of bourgeois liberalism and the Charybdis of right-wing Marxism.*

Revolutionary Christian perspective and praxis pave this middle pathway. They are rooted in the worldview found in the bosom of Afro-American culture and in the major institution which provides refuge from the terror in Afro-American life—Black churches; they are informed by the social analysis and moral impulse of the best of the socialist movement—progressive Marxism; and they build upon, yet go far beyond, the prevailing viewpoint of the vast majority of Afro-Americans—Black liberalism. Revolutionary Christian perspective and praxis incorporate the prophetic dimension of Christianity and eschew the paralyzing liberal outlook. They affirm the libertarian and democratic concerns of Bernsteinian Marxists yet remain critical of their reformist politics. They endorse the Black cultural dignity promoted by Black nationalists but shun their petty provincialism. They support the fervent anti-imperialism of right-wing Marxists and reject their elitist Leninism.

There are signs of hope in the Afro-American community for the institutional expression of revolutionary Christian perspective and praxis. The June 1980 founding of the National Black United Front (NBUF) in the House of the Lord Church, a vibrant Pentecostal church in Brooklyn, New York, pastored by the dynamic Rev. Herbert Daughtry, is a major case in point. Rev. Daughtry, the son of the late Alonzo A. Daughtry (a courageous early breakaway from Daddy Grace's movement in 1930), is a prophetic Black Christian leader, reflective writer, and the talented national chairman of the NBUF. His charismatic leadership and dedicated organization represent a significant attempt to displace Black bourgeois leadership and put a version of revolutionary

Christianity on the Afro-American liberation agenda. With over twenty NBUF branches throughout the country, Rev. Daughtry's movement indeed is worth taking seriously—and supporting.

The establishment of the National Black Independent Political Party (NBIPP) in Philadelphia, Pennsylvania (November 1980), and the merger of the New American Movement (NAM) with the Democratic Socialist Organizing Committee (DSOC) in March 1982 project much potential and present many possibilities for revolutionary Christian perspective and praxis. In addition, numerous noteworthy groups are open to a prophetic Christian, progressive Marxist viewpoint, including Christians for Socialism (CFS), New York Circus (NYC), Theology in the Americas (TIA), Clergy and Laity Concerned (CALC), Black Christian Evangelical Association (BCEA), Black Theology Project (BTP), and Black Seminarians, Inc.[32] Of course, dialogue and coalitions with right-wing Marxist parties can be strategically desirable and may be ultimately inevitable, but such interaction must preclude dogmatic reflections and doctrinaire resolutions.

Revolutionary Christian perspective and praxis must remain anchored in the prophetic Christian tradition in the Afro-American experience which provides the norms of individuality and democracy; guided by the cultural outlook of the Afro-American humanist tradition which promotes the vitality and vigor of Black life; and informed by the social theory and political praxis of progressive Marxism which proposes to approximate as close as is humanly possible the precious values of individuality and democracy as soon as God's will be done.

Until change comes about, let us not forget that Jesus Christ proclaimed:

> The Spirit of the Lord is upon me, because he has anointed me to preach good news to the poor. He has sent me to proclaim release to the captives and recovering of sight to the blind, to set at liberty those who are oppressed.
>
> (Luke 4:18, RSV)

And therefore let us forever remember the plight of the downtrodden in the spirit of resistance and hope.

We wade in the water
America
America

We wade in the bleeding
We wade in the screaming
        in the unemployment
        in the frustrated wives
        & impotent husbands
        of the dying middle
        class,
        in the anger of its
        workers
        its niggers
        its wild intelligent
        spics
        its
        brutalized
        chicanos
        its women out of work, again

AMIRI BARAKA
"Reprise of One of A. G.'s Best Poems!"
boundary 2 6, no. 2 (Winter 1978): 328–29,
https://doi.org/10.2307/302326.

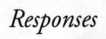

Responses

A Response to Chapter 1
Cultural Alienation and Intellectual Insecurity in the Modern West

SHATEMA THREADCRAFT

Cornel West's "American Africans in Conflict: Alienation in an Insecure Culture" deftly documents the development, anxieties, and exclusions of Europeans, white Americans, and American Africans as they journey through early, middle, late, and postmodernity. West penned *Prophesy Deliverance!* three decades after the end of European modernity. Thus, he tracks several epochs. From the Glorious Revolution to the French Revolution; from the French Revolution to the unification of the German Empire; from the unification of the German Empire to the emergence of the United States as the unquestioned supreme world power, this chapter offers the broader context for Blacks' American theodicy. While early modern culture featured the increasing acceptance of the authority of science, the appearance of a new kind of pagan neoclassicism, and the subjectivist turn in philosophy, the decline of modernity saw a crisis in science, despair in modern paganism, and major attacks on the primacy of the subject. All would have an impact on Black life in the United States.

For Europeans, the chapter reads like a classic Martin Scorsese mob film—it's all fun until the feds come. Consider philosophy and even the subject's wild ride in the text. In the beginning, West says, "philosophy became the queen of the emerging scientific disciplines within this new paradigm" (p. 14). The one discipline to validate them all, it provided the objective grounds for the knowledge claims of physics and other emerging disciplines. "This turn in philosophy granted science a monopoly on truth in the marketplace of ideas, to the dismay of both artists and theologians" (p. 14). West also calls attention to philosophy's subjectivist turn at the origin of European modernity. Initiated by Descartes, the turn centered the subject, the ego, the self and gave "preeminence to the notion of representative knowledge." By the end of the period, however, not only are the "most precious ideals of science, politics, philosophy, and the arts . . . radically called into question," but there are also major attacks on the primacy of the subject (p. 24).

West's analysis of our postmodern period feels as fresh as ever—prescient really—and I was particularly taken by his take on the state of the sciences. He states,

> The crisis in science which emerged in European modernism is now becoming a more widespread crisis in the authority of science, in many ways similar to the crisis in the authority of the church in the Age of Enlightenment. This rudimentary state of demythologizing science relegates scientific descriptions and theories of the self, world, and God alongside rather than above religious, artistic, and moral descriptions and theories of the self, world, and God. . . . This process signifies a deep authority crisis in knowledge, a kind of demonopolizing of science on truth and reality in the marketplace of ideas. It raises the prospect of a possible plurality of epistemic authorities on truth and reality as well as a frightening full-blown relativism or laissez-faire policy regarding access to truth and reality. (p. 28)

West's analysis feels so fresh and particularly relevant to our contemporary moment. We live in a world plagued by the rapid spread of misinformation, accelerated by algorithms honed to precision in the service of surveillance capitalism. We are dealing with vaccine skepticism that both speaks the language of the scientific method—that is, "I just want to do my own research" and "we really just don't have enough data yet"—and owes much to the language of vegan hippie wellness. All of this is fed by inequality and a sense of powerlessness, even if among the white upper-middle class it is only the feeling of losing illegitimate cultural power. As well, I am sensitive to the fact that the Lululemon yoga mom variant of vaccine hesitancy and skepticism, and the turn toward the wellness industry in general and companies like Goop in particular, is partially a result of doctors' dismissal of women's testimony regarding their experiences of pain—which is itself a form of testimonial injustice that is an aspect of epistemic oppression. Beyond calls to "believe women" and "follow the science," the problems we face require collective and therefore political solutions. Women confronted their epistemic injustice regarding such phenomena as sexual harassment, a problem for which we long had no name, through consciousness-raising. People began to believe them once they had the words to believe themselves and organize around their oppression. This is but one story of organizing around knowledge. Plural epistemes are a fact of our lives now, and all that is left to us is to mobilize to empower those we would support.

West tells the story of the rise of white American self-confidence as things fall apart, their movement from self-conscious colonial provinciality "of being American but feeling European, of being provincial but yearning for British cosmopolitanism [which is kind of a funny thing to think about post-Brexit], of being at once incompletely civilized and materially prosperous" (p. 17). Africans in America wrestling with their own liminal fragility confronted a dominant white population in the midst of a full-on anxiety attack, which West argues created an emergent triple consciousness among them. Africans in America were forced to define their identity over against anxious and insecure white provincials empowered to run things—that is, run things right into the ground. And of course, ever plucky and tragic, there are the American Africans, trying at turns to integrate into or radically transform a burning house.

Part of my current research examines the place of lynching in the story of Black peoplehood. It considers how W. E. B. Du Bois and others wrote lynching into the story of Black peoplehood by connecting lynching—through narrative and imagery—to the biblical crucifixion. This means that I now perk up any time I see the word "theodicy"—a term political theorists rarely use. West's concise, clear, and convincing summary of the intellectual, existential, and political reasons Blacks chose Christianity is informed by an ongoing wrestling with the question of divine justice. Intellectually, Africans could see Christianity as a religion for the oppressed. Both the exodus motif and resurrection narrative offer Black folk triumphal narratives of good over evil. Indeed, Black folk in America had and continue to have much evil to overcome. West argues that "the intellectual life of the African slaves in the United States—like that of all oppressed peoples—consisted primarily of reckoning with the dominant form of evil in their lives. The Christian emphasis on against-the-evidence hope for triumph over evil struck deep among many of them" (p. 21). One wonders, given the declining significance of the church in the lives of younger generations of African Americans, what sources will animate Black political struggle moving forward.

I have argued elsewhere that the resurrection narrative and the ways in which Du Bois and others connected lynching to the biblical crucifixion marginalized Black women in politics and among Blacks as a political people. It is my hope that we can find inspiration in old stories that better lend themselves to care for women's suffering. We could do worse here than looking for inspiration in the stories and retellings of Toni Morrison and Saidiya Hartman.

Similarly, Dr. West is convincing with his existential arguments as to why African Americans found succor in evangelical piety—though as a political theorist, feminist, and lapsed Baptist, I see a few loose threads that must be pulled. Consider West's argument that the primary political appeal of Methodists and Baptists was the open access to leadership roles and the loose requirements for membership. Of course, he notes the good and the bad here. The good is the independent control that "produced community-minded political leaders, polished orators, and activist journalists and scholars" (p. 22). The bad is the charismatic, autocratic leadership that favored male leadership and overlooked generations of talented female leaders.

Barbara Ransby speaks of Ella Baker as emerging from a female tradition of missionary service in the Black church. Ransby sees it as an oft overlooked and undervalued alternative to charismatic leadership.[1] There is a reason for this systematic invisibility and undervaluing. As Erica Edwards tells us, "Charisma participates in a gendered economy of political authority in which the attributes of the ideal leader are the traits American society usually conceives as rightly belonging to men or to normative masculinity: ambition, courage, and above all, divine calling." She continues, "It is for this reason, for example, that black female leaders have either been written out of history, or masculinized, or subjected to violent gender policing. The conflation of charisma and normative manliness . . . is an epistemological, conceptual violation that has actual and physical effects."[2]

If we take seriously the critiques of Barbara Ransby and Erica Edwards, then we must interrogate how much the democratic norm of prophetic Christianity depends, in fact, on the dialectic between the male-dominated prophetic traditions in the Black church and the woman-led tradition of missionary service. According to West, "The basic contribution of prophetic Christianity . . . is that every individual, regardless of class, country, caste, race, or sex should have the opportunity to fulfill his or her potentialities" (introduction, p. 2). If this was ever realized within Afro-Protestant communities, it was always and already along gendered lines.

Consider Martin Luther King Jr., whom West considers an exemplar of both Black church tradition and democratic norms. What is democratic about a view of religious leadership that professes,

> Leadership never ascends from the pew to the pulpit, but . . . descends from the pulpit to the pew. . . . The pastor is to be respected and accepted as the central figure around which the policies and programs of the church revolve. He must never be considered a mere puppet for the whimsical and capricious mistreatment of those who wish to show their independence, and "use their liberty for a cloak of maliciousness." It is therefore indispensable to the progress of the church that the official board and membership cooperate fully with the leadership of the pastor.[3]

Moreover, there is the tendency to mistake the prophet for divine leader—members of the Student Nonviolent Coordinating Committee (SNCC) jokingly referred to King as "De Lawd"—and to ignore profound insight because of gendered notions of charisma. Cornel West has written eloquently of the prophetic witness of Ida B. Wells, Frances Beale, and Toni Morrison.[4] Nevertheless, this does not negate the marginalization the women experienced, nor the way this ideal tends, tragically in Baker's view, to take agency away from the people themselves. Again, to quote Erica Edwards, "The charismatic leadership ideal is an ideal that situates authority or the right to rule in one exceptional figure perceived to be gifted with a privileged connection to the divine. The charismatic leader is both gifted and a gift himself; he is given divine authority and power, given to the people, and given for the sake of historical change."[5]

How can we deal with this in order, as critical theorists, to get all we can out of our tradition of Black Christianity? I can only, humbly, suggest that we can only organize our way out of the problem of the divine gift. And, in so doing, we throw our lot in with the overlooked Black female tradition of missionary service to empower people to be the change they seek. The solution here is to constantly highlight and amplify the power the people themselves wield in making change.

A Response to Chapter 2
Reflecting on Modern Racism

KERI DAY

As I write, there are many ideological debates raging over the history of race in America. In Texas, for instance, a group of House Republicans sponsored House Bill 3979, which would ban the teaching of critical race theory and prescribe how teachers can talk about current events.[1] Texas is not alone. Several states across the nation that include Idaho, South Carolina, Mississippi, New Hampshire, and Arizona have passed anti–critical race theory legislation. Underneath these proposals is a sinister desire to whitewash the racial evils of American history and its lingering effects in the present.

In chapter 2, "A Genealogy of Modern Racism," Cornel West offers a genealogy of racism to combat such intentional amnesia. First, West demonstrates that white supremacy is not an aberration of America's otherwise noble intellectual and aesthetic ideals. White supremacy is the result of European categories and ideas that grounded and shaped modern discourses of rationality, morality, and objectivity. Cornel West offers a brief but breathtaking survey of how the natural sciences established ideas of truth and knowledge in the modern West.

For instance, writers, artists, and scholars of the Enlightenment introduced a scientific method that provided a new paradigm of knowledge based on observation and evidence. This method involved "observing, comparing, ordering, and measuring in order to arrive at evidence sufficient to make valid inferences . . . and verify true representations of reality" (p. 39). Modern racism was constituted *through* the humanities and sciences. In the scientific areas of natural history and anthropology, this involved recovering norms and values from classical antiquity (Greek philosophy and art) to measure, compare, and observe other cultures and peoples. Greek notions of logic, beauty, and moderation (morality) would become the cultural and aesthetic ideals against which non-Europeans would be compared and measured.

That which constituted a beautiful face, then, was as much a scientific question as a cultural question in the modern West. These forms of rationality and scientificity would ground and legitimate cultural norms and aesthetic ideals used to oppress and denigrate those deemed nonwhite. In this way, according to Cornel West, the structure of modern discourse excluded the very idea of Black equality, because scientific knowledge itself made European subjects the exemplars of rationality, morality, and beauty. The ideas of Black beauty and Black brilliance were unintelligible inside of this conceptual framework of modern discourse.

Because the discursive structure of modern racism precludes the possibility of Black equality, West makes it clear that we need to discuss the genealogy of racism, not simply its history. Why *genealogy*? As Michel Foucault reminds us, genealogy is an investigation into those things we tend to feel are without history.[2] Another way of saying it: genealogy is an investigation into those things that are presumed to have essences and origins, which assumes their transparency epistemologically (versus complex explanations into its nature, revealing the opacity of knowledge and things). Genealogy is not simply the search for origins or some linear development. Instead, genealogy is a historical technique that questions the commonly understood emergence of various social or philosophical beliefs by attempting to account for their scope and breadth to understand the conditions of their possibility. In terms of race, West wants to think about race away from the reductionistic accounts of racism as personal prejudice or the totalizing Marxian explanations of racism as structural-social. He offers a genealogy to interrogate the conditions that are *discursive* in nature toward understanding modern racism. Why does a genealogy matter today? It matters because we tend to think we know what racism *is*. The average conservative American tends to think that racism is simply personal prejudice and that it is a thing of the past. The average liberal American tends to speak primarily of racism in structural terms. Modern racism is all these things and something *more*. Professor West's genealogical approach provides new intellectual pathways.

For instance, I have written about the erotic life of racism, which focuses on how white discursive practices engender particular forms of intimacy, connections, and repulsions. Taking my cue from Black feminist Sharon Holland, structural racism gains its sustenance, in part, from intense *desires* for white forms of belonging. As she notes, projects of racial belonging have two moments. Through discursive and material practices, the first moment produces presumed "real" biological connections at the level of blood (i.e., blue blood or the "one-drop rule"). The second moment uses such discursive and material practices to establish racial identity and social relations that are reciprocal and mutual, forming a "community" or "nation." This racial community or "peoplehood" requires exclusive patterns of intimacy and belonging, which materializes in separate and often racist relations and structures.[3]

These two moments are worked out in quotidian ways. They inform whom one chooses to sit with on the bus, selects as a mate, elects to hire, as well as assumptions regarding what kinds of people demonstrate higher intellectual promise.[4] Racism, in this sense, can be described as "the emotional lifeblood of race; it is the 'feeling' that articulates and keeps the flawed logic of race in its place."[5] In this way, racism is an everyday practice. It is an erotic practice that maintains white intimacies within unequal structures and institutions.

Considering modern racism as having an erotic life is important because it traces how modern racism is produced through intense forms of desire and how such desire becomes the emotional blood of racism, ensuring its reproduction in cultural and structural contexts. The erotic life of racism can open to scenes of racist welcoming as white discursive practices of intimacy and belonging have been crucial to upholding white supremacist systems. Cornel West's genealogical work on modern racism has helped me theorize racism's erotic life and why desire is important to the question of structural racism.

Although Cornel West focuses on the natural and social sciences as foundational for the cultivation of a particular European aesthetic and intellectual ideal, he laid the groundwork for how theology, too, is rooted in racist European philosophical and aesthetic ideals. Christian theology has certainly participated in the discursive foundations of modern racism. Several scholars have certainly expanded on this in recent years, most notably J. Kameron Carter and Willie Jennings. Stitched into the fabric of theology is an entire discourse of the white Christian subject and the "other" who needs to be saved and civilized. As a result, the religious or cultural other can only be saved through becoming a white Christian subject, accepting the moral, cultural, and aesthetic ideals and values of white European Christians.

While African American male theologians have interrogated the theological underpinnings of modern racism, their projects have not been as effective at addressing the gendered dimensions. It is not merely about "wresting the theological battlefield" from white theology (to use Charles Long's words), because the winner of the battle still operates with the same categories of whiteness, and these categories disallow ways of thinking and being beyond categorical epistemic modes of the West.[6] The task of constructive theology should not be about merely reformulating traditional androcentric ideas of God and the world, ideas steeped in Eurocentric, heteronormative assumptions and logic.

Therefore, constructive theology might take its cue from theologians like Mayra Rivera and Monica Coleman who are challenging the basic set of terms by which we do theology and how we construct the idea of the theological. Rivera's writings on theology and the body reconceptualize ideas of flesh and materiality toward articulating how human flesh and the world are co-constituted. Rivera offers a deep exploration of reality and subjectivity that are not beholden to traditional theological anthropology and its privileging of the human subject. She draws on Black studies, critical theory, and phenomenology to rethink the basic categories of theology away from the traditional, masculinist white normative gaze.[7]

Similarly, Monica Coleman offers a constructive womanist theology grounded in religious multiplicity and interreligious engagement. Coleman speaks of God, suffering, humanity, and the world not through white orthodox categories and heteropatriarchal norms but reenvisions divinity, humanity, and the world's processes through process philosophy and womanist thought.[8] Neither Rivera nor Coleman are seduced by the European ideals and ideas that undergird much of Christian theology in the West. In addition, these insights help to expand the masculinist discursive interpretations of modern racism by thinkers like Cornel West, and subsequently Carter and Jennings.

In terms of revolutionary Black Christian faith (and African American religion more broadly), we must become clear about *our ideals and ideas* in seeking salvation for our communities. Part of our salvation is grasping the complex character of modern racism in America and how Christian theology has propagated *heteropatriarchal* anti-Black racism. So many Black churches remain uncritical of their inherited theological traditions. What would it mean for Black church leaders to discern how certain white hetero Christian ideals reinforce Black denigration? Black feminist and historian of religion Tamura Lomax considers the image of Jezebel and how it has functioned in Black Christian spaces. Cultivated in slavery and preached within contemporary Black churches, the Jezebel archetype has been deployed to describe Black women as lascivious, sexually wanton, and morally undisciplined.[9] One must read Jezebel against the white Victorian ideal. Black women were morally deficient while white women were moral paragons. Central to understanding modern racism is how it articulates itself through Christian theology and its heteronormative notions of purity as well as how Black churches integrate these problematic ideas into their practices of faith.

Black communities must reject these white, heteronormative ideals and envision new ones. Part of our salvation involves articulating alternative religious/theological ideals and ideas that promote our flourishing and thriving as Black communities. Black religious communities like Black churches must disavow and reject white heteropatriarchal ideals and ideas like Jezebel and fashion new images that promote healthy views of self and community. We need authentic Black ideas and ideals of beauty, knowledge, and truth that help Black communities dream of a new world, a new normative center where equality, equity, and flourishing are possible for them.

Despite these gender challenges, one still must consider Cornel West's genealogical retrieval of modern *racism as prophetic speech*. Prophetic speech is critiquing institutions that generate and sustain material inequities. Yet Cornel West proves that prophetic speech also involves how we *demystify* the ideals that marginalize and oppress Black communities. The demystification of European ideals that give racism its power might help us interpret how Black communities might further resist theological categories that contribute to their own undoing. Professor West invites both theological scholarship and religious communities (especially Christian communities) to explore these discursive aspects of modern racism. West's genealogical intervention helps one to also see modern racism and its afterlife. The afterlives of racism involve the way racism inserts itself into cultural and material forms of life, shaping our institutional arrangements as well as the ideals we hold sacred. Discussing modern racism and its discursive character also remains important for theology and Black faith because it helps us to see how theological categories and Black faith practices are often marked by harmful Eurocentric categories and ideals that we must reject if our theological production and faith commitments are to be truly liberative.

These are just a few of the reasons why *Prophesy Deliverance!* continues to be a gift to theological education and religious studies more broadly. The emergence of modern racism is complex and resists reductionist explanations. West helps us to remember that exploring racism's discursive elements helps us *investigate modern racism in ways that reveal its ambiguities, contradictions, and grotesqueries.* We would do well to linger in this complexity as we seek to grasp the unfolding of modern racism within ever new historical and cultural conditions. More importantly, may this book inform another generation so that we might better understand the experiences of the marginalized, vulnerable, and oppressed. In this way, we might prophesy deliverance to our minds, hearts, and the social structures in which we live and breathe.

A Response to Chapter 3
The Four Traditions
of Afro-American Response

BRANDON M. TERRY

It is difficult now, perhaps, to appreciate the sclerotic state of the debate on African American political thought and cultural politics when Cornel West's masterwork, *Prophesy Deliverance!*, exploded upon the intellectual scene. The four decades since have been mostly kind to the study of African American political thought and intellectual history, with long-unsung work of archival retrieval and philosophical reinterpretation buoyed by the need to understand the Barack Obama phenomenon, Black Lives Matter, and authoritarian turn of the contemporary right. While West strained mightily against the prevailing interpretive frameworks of the time, today's students in African American studies and critical theory find themselves exposed to granular descriptions of the "Black radical tradition," allegations of "Afro-pessimism," and genealogies of Black feminism.[1] This propitious situation is due, at least in part, to the book's pathbreaking account of Black political thought and culture in "The Four Traditions of Response."

Throughout the twentieth century, many occasional commentators on Black politics and culture remained in thrall to the view that African American thought is derivative in its fundamentals and, thus, of more tactical than philosophical significance. Condemning the Negro intellectual as a "failure," the irascible sociologist E. Franklin Frazier insisted that most Black political thought "is restricted to sterile repetition of the safe and conventional ideas current in American society."[2]

In *An American Dilemma* (1944), arguably the twentieth century's most influential work of scholarship on African American political life, Gunnar Myrdal summarily declared that

> Negro thinking is almost completely determined by white opinions—negatively and positively. It develops as an answer to the popular theories prevalent among whites by which they rationalize their upholding of caste. In this sense it is a derivative, or secondary, thinking.[3]

"Negro thinking in social and political terms," Myrdal contended, "is . . . *exclusively* a thinking about the Negro problem," chiefly concerned with the proper balance between "accommodation" and "protest," and defending which "social class or group among the whites is chosen as a prospective ally."[4]

While Frazier lamented that Black intellectuals had "never developed a social philosophy, except perhaps a crude and unsophisticated opportunism," Myrdal regarded the supposed imitative and opportunistic quality of Negro thinking as rational and, frankly, fortunate.[5] "The Negroes, the new immigrants, the Jews, and other disadvantaged and unpopular groups," he argued, "could not possibly have invented a system of political ideals which better corresponded to their interests" than the liberal principles Myrdal claimed to discern as the bedrock "American Creed."[6] Indeed, where Black thinkers veered off-script from creedal liberalism, flummoxed social scientists of the Myrdalian breed tended to turn to the rhetoric of therapeutic psychology for assistance. Nationalists and radicals were more likely to be described in the diagnostic concepts of rage, frustration, and "make-believe" than in terms demanding reasoned argument and philosophical reconstruction.[7]

Fortunately, other Black intellectuals produced more sophisticated (and sympathetic) mappings of Black political thought and culture. In *The Souls of Black Folk* (1903), W. E. B. Du Bois offered a tripartite typology of "revolt and revenge," "adjustment and submission," and "assimilation through self-realization" as key traditions. Midcentury scholars like Ralph Bunche and Rayford Logan dropped Du Bois's romanticism to proceed with more conventional terms from political science—conservatism, "moderate" liberalism, and radicalism.[8] These early framings eventually yielded ground, however, to what became the most enduring and influential interpretive framework for Black political thought: a struggle between *integrationism* and *nationalism*.

The most authoritative defense of this binary was Harold Cruse's 1967 classic, *The Crisis of the Negro Intellectual*, released during the crystallization of the Black Power movement and the recruitment of unprecedented numbers of Black students and scholars—including Cornel West—into predominantly white universities. Projecting backward from the "new wave" of "Negro Nationalism" that he identified as the most important mid-twentieth-century development in American "race relations," Cruse insisted that tensions between figures like Malcolm X and civil rights movement liberals were part of a nationalist-integrationist contretemps dating back to the 1850s.[9] As the United States barreled toward civil war in that portentous decade, Black intellectuals like Frederick Douglass and Martin Delany openly sparred over the prospects for a multiracial republic, the wisdom of Black emigration from the United States, and whether anti-Black racism was intractable. Though Cruse was undoubtedly correct to note the persistence of Black nationalism and the trouble it caused for the analytical categories of political science, his insistence on this binary ultimately flattened the very complexity of debate that the *Crisis* promised to clarify.

Cramming questions about political economy, gender, and imperialism into ill-fitting categories, these successive images of Black political thought were rendered more plausible by deep, structural constraints on Black political organizing and expression. Black marginalization in mainstream media and public forums, systematic disenfranchisement in the South and machine capture in the North, widespread discrimination in civil society (including unions and universities), and outright repression left the space for Black political expression *over*determined by what breaks through to public notoriety on the back of philanthropic tastes, charismatic spokespersons, and racial ideology. Under such conditions, it was easy even for thoughtful students of Black political thought to reduce its crucial debate to the most effective strategies for what West calls "inclusion within the rapidly expanding American capitalist order" (p. 25) and partition accordingly.

Against this background, one of the outstanding contributions of *Prophesy Deliverance!* is its frontal assault on these once-dominant cartographies of Black political thought. Offering up a strikingly original attempt to remap the contours and content of Black political culture, West argues that the critical questions of Black political life are not integration or nationalism, but "self-image" and "self-determination." This widening of the aperture through which we might view the thematic preoccupations of Black political thought stems from West's willingness to pare back the debate to a sparer level and restate its most basic questions. How do we conceive of "Blacks," and what are the stakes of that group conception for us as individuals? What forms of identification, acknowledgment, or recognition do such conceptions require? What would it mean—socially, politically, culturally, psychologically—for Afro-modern subjects or peoples to exercise meaningful direction throughout their lives absent domination or usurpation? What, if any, democratic, identitarian, or solidaristic commitments and practices follow from these claims?

The recovery of these questions is parasitic on two other moves— one historiographical, the other anthropological. West's historical claim is that the "modern" era of Black political life was eclipsed by a "postmodern" one, where *formal* legal inclusion and public norms of liberal tolerance (e.g., against racism, sexism, homophobia) are rendered precarious and paradoxical by cascading crises of postindustrial capitalism. These crises include the collapse of European empire, the volatile attempt to secure American hegemony, and the deterioration of scientific and other traditional forms of epistemic authority. These developments accelerated the fragmentation of Black communities across gender, geographical, and class lines. In Cornel West's view, such transformations, local and geopolitical, have "rendered the framework of the Du Bois–Washington debate obsolete" (p. 30). West's sense of the glaring inability of this older inheritance to speak to the "problem-space" of the present allows him to rethink the Black political tradition anew and ask whether its constituent elements can produce a new synthesis appropriate to problems besetting *our* form of life.[10]

Anthropologically, West also moves from the conventional political science project of mapping *ideologies* to a broader category of "*traditions of cultural response*" because "culture is more fundamental than politics in regard to Afro-American self-understanding" (p. 55). West argues that political consciousness will be "shaped and molded" by judgments made by Black people about whether the group has the "resources and resiliency" within its *cultural* traditions to meet the constitutive problems of its form of life, including problems of meaning, self-assurance, and purposiveness (p. 55). At the outset, West describes his revisionist project as influenced by studies of Jewish, Spanish, and women intellectuals, suggesting a still-underappreciated template for the *comparative* study of the "ethics of the oppressed" around the globe and a critique of methodological nationalism and parochialism in the study of Black thought.[11]

The generative nature of these methodological innovations is most evident in the novelty of West's mapping of "four traditions of response" in Black political thought and culture. First, West identifies an *exceptionalist* tradition, evidenced by Black nationalists and W. E. B. Du Bois's early cultural expressivism. Exceptionalists, West argues, fetishize the uniqueness of African American culture and "personality," often indulging extravagant claims about Black particularity and the normative demands of Black solidarity (e.g., obligations to practice endogamy, maintain residential separation, hold particular cultural tastes). While the traditional concern with exceptionalism is its propensity toward out-group hostility, West echoes Frantz Fanon's more subtle critique about the power of such discourse to generate and protect economic interests for a petite bourgeoisie that seeks to invest their quest for consumer loyalty, government set-asides, and market leverage with the intensity of race pride.[12]

Second, West describes an *assimilationist* tradition, which diagnoses the greatest remaining obstacle to Black flourishing as the pervasiveness of pathological forms of culture *and* politics which prevent assimilation to the norms that govern putatively "healthy" segments of American (or modern, Western, middle-class) society. While this tradition is often (rightly) associated with the Black conservative critique of the "deviance" of the ghetto poor, West directs our attention to E. Franklin Frazier's theory that American chattel slavery and Jim Crow obliterated African traditions and lodged forms of self-contempt, social disorganization, cultural emptiness, and underdevelopment at the heart of Black life. These crises, he argued, were evident in the growing "pathology" of the urbanizing poor and the "deep-seated inferiority complex" of a Black middle class he judged intellectually vapid, hypersensitive, and obsessed with cultivating hierarchical markers of distinction *among* Blacks based on skin color, conspicuous consumption, and status.[13]

In contrast to the assimilationist's quest for high-status absorption, the third, *marginalist* tradition lives in more liminal spaces. While it issues a derisive disavowal of mainstream American society's oppressive mores and machinery, it also tends to treat African American politics and culture as unduly restrictive, constraining our individuality, creativity, and freedom. West associates this tradition with creative artists like Richard Wright, James Baldwin, and Toni Morrison.[14]

In West's account, this tradition has the flavor of bourgeois existentialism. Its politics are moralistic and often melodramatic forms of sermonizing criticism, preoccupied with the heroic revolt of individuals against unbearably conformist and repressive communities. However liberating creatively and critically, West sees the tradition ultimately as self-undermining. It so persistently fails to theorize the complexity of collective action and institutional life that West treats marginalism alone as a transitional tradition that cannot sustain itself.

This characterization, however, downplays the constructive—and dare I say, *prophetic*—dimensions of so-called marginalism. Despite West's interest in competing accounts of African American culture, *Prophesy* sometimes proceeds without acknowledging how deeply these renderings of who "we" are and how "we" have gone awry in some way, are *themselves* part of the work of cultural construction.[15] The marginalist's provocation is to present an image or account of the group that, on considered reflection, its members will feel constricted in or chagrined by. As the legacy of the feminist and queer-of-color writers whom West associates with this tradition suggests, when such work succeeds in *implicating* us in injustice or cruelty, the intervention can spur efforts to progressively remake the group itself—including its constitutive scripts, norms, and forms of solidarity.[16]

Even if West might concede this critical power, he certainly thinks the best outcome is a final transition into his favored category, the *humanist*. This tradition rejects claims of Black exceptionalism and abjection, instead seeking out, articulating, and distilling "the universal human core" within African American freedom struggles and expressive culture (especially music). Here, West attempts a tightrope act. He connects the Black musical tradition (e.g., spirituals, blues, and jazz) and its literary manifestation in the work of Jean Toomer, Zora Neale Hurston, and Ralph Ellison to radical ideals of *individuality* and *democracy* shot through with the tragic sensibility of "the small yet cumulative struggles of human beings against overwhelming odds, [including] the creation of both supportive values and stifling mores" (p. 72). Left unresolved is the uncomfortable fact that Hurston, Ellison, and many of these artists make clear their disagreements with the defenders of Black radicalism and democratic socialism that West *also* connects with the humanist tradition (e.g., the later Du Bois, King, Malcolm, and the Black Power left).[17] Part of the viability of West's philosophical vision, therefore, in *Prophesy* and beyond, turns not just on the attempt to tether Christianity to Marxism, but on whether we can reconcile Black writers' celebration of individuality, creativity, nonconformity, and personal dignity with Black activists' insistence that such values need militant, disciplined social movements and in the creation of a democracy robust enough to extend into economic control.[18]

Though the philosopher Robert Gooding-Williams raises important worries about the "adequacy" of any classificatory scheme for Black political thought, given the "scheme-exceeding complexity and specificity" of the tradition's best, West's efforts remain instructive.[19] To emphasize the connections, for example, between Marcus Garvey and W. E. B. Du Bois, Toni Morrison and Richard Wright, or Angela Davis and Martin Luther King, is to decisively scramble the easy categories and tired oppositions we have inherited to think about Black art and politics. If, as Gooding-Williams argues, our contemporary political theorizing needs to "step back" and gain novel perspectives on our contemporary problems, West's still underappreciated gambit remains a promising point of entry four decades later.

Questions for us, however, remain. How do West's categories need to be revised or rejected in light of the unexpected set of mutations Black political life has experienced since 1982, including: Barack Obama's meliorist liberalism, the Black feminist renaissance, market-obsessed Black neoliberalism, Afro-pessimist nihilism, police and prison abolitionism, the self-proclaimed "radicalisms" of Black Lives Matter, and the hardly studied currents of masculinist populism and nationalism living mainly on the internet? More complicated is whether the turn to "cultural traditions of response" forces a confrontation with knottier problems of psychology. Do the interpretive ambitions of West's critical theory make it even more vital to know more about, as Richard Wright put it, "the psychological reactions of oppressed peoples" and what drives them to different responses? Wright, for instance, is skeptical of political typologies in part because he thinks *emotion* "precedes the idea . . . [and] attitudes select the kind of ideas in question."[20] If something akin to this is correct, references to the "politics of conversion" in West's *Race Matters* (1993) become crucial.

The project of humanist radicalism suggests the need not simply for rich description and sweeping critique, but comprehensive practices of organization, intimacy, and persuasion, which take aim at the dispositions, anxieties, pleasures, and affective investments that attach us to self-undermining forms of response. If realism or pluralism makes hopes for mass "conversion" politics implausible, however, perhaps there still may be room for a chastened politics built upon West's cartography. This politics, admittedly, has none of the flair of prophesy delivered, but does suggest a modus vivendi between competing traditions of response, seeking out narrow, but not inconsequential, grounds of solidarity that contest the most severe forms of oppression and stigma, if nothing else.

A Response to Chapter 4
On Capitalism, Christianity, and Culture

COREY D. B. WALKER

It is no secret that the question of liberation raised a series of provocative encounters in the wake of the modern Black freedom movement. We need look no further than on the pages of *The Black Scholar* in 1975 where William Strickland raised the important question "Whatever happened to the politics of Black liberation?"[1] Strickland's question was grounded in a critical analysis of the fracture and waning of a Black freedom movement that had galvanized the Black community in moving toward a fundamental reevaluation of American democracy. It was a question that was not of mere academic or parochial interest. It went to the very heart of a political malaise that had captured the revolutionary intent of a Black politics and a Black imagination that was arrested in its development. In its wake, a panoply of political philosophies and ideologies ranging from Black nationalism to Pan-Africanism to Black feminism to Marxist-Leninist-Maoism sought to respond to the original and creative thrust of Black freedom politics.

It is in this context that a critical intellectual confrontation between Marxism and African American religious criticism was staged. Cornel West joined a tradition of African American thinkers who engaged the broad and diverse streams of Marxist thought across the twentieth century. Yet West is distinctive in his commitment to bring Marxism into sustained conversation with African American religious thought, culture, and experience. Unlike classical social gospel adherents Walter Rauschenbusch and Washington Gladden and African American religious socialists George Washington Woodbey and Reverdy Ransom, West set out to examine the contours of Marxist thought toward developing a critical analytic to power a prophetic vision of Christianity born out of African American experience and culture.[2] In so doing, he created a unique synthesis of Marxism and Christianity as *parrhesia*—"fearless speech"—elegantly captured in the title of his pioneering text *Prophesy Deliverance!*[3]

Prophesy Deliverance! can be thought of as the third in a trinity of texts that stage a critical engagement between Marxist thought and African American experience in the wake of the Black freedom movement.[4] Published in 1981, Manning Marable's *Blackwater: Historical Studies in Race, Class Consciousness and Revolution* opens with a series of essays that engage radical Black thinking and revolutionary Black religion in the service of liberation.[5] From Nat Turner to African American religious spirituals to the religious dimensions of Black radical thought, *Blackwater* engages in a dialectical investigation between Marxism and Black history. Angela Davis's *Women, Race and Class* plumbs the depths of Black women's experience in the Black freedom struggle and the women's liberation movement.[6] Davis recovers the marginalized voices, perspectives, and ideas of Black women in charting how they sought to transform a racist, sexist, and classist capitalist society. Davis does not shy away from deploying a critical Marxist hermeneutic and uncovering the class dimensions of Black women's oppression in these liberatory movements as well as recovering the critical movements by Black women to open up another terrain of freedom. Cornel West's *Prophesy Deliverance!* makes a distinctive contribution to the engagement of Marxist thought in African American intellectual and political circles by linking a progressive vision of African American Christianity with a Marxist critique of American capitalist and white supremacist society. In so doing, *Prophesy Deliverance!* articulated a philosophically astute project of the radical and revolutionary potential of African American Christianity that would complement the formidable theological challenge of the prevailing intellectual and political regime of American life and culture—Black theology.

The publication of James H. Cone's *Black Theology and Black Power* in 1969 marked a pivotal moment in theological and political discourse. *Black Theology and Black Power* was part of a flowering of theological works in a period of intense theological reflection on the philosophies and practices of Black Power. The year prior to the publication of Cone's text witnessed the appearance of Albert Cleage's theologically revolutionary collection of sermons *The Black Messiah*, C. Eric Lincoln's theological update of Rayford Logan's 1944 collection of social criticism *What the Negro Wants* in *Is Anybody Listening to Black America?*—with James Cone's first published essay "Christianity and Black Power" as the lead in the collection—and Tom Skinner's evangelical memoir and manifesto *Black and Free.*[7] But Cone's text was the first formal theological work to take up the politically resonant message of Black Power. In so doing, it effected a veritable sea change in the role, function, and identity of theological discourse. The book aimed at nothing less than to capture in theological discourse what Lerone Bennett termed the "cataclysmic shift in the mood of Negroes."[8]

However, the book entered a dominant social and intellectual context whereby it could only be misread. Theologians did not know what to make of a phenomenon that wedded ultimate claims with the existential and material conditions of African Americans. Scholars did not understand the poaching of the language of Black Power within theological discourse. The foundational misreading was further exacerbated by the prevailing regime of thought that rendered humanity as existing within the limits of whiteness alone. Hence Cone's text was an ontological violation. Moreover, by bringing together theology and Black Power—thus making explicit the always already conflict of sovereignties that lie at the heart of the project of the modern nation-state— the text instantiated a political violation of the conceptual universe of democracy proper. The frustration the text caused is exquisitely captured in the question posed by liberal theologian Paul Lehmann to James H. Cone during Cone's interview for a faculty appointment at Union Theological Seminary, "Why in the hell did you write that book—*Black Theology and Black Power*?"[9]

The emergence of Black Power further destabilized the liberal consensus that governed American race relations. "*Black Theology and Black Power*," as Cone reminds us in his 1989 preface to a twentieth-anniversary edition of the book, "was a product of the Civil Rights and Black Power movements in America during the 1960s, reflecting both their strengths and weaknesses." The text not only facilitated a critical questioning of the liberal consensus that governed American race relations, it also injected a deep critique into the theological underpinnings that supported American democracy. Calling into question the American theo-political project, Cone's project brought into the open new categorical alternatives to Christianity and democracy—Black theology and Black Power. Yet, despite Black theology's determined gaze on the epistemic imperialism of white theology and its culture of white power, it left unassailed the challenges presented by a rapacious capitalism and the arbitrary and absolute proclivities of an American imperialism that laid waste to peoples and cultures across the world.

Cornel West recognized the imperative to critically address the formidable challenges of American capitalism while maintaining the powerful and transformative critique of progressive African American Christianity. In many ways, West extends the deep and probing critique of Martin Luther King Jr. King's call for a transformation of values was not merely rhetorical wordplay to rearrange American capitalist imperium, rather it was a fundamental *critique* of the existing order of things. In commenting on King's last protest with the Memphis sanitation workers, Brandon Terry reminds us of the biting critique of King,

> King sought to link our inability to recognize the dignity of such work and the people who performed it to forms of reification and ideology that we inherited from a sordid history of coerced labor and economic exploitation. In his last presidential address to the Southern Christian Leadership Conference in 1967, King insisted that "[a] nation that will keep people in slavery for 244 years will 'thingify' them and make them things. And therefore, they will exploit them and poor people generally economically."
>
> . . . Our attributions of value (the cost of commodities, the worth of labor) or the ways we treat our fellows more like objects, things, or commodities than equal persons, are embedded in and overdetermined by social structures that constantly impose such relations as natural, inevitable, or rational.[10]

West creatively develops the force of King's critique in a potent philosophical discourse that creatively blends key aspects of the discourses of Marxism and Black theology.

In his lead essay in the 1977 double issue of *Philosophical Forum* on "Philosophy and the Black Experience," edited by the pioneering radical philosopher Jesse McDade, West posits a definition of Afro-American philosophy that is acutely instructive for understanding the critical encounter he stages between Marxism and Black theology in this chapter: "Afro-American philosophy is the interpretation of Afro-American history, highlighting the cultural heritage and political struggles, which provides desirable norms that should regulate responses to particular challenges presently confronting Afro-Americans."[11] In this formulation, African American historical experience offers up the opportunity

to engage in a critical interpretation, adjudication, affirmation, and justification of ideas, norms, and perspectives in response to "existential
and political dilemmas currently besetting a cultural way of life." West
deploys a Gramscian philosophy of history and culture in developing a
practice of cultural criticism that holds the promise of sustaining efforts
and visions of a more just, humane, and democratic existence.

West's article, particularly as it forms and informs the critical basis
of this chapter of *Prophesy Deliverance!*, also reminds us of the work of
an earlier philosopher who stages an ethically inflected confrontation
between Marxism and Black experience. Howard University philosopher Eugene C. Holmes engages the broad currents of Marxist thought
and African American culture in advancing a philosophical vision that
seeks to respond to the revolutionary dynamics afloat in the world and
the precarity that defines African American existence in the United
States.[12] For Holmes, humanist and ethical commitments demand
pressing philosophy to respond to the very problems of life and society.
Holmes turns to Marx, particularly the early Marx engaging Feuerbach
and Proudhon. This humanist Marx guides him to the rich terrain of
culture and an ongoing engagement with the philosophical midwife of
the Harlem Renaissance and Howard University colleague Alain Locke.
Culture becomes a rich repository of ideas that express the meanings
of the lifeworlds, self-understandings, and self-representations of African Americans. It is this attention to culture and liberatory aspirations
of African Americans that would critically inform Holmes's germinal
1965 paper "A General Theory of the Freedom Cause of the Negro
People" delivered at the meeting of the American Philosophical Association where he would advance the argument that "there would be no
human liberation without the liberation of Black people."[13]

For West, Marxism is not a science of eternal laws nor is it dogma
expressed in formulaic doctrine. Such forms of Marxism deny the
integrity and vitality of culture. West draws on the Marxist tradition
represented by György Lukács and Antonio Gramsci. This Marxist
tradition underscores the critically important matter of culture that is
distinctive and central to modern life in general and African American
life in particular. Indeed, culture and politics are inseparable and must
be critically and creatively thought together through a sophisticated
methodology that does not reduce one to the other. In this chapter,
West's engagement of Marxism and Black theology facilitates a more
critical probing of the contours of Black experience under hegemonic
white supremacy, misogynist male sexism, and exploitive neoliberal

capitalism. West's recourse to Marxism facilitates a critical recognition that a change in the order of things is not only possible but indeed fundamental to realizing a new humanity and a new world. In pursuing this vision, religion is a rich and resplendent resource that can inform this liberatory quest. West stages the encounter between Black theology and Marxism in order to precipitate a cognitive renewal of human possibility and dignity that may help to transform reality and initiate a radical and deep democracy.

The confrontation between Black theology and Marxism yields a critical expression of Afro-American thought able to grapple with the depths of the intellectual and empirical dictates of Western modernity. In *Minima Moralia: Reflections on Damaged Life*, Theodor Adorno provocatively suggests, "The only philosophy which can be responsibly practiced in the face of despair is the attempt to contemplate all things as they would present themselves from the standpoint of redemption. Knowledge has no light but that shed on the world by redemption: all else is reconstruction, mere technique."[14] For Adorno, the task of thinking is not one of technique, but rather a deliberate and considered practice whereby new concepts, categories, and languages are developed that illuminate the contingencies and contradictions, the ironies and erasures of the dominant political protocols and intellectual logics and technologies of the West.

Theology is barbaric. Marxism is debased. *Prophesy Deliverance!* is a critical response, in form and in content, of attempting to write and think and enact a new world in this wake. By bringing together prophetic modes of Afro-Christian thought and progressive Marxism, West demonstrates their reciprocal and dialectical power and praxis for life and thought. It is this project of Afro-American revolutionary Christianity that may offer a new spirit of hope in the struggle for deep democracy. Perhaps, it is the only philosophy possible. Then and now.

A Response to Chapter 5
Afro-American Revolutionary Christianity

MYISHA CHERRY

In 2010, Princeton University scholar of religion Eddie Glaude proclaimed in a *Huffington Post* article that "the Black Church, as we've known it or imagined it, is dead." For Glaude, "The idea of this venerable institution as central to Black life and as a repository for the social and moral conscience of the nation has all but disappeared."[1] There are several reasons for thinking that what we have thought or simply imagined the Black church to be (i.e., always progressive, central, and socially relevant) has not empirically lived up to this imaginative heuristic shorthand.

First, Glaude claims that while it's easy to think that the Black church has always been a progressive and prophetic institution, this is not the case. Such thinking obscures the fact that a lot of Black churches have also been and are conservative. So even though the concept of the Black church may evoke progressive images like Martin Luther King Jr. and Adam Clayton Powell Jr., it only tells a partial story since the same imagining doesn't also bring to mind conservative figures like those from the National Baptist Convention, USA. Also, the Black church is no longer at the center of Black communal life. There are other nonreligious institutions that play a specialized role in the lives of Black folk. There are also white religious institutions that serve as a refuge for Black parishioners. And Glaude cites the increasing attendance of Blacks at white megachurches as an example. More important, for Glaude, is what he refers to as the "routinization of black prophetic witness." He worries that the Black church has rested on its laurels, content with pointing to its past prophetic deeds as justification and evidence of its power in the contemporary moment. However, when the church does this, Glaude claims that it loses its power instead. This is because memory becomes sufficient for future-oriented work. Present-day transformation waits for us to rise from our confident neglect.

He then asks, What would be the role of *prophetic* Black churches? He believes that their apt role has been obscured and interrupted by distracting invitations to financial empowerment conferences and other gatherings, in contrast to mobilization in public around "pressing issues of our day." Recognizing this lack of the prophetic he asks, "Where are the press conferences and impassioned efforts around black children living in poverty, and commercials and organizing around jobs and healthcare reform?" While he believes that "prophetic energies . . . can't be passed down," but can be embraced and expressed again, one must wonder if Black churches have given up their prophetic energy in exchange for profit(able) energy.

This worry is not just unfounded anxiety. It can be backed up by empirical studies of Black American life. In their article "The Faith of Black Politics," Eric McDaniel, Maraam Dwidar, and Hadill Calderon note, "Just as Black politics has witnessed a declining commitment to racial and class equality, the Black church's message of social and spiritual salvation is losing its prominence to a theology that emphasizes individual faith and material accumulation."[2]

They found that religious beliefs are associated with difference in group identity and support of strategies to achieve racial equality. For example, researchers have linked the prosperity gospel to the rise of racial conservatism among Blacks and neoliberalism among Black elites. According to the prosperity gospel, people with faith will be rewarded with wealth and health in this world and the world to come. Christians with faith will be divinely favored with material possessions, while those who lack it will be punished. Researchers have found that Blacks are significantly more supportive of the prosperity gospel than whites.[3] And as a result, this influences how they view the underlying causes of poverty and its solutions. This has led some adherents to believe that racism and classism are products of poor faith as opposed to social structures; that poverty is a result of sinful behavior; and that inequality can be prayed away.[4]

Similarly, recent celebration of the Black masses in regard to a select few reaching billionaire status—as if it will equate to Black liberation—is telling of our culture's obsession with capitalism and neoliberalism. In 2020 and 2021, *Forbes* magazine reported that musician Rihanna is worth $1.7 billion (second only to Oprah Winfrey as the richest female entertainer), and that Tyler Perry is worth $1 billion due to his creative projects in film, television, and the stage. When *Forbes* failed to report that rapper Kanye West had reached the $1 billion mark, he accused them of trying to suppress his self-made narrative because of his race. In response, he provided receipts, and was eventually declared a billionaire. But then Kanye noted on Twitter: "It's not a billion. It's $3.3 billion since no one at *Forbes* knows how to count." Black cultural rhetoric seems to embody Perry's misguided words expressed in an interview with *Forbes* that "ownership changes everything," as phrases such as "get the bag" and "we might be Black billionaires in the making" become not just part of Black vernacular speech, but a large part of Black aspirations for many.

As I have previously claimed, the Black church as always progressive, central, and socially relevant is not a universal fact but an ideal image of the past and our present. Similarly, we might say that West's Afro-American Christianity as described in his 1982 text is also an ideal. Given its features and the historical record, if it had been practiced during the late 1970s and early 1980s, its practitioners were the minority. Perhaps West looked at Black evangelical history through a similar nostalgic lens as many have done with the Black church. For example, while West points to a particular Black church as an example of the revolutionary Christian perspective, such as the National Black United Front in the House of the Lord Church in Brooklyn, New York, it is described as a "sign of hope" rather than a realized example pointing to a widespread phenomenon. When it seems that he offers examples of political organizations active during the early 1980s as evidence of the existence of Afro-American revolutionary Christianity, such as the Black Theology Project, Theology in the Americas, and Black Seminarians, Inc., he describes them as "open to a prophetic Christian, progressive Marxist viewpoint" (p. 126) rather than exemplars of it. This is not to say that West's claims have no empirical evidence to back them up. It is only to say that it's possible that what he proposed may not be something we need to return to or do as those who have come before us. Rather it is something we need to actualize and become examples of in the present moment. Even if Afro-American revolutionary Christianity is—like Glaude's Black church—an ideal, still West's account of it provides us with something to live up to and a blueprint to put into action as we face a Christianity lacking in revolutionary power, prophetic power, and progressive Marxism.

Even forty years after its publication, *Prophesy Deliverance!* provides an essential intervention. "The last task of Afro-American religious philosophy," West writes, "is to provide a *political prescription* for—or strategic intervention into—*the specific praxis* in the present historical moment of the struggle for liberation" (introduction, p. 9; italics added). The prescription he offers (which is a way of thinking and acting) is "Afro-American Revolutionary Christianity." And in chapter 5 of the text, he highlights the practical and programmatic dimensions of this revolutionary Christian perspective and praxis.

Revolutionary Christian perspective and praxis is a combination of *prophetic Christianity* and *progressive Marxism* that is lacking in the aforementioned examples. West notes that *prophetic Christianity* is concerned with existential freedom and social freedom. It is guided by "profound conception of human nature and human history, a persuasive picture of what one is as a person, what one should hope for, and how one ought to act" (introduction, p. 2). This prophetic feature "imbues Afro-American thinking with the sobriety of tragedy, the struggle for freedom, and the spirit of hope," but it also calls us to "negate what is and transform prevailing realities against the backdrop of the present historical limits" (introduction, pp. 5–6).

Progressive Marxism is anticapitalist and anti-imperialist. It offers powerful critiques via the dialectical method and engages in praxis. It is neither dogmatic nor elitist. It rejects bourgeois electoral activity. It is the opposite of political liberalism. Liberalism affirms the capitalist vision of society; it focuses on political and economic integration into the mainstream of American life. This in turn creates a viewpoint that "clamors for a bigger piece of the ever-growing American pie" (p. 98).

This brand of individuality is not the kind that promotes a selfish, anticommunity, self-made perspective. Rather, for West, it is one that is concerned with our salvation, as well as our dignity as persons, and our agential capacities to transform the world in which we live. It "reinforces the importance of community, common good, and the harmonious development of personality" (introduction, p. 3). This commitment to democracy is one that is concerned with "the people" having control over the leaders and institutions that serve them. Therefore, it's a democracy that "requires that accountability—of institutions to populace, of leaders to followers, of preachers to laity—be the center of any acceptable social vision" (introduction, p. 4).

This prophetic Afro-American revolutionary Christianity with its combination of prophetic Christianity and progressive Marxism dedicated to the norms of individuality and democracy is needed. As West writes, "For Americans, especially Afro-Americans, adopting a particular Marxist perspective and praxis is an act of desperation, yet we live in desperate times." And since the absence of it has not created a better world, it's understandable that "it proceeds from a persistent pessimism regarding the American way of life, yet such pessimism is, for the most part, warranted" (p. 114).

West notes that this Afro-American revolutionary Christianity can "weaken the hegemony of liberalism over the Afro-American community" (p. 120). This hegemony has led the African American community to rarely ask fundamental questions about why the American pie is never sliced equally or how it is baked. It has thus contributed to many remaining "silent about class divisions" and "how unequal distribution of goods . . . undergird[s] discrimination against regions, impose[s] ceilings on upward social mobility, and foster[s] racism, sexism, and ageism" (p. 98). Thus, adopting it will allow us to understand "in order to enhance and enrich the lives of Afro-Americans" (p. 75).

What results is that we will come closer to figuring out the fundamental determinant of Black oppression and create effective strategies to alleviate it. It will help us to refrain from equating liberation with inclusion and American middle-class status, and a well-paying job with power. It will allow us to address unequal distribution, and work to ensure that oppressive capitalist systems do not stay intact. Without focusing on this prophetic/progressive relationship, Cornel West reminds us that "it becomes extremely difficult to present an idea of liberation with socioeconomic content." Thus, the progressive merging with the prophetic allows for an "emergence of any substantive political program or social vision" informed by a clear-cut social theory in addition to the moral norms thus described (94).

While I think there are less signs of hope for the *institutional expression* of revolutionary Christian perspective and praxis today than West lays out at the end of chapter 5, I believe that it is still needed. But some questions remain. Should we give up this institutional hope, given the consistent failure of Black church leadership and the mass exodus of Black people from Black churches? Perhaps West's single church example, as explained in section 1, is indicative of the fact that this institutional hope may be merely a "sign of hope" but only a sign nonetheless. That is to say, perhaps we should imagine Afro-American revolutionary Christianity beyond the church as an institution. This is not to commit the "spiritual, but not religious" move. Rather it's to suggest that we should begin to reimagine prophetic transformation beyond traditional institutions. If so, where should this hope lie? It should lie in ordinary folk who aim to live out their Christian commitments in the world. The people are the church. Thus, we are reminded always that power belongs to the people. Absent of this power Afro-American revolutionary Christianity will simply be empty, a bureaucratic, soulless enterprise. Will individual expression alone weaken the power and reach of Black revolutionary Christianity? I do not think so. I think individuals can be walking expressions of Black revolutionary Christianity. This is not to deny the power of collective and communal organizing. It's only to suggest that membership is not the only means for revolution, nor are imaginary concepts like "the Black church."

What is the hope for African Americans who have left the Christian church or the Christian faith (although it has not left them)—disillusioned by the lack of the prophetic and progressive found there? Have they—by definition—lost access to this perspective and praxis too? No! Perhaps they may have something to offer us all, for they have seen firsthand the frustration with and dangers of being content in myths and pure imaginings, and thus may have, in addition to the emotional motivation, the spiritual and political tools to help us see what has been missing and what needs to be done if we are to take seriously the features and demands of Afro-American revolutionary Christianity.

The combination of loss of prophetic energy, the ignoring and obscuring of the root causes of suffering, and obsessions with wealth-as-freedom makes *Prophesy Deliverance!* not only still relevant but necessary for our times. As the prosperity gospel infiltrates Black churches, and neoliberalism seduces Black culture, still, Black people are being killed, the poor are being oppressed, trans folk are being attacked, those in developing countries are being exploited, and the marginalized are being ignored. A different, more revolutionary vision and strategy for liberation is needed.

Notes

Introduction

1. For the conception of philosophy as a kind of writing, rather than a science in search of certainty or professional area of study with a distinct subject matter, see Richard Rorty, "Philosophy as a Kind of Writing: An Essay on Derrida," *New Literary History* 10, no. 1 (Autumn 1978): 141–60. Needless to say, my perspective is deeply influenced by Richard Rorty's brilliant work, *Philosophy and the Mirror of Nature* (Princeton, NJ: Princeton University Press, 1979). For my sympathetic yet hard-hitting critique of this book, see my review in *Union Seminary Quarterly Review* 37, nos. 1–2 (Fall–Winter 1981–1982): 179–85.

2. For the best full-length treatment of this neglected phenomenon, see Albert J. Raboteau, *Slave Religion: The "Invisible Institution" in the Antebellum South* (New York: Oxford University Press, 1978).

3. It is important to note that Black churches in the United States evolved as independent churches, separate from any white control. Therefore Black religious leadership and Black theological reflection could arise autonomous (or at least, relatively so) from white censorship, as is not the case for Black people in Catholic and Anglican churches in Latin America and Africa. It is no accident that Pentecostalism—the denomination that vigorously promotes the development of indigenous religious leadership free from the control of church bureaucracies—was founded by Black Baptists, principally Rev. W. J. Seymour in Los Angeles, California, in 1906. Pentecostalism is the only denomination of the Christian faith founded by Black people and is one of the fastest-growing denominations in the world, especially among oppressed peoples. See James S. Tinney, "Black Origins of the Pentecostal Movement," *Christianity Today*, October 8, 1971, 4–6, and Richard Quebedeaux, *The New Charismatics* (Garden City, NY: Doubleday, 1976), 25–51.

4. For the complex relationship between the conception of a person and moral norms, see the superb essays by Samuel Scheffler, "Moral Skepticism and Ideals of the Person," and Norman Daniels, "Moral Theory and the Plasticity of Persons," *The Monist: An International Journal of General Philosophical Inquiry* 62, no. 3 (July 1979): 288–303 and 266–87. I also touch on this difficult issue in "Ethics, Historicism and the Marxist Tradition" (PhD diss., Princeton University, 1980), 3–26, 127–45, 259–74.

5. This claim is partly derived from Hegel's insight regarding the Christian principle of self-consciousness or subjectivity in his *The Philosophy of History,* trans. J. Sibree (New York: Dover Publications, 1956), 19, 319, 334. See also Colin Morris, *The Discovery of the Individual, 1050–1200* (New York: Harper & Row, 1972), 10–13.

6. For interesting treatments of Marx's own Romantic sensibilities as a young literary artist and thinker, see William M. Johnston, "Karl Marx's Verse of 1836–1837 as a Foreshadowing of His Early Philosophy," *Journal of the History of Ideas* 28 (1967): 259–68; Leonard P. Nessell, "Marx's Romantic Poetry and the Crisis of Romantic Lyricism," *Studies in Romanticism* 16, no. 4 (Fall 1977): 509–34; Donald R. Kelley, "The Metaphysics of Law: An Essay on the Very Young Marx," *American Historical Review* 83, no. 2 (April 1978): 350–67. Marx's own deep concern for individuality can be seen in the following three passages from three major works:

> In bourgeois society, therefore, the past dominates the present; in Communist society, the present dominates the past. In bourgeois society capital is independent and has individuality, while the living person is dependent and has no individuality. . . . In place of the old bourgeois society, with its classes and class antagonisms, we shall have an association, in which the free development of each is the condition for the free development of all. (Karl Marx, "Manifesto of the Communist Party," in *The Marx-Engels Reader,* ed. Robert C. Tucker [New York: W. W. Norton, 1972], 347, 353.)

> The communal relationship, into which the individuals of a class entered and which was determined by their common interests over against a third party, was always a community to which these individuals belonged only as average individuals, only insofar as they lived within the conditions of existence of their class—a relationship in which they participated not as individuals but as members of a class. On the other hand, it is just the reverse with the community of revolutionary proletarians who take their conditions of existence and those of all members of society under their control. The individuals participate in this community as individuals. (Karl Marx, *The German Ideology: Writings of the Young Marx on Philosophy and Society,* trans. and ed. Lloyd D. Easton and Kurt H. Guddat [Garden City, NY: Doubleday, 1967], 460.)

> The barrier to capital is that this entire development proceeds in a contradictory way, and that the working-out of the productive forces, of general wealth, etc., knowledge etc., appears in such a way that the working individual alienates himself [*sich entäussert*]; relates to the conditions brought out of him by his labour as those not of his own but of an alien wealth and of his own poverty. But this antithetical form is itself fleeting, and produces the real conditions of its own suspension.

The result is: the tendentially and potentially general development of the forces of production—of wealth as such—as basis; likewise, the universality of intercourse, hence the world market as a basis. The basis as the possibility of the universal development of the individual, and the real development of the individuals from this basis. (Karl Marx, *Grundrisse: Foundations of the Critique of Political Economy,* trans. Martin Nicolaus [New York: Random House, 1973], 541–42.)

7. M. H. Abrams, *Natural Supernaturalism: Tradition and Revolution in Romantic Literature* (New York: W. W. Norton, 1971). For his conception of Marx's "Romantic humanism" in the early *Manuscripts,* see 313–16.

8. This central contrast—as well as the elaboration of the notion of individuality—is the major point of departure in the writings of C. B. Macpherson. This important Canadian political theorist deserves much more attention than he has received. See his *The Political Theory of Possessive Individualism: Hobbes to Locke* (Oxford: Oxford University Press, 1962); *The Real World of Democracy* (Oxford: Oxford University Press, 1966); *Democratic Theory: Essays in Retrieval* (Oxford: Oxford University Press, 1973).

9. A distinctive feature of prophetic Afro-American Christianity is the African encounter with the absurd in the United States: an existential situation in which no reasons suffice to make any kind of sense or give any type of meaning to the personal circumstances and collective condition of Afro-Americans. With the "death of the African gods," the African appropriation of the Christian worldview transformed a prevailing absurd situation into a persistent and present tragic one—a kind of "Good Friday state of existence"—with the hope for a potential and possible triumphant state of affairs. The relationship between this stress on the tragic and the relative absence of tragic themes in the ancient oral narratives of Dahomey (as noted by Melville Herskovits) remains unexplored. This creative appropriation, with African styles and forms within a new faith context, made new sense of the circumstances and gave new meaning to the lives of Afro-Americans by promoting a worldview in which the problem of evil—the utterly tragic character of life and history—sits at its center. Prophetic Afro-American Christianity is not simply an escapist pie-in-the-sky religion, nor a sophisticated political ideology in religious veil. Rather, it contains elements of both, plus an enduring emphasis on the deeply tragic quality of everyday life of a culturally degraded, politically oppressed, and racially coerced labor force and unique individuals who face the ultimate facts of human existence: death, disease, disappointment, dread, and despair. In fact, I suggest that the radically comic character of Afro-American life—the pervasive sense of joy, laughter, and ingenious humor in the Black community—flows primarily from the Afro-American preoccupation with tragedy, a preoccupation significantly colored by the Black Christian worldview. For as Walter Kerr has rightly noted: "Comedy is never the gaiety of things; it is the groan made gay. Laughter is not man's first impulse, he cries first. Comedy always

comes second, late, after the fact and in spite of it or because of it." (Walter Kerr, *Tragedy and Comedy* [New York: Simon & Schuster, 1967], 19.) Furthermore, as Prof. Dennis Dickerson, of Williams College, conveyed to me in conversation, the African sense of time, with its paradoxical poles of urgency and belatedness, in conjunction with this stress on tragedy may partly account for the phenomenon so deeply rooted in Afro-American Christian thought and practice: the aggressive waiting (or what I call revolutionary patience) for the Lord to intervene and the Kingdom of God to come. This "waiting" is not of the quietistic sort, but rather encourages action while tempering one's exorbitant expectations. I explore this matter as a pillar (among others) for a theory of Afro-American culture in my as yet unpublished essay (delivered at Haverford College), "Afro-American Christianity and the Quest for Cultural Identity."

10. For a recent philosophical plea for the importance of American pragmatism, see Richard J. Bernstein, "In Defense of American Philosophy," in *Contemporary American Philosophy,* 2nd series, ed. John E. Smith (New York: Humanities Press, 1970), 293–311. For historical analyses of American pragmatism, see H. S. Thayer's detailed work, *Meaning and Action: A Critical History of Pragmatism* (Indianapolis: Bobbs-Merrill, 1968), and John Dewey's classic essay "The Development of American Pragmatism," in his *Philosophy and Civilization* (New York: Peter Smith, 1963), 13–35. It is interesting that one of the leading African philosophers, Kwasi Wiredu, of the University of Ghana, is deeply influenced by American pragmatism—especially that of John Dewey. See his noteworthy book, *Philosophy and an African Culture* (Cambridge: Cambridge University Press, 1980).

11. I have in mind John Dewey's formulations in *Reconstruction in Philosophy* (Boston: Beacon Press, 1949). For a comparison to the work of Heidegger and Wittgenstein, see Cornel West, "Philosophy and the Afro-American Experience," *Philosophical Forum* 9, nos. 2–3 (Winter 1977–78): 117–48.

12. For a penetrating critique of the neglect of the self in pragmatism, especially in the work of John Dewey (and treatment by the pragmatic psychologist George Mead), see Gordon Allport, "Dewey's Individual and Social Psychology," in *The Philosophy of John Dewey,* ed. Paul Arthur Schilpp (Evanston, IL: Northwestern University, 1939), 265–90. For the pragmatic movement's refusal to take seriously class struggle, the early Sidney Hook's work is unsurpassed. As the work of a student and disciple of Dewey and a self-styled Marxist, Hook's writings in the 1930s serve as a corrective to Dewey's. See Sidney Hook, "John Dewey and His Critics," *New Republic* 67 (June 3, 1931): 73–74; *Towards the Understanding of Karl Marx* (New York: John Day, 1933); "Experimental Naturalism," in *American Philosophy Today and Tomorrow,* ed. Horace M. Kallen and Sidney Hook (New York: Lee Furman, 1935), 205–25; and for a brief examination of the early Hook's work, note the critical essay by Lewis S. Feuer, "From Ideology to Philosophy: Sidney Hook's Writings on Marxism," in *Sidney Hook and the Contemporary World: Essays on the Pragmatic Intelligence,* ed. P. W. Kurtz (New York: John Day, 1968), 35–53. Other noteworthy treatments of the

intersection of American pragmatism (especially Dewey) and Marx are Max Eastman's polemic response to the early Hook, "The Americanization of Marx," in his *Marxism: Is It Science?* (New York: W. W. Norton, 1940), 299–348; William English Walling, *The Larger Aspects of Socialism* (New York: Macmillan, 1913), 1–29, 373–85; Jim Cork, "John Dewey and Karl Marx," in *John Dewey, Philosopher of Science and Freedom,* ed. Sidney Hook (New York: Dial Press, 1950), 331–50; Harry K. Wells, *Pragmatism: Philosophy of Imperialism* (New York: International Publishers, 1954); Howard Selsam, *Philosophy in Revolution* (New York: International Publishers, 1957), 102–14, 146–48; George Novack, *Pragmatism vs. Marxism: An Appraisal of John Dewey's Philosophy* (New York: Pathfinder Press, 1975); and the fine treatment by Richard J. Bernstein, *Praxis and Action: Contemporary Philosophies of Human Activity* (Philadelphia: University of Pennsylvania Press, 1971), 80–83, 227–29. I believe Bernstein hits the nail on the head when he writes, "The dialectic that can take place between Marx and Dewey is the political dialectic of our time" (80). Lastly, for the pragmatic movement's veneration of scientific method (much more Peirce, Dewey, and Mead than James), see the standard critical treatment of this issue by Jürgen Habermas, *Knowledge and Human Interests* (Boston: Beacon Press, 1971), 113–39.

13. A particular conception of the Afro-American self-image deeply affects the political strategy of Afro-American self-determination. Yet we must not assume *a priori* that certain correlations necessarily hold, such as that a positive self-image will always accompany the acquisition of power, or a negative self-image the absence of power. Afro-American philosophy must preserve the delicate symbiotic relationship between culture and politics without resorting to a simplistic and all too often incorrect reductionism.

14. Based on my conception of Afro-American philosophy, there have been few instances of it. Of course, there have been Afro-American philosophers, such as Alain Locke, Eugene Holmes, and William Fontaine, but, like most Afro-American intellectuals, they have exerted their energies either trying to convince the Black middle class that the world of ideas should be taken seriously, serving as an ideologue for a particular political or cultural movement, or attempting to gain acceptance in the predominantly white academy. All three activities are essential for a potent intelligentsia, but leave little time for reflecting upon the basic assumptions of the theoretical frameworks wherein thinkers speculate. Effective propagandists and insecure academicians rarely question basic frameworks or ask fundamental questions with seriousness.

Chapter 1: American Africans in Conflict

1. This claim is based on a particular periodization of the development of the Western world persuasively argued in Ernest Cassirer's *The Philosophy of the Enlightenment,* trans. Fritz C. A. Koelin and James P. Pettegrove (1932); Ernst Troeltsch's *The Social Teaching of the Christian Churches,* trans. Olive Wyon

(New York: Macmillan, 1931), vol. 1, 23–34, and his *Protestantism and Progress: A Historical Study of the Relation of Protestantism to the Modern World,* trans. W. Montgomery (1912); and Peter Gay's magisterial work, *The Enlightenment: An Interpretation* (New York: Alfred A. Knopf, 1966), vol. 1. For the classic Marxist treatment of the Enlightenment, see Max Horkheimer and Theodor Adorno, *Dialectic of Enlightenment,* trans. John Cumming (New York: Herder & Herder, 1972), esp. 3–42.

2. For a classic treatment of this problematic of provinciality in the beginnings of the United States, see Merle Curti, *The Growth of American Thought,* 2nd ed. (New York: Harper & Brothers, 1951), 3–126. Note also Max Lerner, *America as a Civilization* (New York: Simon & Schuster, 1957), 3–73. My own theory of the development of American provinciality is based in part on the seminal treatment of American culture by Geoffrey Thurley, *The American Moment: American Poetry in the Mid-Century* (New York: St. Martin's Press, 1978), esp. 3–32.

3. Alexis de Tocqueville, *Democracy in America,* ed. Phillips Bradley (New York: Alfred A. Knopf, 1945), vols. 1 and 2; George Santayana, *The Genteel Tradition,* ed. Douglas L. Wilson (Cambridge, MA: Harvard University Press, 1967); Van Wyck Brooks, *America's Coming-of-Age* (New York: B. W. Heubsch, 1915). The best secondary literature on de Tocqueville's unsurpassed analysis of American culture remains the superb extended essays by John Stuart Mill which accompany the de Tocqueville volumes. For insightful interpretations of Santayana's work, especially his classic 1911 essay, "The Genteel Tradition in American Philosophy," originally given at the Philosophical Union of the University of California at Berkeley and first published in his *Winds of Doctrine* (New York: Scribner's Sons, 1913), 186–215, see Danforth Ross, "The Genteel Tradition: Its Characteristics and Its Origins" (PhD diss., University of Minnesota, 1954); Douglas L. Wilson, "Introductory," in *Genteel Tradition,* 1–25, and Morton White, *Science and Sentiment in America: Philosophical Thought from Jonathan Edwards to John Dewey* (New York: Oxford University Press, 1972), 241–46. The best recent books on the long and winding career of Van Wyck Brooks are James Hoopes, *Van Wyck Brooks: In Search of American Culture* (Amherst: University of Massachusetts Press, 1977), and Raymond Nelson, *Van Wyck Brooks: A Writer's Life* (New York: E. P. Dutton, 1980).

4. William James's notions were put forward in his address to the Anti-Imperialist League in 1903. See the Report of the Fifth Annual Meeting of the New England Anti-Imperialist League, November 28, 1903, with excerpts in Ralph Barton Perry, *The Thought and Character of William James,* Briefer Version (Cambridge, MA: Harvard University Press, 1948), 246–47. For a theory of American culture based directly on James's notions, see H. S. Thayer, *Meaning and Action: A Critical History of Pragmatism* (Indianapolis: Bobbs-Merrill, 1968), 437–45. For a fine dramatic simplification of this theory, see Philip Rahv's well-known essay, "Paleface and Redskin," in his *Image and Idea* (New York: New Directions, 1957), 1–6.

5. Herbert W. Schneider, *A History of American Philosophy,* 2nd ed. (New York: Columbia University Press, 1963), 23–26; Joseph L. Blau, *Men and Movements in American Philosophy* (Englewood Cliffs, NJ: Prentice-Hall, 1952), 27–35.

6. Garry Wills, *Inventing America: Jefferson's Declaration of Independence* (Garden City, NY: Doubleday, 1978), esp. 167–319.

7. Schneider, *History of American Philosophy,* 55–61; Blau, *Men and Movements,* 114. See also Andrew Delbanco, *William Ellery Channing: An Essay on the Liberal Spirit in America* (Cambridge, MA: Harvard University Press, 1981).

8. Winthrop Jordan, *White over Black: American Attitudes toward the Negro, 1550–1812* (New York: W. W. Norton, 1968), pts. 1–3, pp. 44–98, 179–265; Thomas F. Gossett, *Race: The History of an Idea in America* (Dallas: Southern Methodist University Press, 1965), 17–31.

9. W. E. B. Du Bois, *The Souls of Black Folk* (Greenwich, CT: Fawcett Publications, 1961), 16–17. The best secondary treatment of this classic text can be found in Arnold Rampersad, *The Art and Imagination of W. E. B. Du Bois* (Cambridge, MA: Harvard University Press, 1976), 68–90, and Robert B. Stepto, *From behind the Veil: A Study of Afro-American Narrative* (Urbana: University of Illinois Press, 1979), 52–91.

10. The most important work on the retention of African practices among Black people in the United States (and New World) remains Melville J. Herskovits's *The Myth of the Negro Past* (Boston: Beacon Press, 1958). For a superb recent treatment of this phenomenon, see Albert J. Raboteau, *Slave Religion: The "Invisible Institution" in the Antebellum South* (New York: Oxford University Press, 1978), 4–92.

11. M. H. Abrams, *The Mirror and the Lamp: Romantic Theory and the Critical Tradition* (New York: Oxford University Press, 1953), chap. 7, pp. 156–83, and chap. 8, pp. 184–225. See also the influential essays by Harold Bloom, "The Internalization of Quest-Romance," in *Romanticism and Consciousness: Essays in Criticism,* ed. Harold Bloom (New York: W. W. Norton, 1970), 3–24, and "'To Reason with a Later Reason': Romanticism and the Rational," in *The Ringers in the Tower: Studies in Romantic Tradition* (Chicago: University of Chicago Press, 1971), 323–37.

12. Jacques Barzun, *Classic, Romantic and Modern* (Boston: Little, Brown, 1961), 1–17, 96–114.

13. M. H. Abrams, *Natural Supernaturalism: Tradition and Revolution in Romantic Literature* (New York: W. W. Norton, 1971), 11–140, 327–72, 411–62.

14. For the classic text on this subject, see F. O. Matthiessen, *The American Renaissance* (New York: Oxford University Press, 1941). Other notable works include V. L. Parrington, *Main Currents in American Thought,* vol. 2 (New York: Harcourt, Brace, 1954), 427–65; D. H. Lawrence, *Studies in Classic American Literature* (New York: T. Seltzer, 1923); R. W. B. Lewis, *The American Adam: Innocence, Tragedy, and Tradition in the Nineteenth Century* (Chicago: University

of Chicago Press, 1955), esp. the prologue, 1–10; Richard Chase, *The American Novel and Its Tradition* (Garden City, NY: Doubleday, 1957), esp. 1–22; and Ihab Hassan, *Radical Innocence: Studies in the Contemporary American Novel* (Princeton, NJ: Princeton University Press, 1961), 34–60. This American search for newness is captured by the words of the two major literary figures of the period: Ralph Waldo Emerson and Herman Melville. In his renowned essay "Circles," Emerson states that "I am only an experimenter . . . I simply experiment, an endless seeker, with no past at my back" (*Selected Writings of Ralph Waldo Emerson,* ed. William H. Gilman [New York: New American Library, 1965], 304). In his famous essay "Hawthorne and His Mosses," Melville writes, "Let us boldly contemn all imitation, though it comes to us grateful and fragrant as the morning, and foster all originality, though at first, it be crabbed and ugly as our own pine knots" (Herman Melville, *Moby-Dick,* ed. Harrison Hayford and Hershel Parker [New York: W. W. Norton, 1967], 546, 550).

15. Raboteau, *Slave Religion,* 128–32. Note also Lawrence W. Levine, *Black Culture and Black Consciousness: Afro-American Folk Thought from Slavery to Freedom* (New York: Oxford University Press, 1977), 60–61.

16. Herskovits, *Myth of the Negro Past,* 232–35. The material conditions under which many Africans in the United States became Christians are worth noting: the structure of domination was that of a pre-industrial form of slavery; a lower ratio of Africans to whites than that in Latin America facilitated more frequent and intense African-white interaction; and though only 4.5 percent of all Africans imported to the Western Hemisphere came to the United States and Canada, an incredibly high rate of natural increase soon quadrupled this percentage figure. Therefore most converts (though not all, such as the poet Phillis Wheatley) were American-born Africans struggling to make sense of and give meaning to life without an immediate relation to African customs and world views. For further elaboration on this matter, see Raboteau, *Slave Religion,* 87–92.

17. Raboteau, *Slave Religion,* 59–75.

18. This point is accented by E. Franklin Frazier, *The Negro Church in America* (New York: Schocken Books, 1964), 30–34. For a more dialectical treatment—which highlights the liberating and debilitating aspects of the Black Christian churches—see Eugene D. Genovese, *Roll, Jordan, Roll: The World the Slaves Made* (New York: Random House, 1974), 159–284. See also the first-rate dissertation of James M. Washington which is a pioneering study of the separate Black Baptists, "The Origins and Emergence of Black Baptist Separatism, 1863–1897" (PhD diss., Yale University, 1979).

19. Lionel Trilling, *Beyond Culture: Essays on Literature and Learning* (New York: Viking Press, 1965), 3. In a famous essay entitled "The Idea of the Modern," in *The Idea of the Modern in Literature and the Arts,* ed. Irving Howe (New York: Horizon Press, 1967), Irving Howe writes, "Nihilism lies at the center of all we mean by modernist literature, both as subject and symptom, a demon overcome and a demon victorious" (39). For a more affirmative view of modernism, see Peter

Gay, *Freud, Jews and Other Germans: Masters and Victims in Modernist Culture* (New York: Oxford University Press, 1978). The best general treatment of modernism is Malcolm Bradbury and James McFarlane, eds., *Modernism: 1890–1930* (Middlesex: Penguin Books, 1976), and the classic Marxist perspective is put forward by Georg Lukacs in his influential essay "The Ideology of Modernism," in *Marxism and Human Liberation,* ed. E. San Juan Jr. (New York: Dell Press, 1973), 277–307.

20. Virginia Woolf, "Mr. Bennett and Mrs. Brown," in *Collected Essays,* vol. 1 (London: Hogarth Press, 1966), 321.

21. The major texts on the industrial provincial stage of American culture are Henry F. May, *The End of American Innocence: A Study of the First Years of Our Own Time, 1912–1917* (New York: Alfred A. Knopf, 1959); Robert H. Wiebe, *The Search for Order, 1877–1920* (New York: Hill & Wang, 1967); Samuel P. Hays, *The Response to Industrialism, 1885–1914* (Chicago: University of Chicago Press, 1957); Chase, *American Novel and Its Tradition,* 117–236; Hassan, *Radical Innocence,* 61–95; and the seminal essay by Herbert G. Gutman, "Work, Culture, and Society in Industrializing America, 1815–1919," in *Work, Culture, and Society in Industrializing America: Essays in America's Working Class and Social History* (New York: Vintage Books, 1977), 3–78.

22. Alfred Kazin, *On Native Grounds: An Interpretation of Modern American Prose Literature* (Garden City, NY: Doubleday, 1956), ix.

23. This formulation follows Richard Rorty's brilliant contemporary remake of Santayana's essay, entitled "Professionalized Philosophy and Transcendentalist Culture," in *Georgia Review,* 30th anniversary, Winter 1976, 757–69. For a broader characterization of the pragmatist attack on idealism, see Morton White, *Social Thought in America: The Revolt against Formalism* (Boston: Beacon Press, 1957). Note also Bruce Kuklick, *The Rise of American Philosophy: Cambridge, Massachusetts, 1860–1930* (New Haven, CT: Yale University Press, 1977), 129–227, 233–401. Related treatments on the phenomenon of professionalism in American culture are Burton J. Bledstein, *The Culture of Professionalism: The Middle Class and the Development of Higher Education in America* (New York: W. W. Norton, 1976), esp. 80–128, 287–334, and David F. Noble, *America by Design: Science, Technology, and the Rise of Corporate Capitalism* (New York: Alfred A. Knopf, 1977).

24. August Meier, *Negro Thought in America, 1880–1915: Racial Ideologies in the Age of Booker T. Washington* (Ann Arbor: University of Michigan Press, 1963), 161–278; S. P. Fullinwider, *The Mind and Mood of Black America: 20th-Century Thought* (Homewood, IL: Dorsey Press, 1969), 47–71; Abby Arthur Johnson and Ronald Maberry Johnson, *Propaganda and Aesthetics: The Literary Politics of Afro-American Magazines in the Twentieth Century* (Amherst: University of Massachusetts Press, 1979), 1–63; and Julius Lester, "Du Bois and Washington," in his fine introduction to *The Seventh Son: The Thought and Writings of W. E. B. Du Bois,* ed. Julius Lester, vol. 1 (New York: Random House, 1971), 41–52.

25. This insight is but one of many in the superb essay by Harold Cruse, "Behind the Black Power Slogan," in his *Rebellion or Revolution?* (New York: William Morrow, 1969), 193–260.

26. For actual reprints of articles from *The Messenger,* see *Voices of a Black Nation: Political Journalism in the Harlem Renaissance,* ed. Theodore G. Vincent (San Francisco: Ramparts Press, 1973), 43–51, 113–22. Reliable treatment of Owen and Randolph can be found in Philip Foner, *American Socialism and Black Americans: From the Age of Jackson to World War II* (Westport, CT: Greenwood Press, 1977), 265–87; Johnson and Johnson, *Propaganda and Aesthetics,* 57–63; and Henry Williams, *Black Response to the American Left: 1917–1929* (Princeton, NJ: Princeton University Press, 1973), 80–93. For a fuller examination of Randolph, see Jervis Anderson, *A. Philip Randolph: A Biographical Portrait* (New York: Harcourt Brace Jovanovich, 1972).

27. Similarly, reproductions of articles from *The Crusader,* the periodical of the African Blood Brotherhood, are in Vincent, *Voices of a Black Nation,* 123–36. Detailed treatments of this fascinating group are difficult to find. The best ones I know are Harry Haywood, *Black Bolshevik: Autobiography of an Afro-American Communist* (Chicago: Liberator Press, 1978), 122–31; Foner, *American Socialism and Black Americans,* 309–11; Mark Solomon, "Red and Black: Negroes and Communism" (PhD diss., Harvard University, 1972), 79–84; and Mark Naison, "The Communist Party in Harlem, 1928–1936" (PhD diss., Columbia University, 1975), chaps. 1 and 2.

28. N. R. Hanson, *Patterns of Discovery* (Cambridge: Cambridge University Press, 1958); Michael Polanyi, *Personal Knowledge: Towards a Post-Critical Philosophy* (Chicago: University of Chicago Press, 1958); Thomas S. Kuhn, *The Structure of Scientific Revolutions,* 2nd ed. (Chicago: University of Chicago Press, 1970), and "Reflections on My Critics," in *Criticism and the Growth of Knowledge,* ed. Imre Lakatos and Alan Musgrave (Cambridge: Cambridge University Press, 1970), 231–78; Imre Lakatos, "Falsification and the Methodology of Scientific Research Programmes," in *Criticism and the Growth of Knowledge,* 91–196; Paul Feyerabend, *Against Method* (New York: Schocken Books, 1975) and *Science in a Free Society* (New York: Schocken Books, 1978). For serious critical responses to the demythologizing of science, see Israel Scheffler, *Science and Subjectivity* (Indianapolis: Bobbs-Merrill, 1967), and "Vision and Revolution: A Postscript on Kuhn," in *Philosophy of Science* 39, no. 3 (September 1972): 366–74; Larry Laudan, *Progress and Its Problems: Towards a Theory of Scientific Growth* (Berkeley: University of California Press, 1977); and Clark Glymour, *Theory and Evidence* (Princeton, NJ: Princeton University Press, 1980).

29. Ihab Hassan, *The Literature of Silence: Henry Miller and Samuel Beckett* (New York: Alfred A. Knopf, 1968); Hassan, *The Dismemberment of Orpheus: Toward a Postmodern Literature* (New York: Oxford University Press, 1971); Hassan, *Paracriticisms: Seven Speculations of the Times* (Urbana: University of Illinois Press, 1975); Hassan, *The Right Promethean Fire: Imagination, Science and*

Cultural Change (Urbana: University of Illinois Press, 1980); Raymond Older-man, *Beyond the Waste Land: A Study of the American Novel in the Nineteen-Sixties* (New Haven, CT: Yale University Press, 1972); Christopher Lasch, *The Culture of Narcissism* (New York: W. W. Norton, 1978); Heinz Kohut, *The Analysis of the Self* (New York: International Universities Press, 1971); Kohut, *The Restoration of the Self* (New York: International Universities Press, 1977); *The Search for the Self: Selected Writings of Heinz Kohut, 1950–1978*, 2 vols., ed. Paul H. Ornstein (New York: International Universities Press, 1978); Jerome Klinkowitz, *Literary Disruptions: The Making of a Post-Contemporary American Fiction,* 2nd ed. (Urbana: University of Illinois Press, 1981). Relevant Marxist responses to and analyses of postmodernism include Fredric Jameson, *Marxism and Form: Twentieth-Century Dialectical Theories of Literature* (Princeton, NJ: Princeton University Press, 1971); Jameson, *Fables of Aggression: Wyndham Lewis, the Modernist as Fascist* (Berkeley: University of California Press, 1979); Jameson, *The Political Unconscious: Narrative as a Socially Symbolic Act* (Ithaca, NY: Cornell University Press, 1981), and his insightful essay "Reification and Utopia in Mass Culture," *Social Text,* Winter 1979, 130–48; Russell Jacoby, *Social Amnesia: A Critique of Conformist Psychology from Adler to Laing* (Boston: Beacon Press, 1975); and Stuart Ewen, *Captains of Consciousness: Advertising and the Social Roots of the Consumer Culture* (New York: McGraw-Hill, 1976). For a critical, even polemic, treatment of postmodernism, see Gerald Graff, "The Myth of the Postmodernist Breakthrough," *Tri-Quarterly* 26 (Winter 1973): 383–417, and his controversial book *Literature against Itself: Literary Ideas in Modern Society* (Chicago: University of Chicago Press, 1979). Of course, the basis of scholarship on postmodernism and mass culture was laid by the pioneering work of Max Horkheimer and Theodor Adorno with their classic essay "The Culture Industry: Enlightenment as Mass Deception," in *Dialectic of Enlightenment,* 120–67, and the writings of David Riesman in his (along with Nathan Glazer and Reuel Denney) *The Lonely Crowd: A Study of the Changing American Character,* abr. ed. (New Haven, CT: Yale University Press, 1961); Riesman, *Individualism Reconsidered* (Garden City, NY: Doubleday, 1955), esp. 12–27, 126–63; and Riesman, *Abundance for What? and Other Essays* (Garden City, NY: Doubleday, 1964), 103–367.

30. This leadership fulfills the prophecy of Thomas Mann, the major German modernist writer, who writes in the last paragraph of his famous 1938 lecture given on his coast-to-coast tour, "I believe, in fact, that for the duration of the present European dark age, the centre of Western culture will shift to America" (*The Coming Victory of Democracy,* trans. Agnes E. Meyer [New York: Alfred A. Knopf, 1938], 66–67). Note also William Barrett's words regarding the situation of American intellectuals in 1945, "We were probably the last American generation to go through this old rite of looking toward Europe for our culture . . . that older exclusive filial relation to Europe—the sense of Europe as a unique treasure on which Americans must depend—was on the way out" (*The Truants: Adventures among the Intellectuals* [Garden City, NY: Doubleday, 1982], 130).

31. Kuklick, *Rise of American Philosophy,* 565–72. See also Richard Rorty's introduction in *The Linguistic Turn,* ed. Richard Rorty (Chicago: University of Chicago Press, 1967), 1–39. For a slightly different perspective, note my essay "Nietzsche's Prefiguration of Postmodern American Philosophy," *Boundary 2,* vol. 9, no. 10 (Spring–Fall 1981): 241–70.

Chapter 2: A Genealogy of Modern Racism

1. This second theoretical moment of Afro-American philosophy constitutes its Foucaultian elements: the exploration of the complex relationship between knowledge and power, discourse and politics. For a similar yet more ambitious project, see Edward Said, *Orientalism* (New York: Pantheon Books, 1978). Note that my aim is not to endorse the discursive idealism of Michel Foucault, but rather to incorporate some of his powerful insights into a more sophisticated Marxist analysis of the emergence of modern racism. I have just embarked on a huge project that deepens my concern in this chapter into a full-fledged volume.

2. Friedrich Nietzsche, *On the Genealogy of Morals,* trans. Walter Kaufmann and R. J. Hollingdale (New York: Vintage Books, 1967); Michel Foucault, "Nietzsche, Genealogy, History," in *Language, Counter-Memory, Practice: Selected Essays and Interviews,* trans. Donald F. Bouchard and Sherry Simon (Ithaca, NY: Cornell University Press, 1977), 139–64.

3. Cf. Louis Althusser, "Marx's Relation to Hegel," in *Politics and History* (New York: Schocken Books, 1972), 181–83. For trenchant criticisms of Althusser, see Stanley Aronowitz, *The Crisis in Historical Materialism: Class, Politics, and Culture in Marxist Theory* (New York: Praeger, 1981), 68–69, 120–21, 325–27.

4. This insight bears the stamp of Foucault's long-drawn-out quarrel with vulgar Marxism. See Michel Foucault, *The History of Sexuality,* vol. 1, trans. Robert Hurley (New York: Random House, 1980), 92–98; Foucault, *Power/ Knowledge: Selected Interviews and Other Writings, 1972–1977,* ed. Colin Gordon (New York: Pantheon Books, 1980), 109–45.

5. For the "classicism plus science" view of the Enlightenment, see Peter Gay, *The Enlightenment: An Interpretation,* vol. 1 (New York: Alfred A. Knopf, 1966), 3–27, 313–21. For the importance of the Cartesian transformation of philosophy, see Richard Rorty's insightful metaphilosophical claims in *Philosophy and the Mirror of Nature* (Princeton, NJ: Princeton University Press, 1979), esp. 8–12, 45–51, 54–69, 136–40.

6. This understanding of the Renaissance derives from Aby Warburg's notion of *Ausgleichsformel* (compromise formula); and for Galileo's and Newton's protomodern worldviews, see Gay, *Enlightenment,* 269–77.

7. Benjamin Farrington, *Francis Bacon: Philosopher of Industrial Science* (New York: Collier Books, 1961), 78–106; Bertrand Russell, *A History of Western Philosophy* (New York: Simon & Schuster, 1945), 544.

8. Martin Heidegger, "The Age of the World View," trans. Marjorie Grene, *Boundary 2,* vol. 4, no. 2 (Winter 1976): 348–49.

9. Gay, *Enlightenment,* 310–11.

10. Rorty, *Philosophy and the Mirror of Nature;* M. H. Abrams, *The Mirror and the Lamp: Romantic Theory and the Critical Tradition* (New York: Oxford University Press, 1953).

11. This claim, as well as my general argument, derives in part from the seminal study by George L. Mosse, *Toward the Final Solution: A History of European Racism* (New York: Howard Fertig, 1978). This neglected work deserves much more attention than it has heretofore received.

12. Mosse, *Toward the Final Solution,* 10.

13. Mosse, *Toward the Final Solution,* 10.

14. Winthrop Jordan, *White over Black: American Attitudes toward the Negro, 1550–1812* (New York: W. W. Norton, 1968), 3–98; Thomas F. Gossett, *Race: The History of an Idea in America* (Dallas: Southern Methodist University Press, 1965), 3–31.

15. Michel Foucault, *The Order of Things: An Archaeology of the Human Science* (New York: Pantheon Books, 1970), 132, 158.

16. Jordan, *White over Black,* 217–18; Gossett, *Race,* 32–34; Ashley Montagu, "The Origin of the Concept of 'Race,'" in *Man's Most Dangerous Myth: The Fallacy of Race,* 5th ed. (New York: Oxford University Press, 1974), 46ff.

17. Jordan, *White over Black,* 220.

18. Jordan, *White over Black,* 220–21.

19. Gossett, *Race,* 36.

20. For their defenses of Blumenbach, see Jordan, *White over Black,* 223, 507; Gossett, *Race,* 39; Montagu, *Man's Most Dangerous Myth,* 41–45. Support for my viewpoint is found in Mosse, *Toward the Final Solution,* 11, 21.

21. Most notably in the United States, Dr. John Augustine Smith, president of the College of William and Mary, and the famous naturalist Dr. Samuel George Morton of Philadelphia—both fervent proponents of Black inferiority. Jordan, *White over Black,* 505–6; Gossett, *Race,* 58–59.

22. Mosse, *Toward the Final Solution,* 22.

23. Mosse, *Toward the Final Solution,* 25.

24. Mosse, *Toward the Final Solution,* 25.

25. Jordan, *White over Black,* 486ff., 514.

26. Jordan, *White over Black,* 515.

27. Jordan, *White over Black,* 515.

28. Jordan, *White over Black,* 515–16.

29. Jordan, *White over Black,* 520.

30. Jordan, *White over Black,* 520.

31. David Brion Davis, *The Problem of Slavery in Western Culture* (Ithaca, NY: Cornell University Press, 1966), 403.

32. Gossett, *Race,* 45.

33. Richard H. Popkin, "Hume's Racism," *Philosophical Forum* 9, nos. 2–3 (1977): 213.

34. Jordan, *White over Black,* 436–37.

35. Popkin, "Hume's Racism," 218.

36. Popkin, "Hume's Racism," 218.

37. Gay, *Enlightenment,* 34.

38. Frank M. Snowden Jr., *Blacks in Antiquity: Ethiopians in the Greco-Roman Experience* (Cambridge, MA: Belknap Press, 1970), 178–79.

39. Snowden, *Blacks in Antiquity,* 179.

40. E. E. Sikes, *The Anthropology of the Greeks* (London: D. Nutt, 1914); W. L. Westermann, *The Slave Systems of Greek and Roman Antiquity,* Memoirs of the American Philosophical Society 40 (Philadelphia: American Philosophical Society, 1955); Moses Hadas, *Hellenistic Culture: Fusion and Diffusion* (New York: Columbia University Press, 1959); Adrian N. Sherwin-White, *Racial Prejudice in Imperial Rome* (Cambridge: Cambridge University Press, 1967).

Chapter 3: The Four Traditions of Response

1. These four ideal types represent the basic responses of any group, community, or nation entering modernity. In the American context, they are found among emerging Irish, Italian, Polish, Jewish, etc., communities beginning to interact with the dominant WASP culture and society. In the European context, these traditions are salient in early nineteenth-century Germany, late nineteenth-century Russia, early twentieth-century Spain, etc. They are presently forming in Third World countries. The best recent studies on this problematic of groups entering modernity are those of John Cuddihy on Jewish intellectuals, Rockwell Gray on Spanish thinkers (esp. Ortega y Gasset), and Elaine Showalter on British women novelists. For samples of their work, see John Cuddihy, *The Ordeal of Civility: Freud, Marx, Lévi-Strauss, and the Jewish Struggle with Modernity* (New York: Basic Books, 1974); Rockwell Gray, "Ortega y Gasset and Modern Culture," *Salmagundi* 35 (Fall 1976): 6–41; Elaine Showalter, *A Literature of Their Own: British Women Novelists from Brontë to Lessing* (Princeton, NJ: Princeton University Press, 1977).

2. Antonio Gramsci defends this viewpoint in his important essay "Problems of Marxism," in *Selections from the Prison Notebooks,* trans. and ed. Quintin Hoare and Geoffrey Nowell Smith (London: Lawrence & Wishart, 1971).

3. W. E. B. Du Bois, "The Conservation of Races," in *The Seventh Son: The Thought and Writings of W. E. B. Du Bois,* ed. Julius Lester, vol. 1 (New York: Random House, 1971), 180.

4. W. E. B. Du Bois, *The Souls of Black Folk* (Greenwich, CT: Fawcett Publications, 1961), chap. 1.

5. This remark is quoted from S. P. Fullinwider's seminal work, *The Mind and Mood of Black America: 20th Century Thought* (Homewood, IL: Dorsey Press, 1969), 60.

6. *The Book of American Negro Poetry,* ed. James Weldon Johnson (New York: Harcourt, Brace and Co., Inc., 1922), 10.

7. Manuscript of speech delivered to the Washington, DC, branch of the NAACP, 1924, Johnson papers, James Weldon Johnson Collection, Yale University Library. Quoted from Fullinwider, *Mind and Mood of Black America,* 89.

8. R. R. Wright Jr., "Unlynchable Facts," *Christian Recorder* 64 (November 16, 1916): 4.

9. R. R. Wright Jr., "African Methodism and the Second Century," *Christian Recorder* 64 (April 13, 1916): 4.

10. Amy-Jacques Garvey, *Garvey and Garveyism* (New York: University Place Book Shop, 1963), 98.

11. *Black Nationalism in America,* ed. John H. Bracey Jr., August Meier, and Elliott Rudwick (Indianapolis: Bobbs-Merrill, 1970), 193.

12. Martin Luther King Jr., "A Mighty Army of Love," *SCLC Newsletter* 2 (October–November 1964): 7.

13. This interpretation puts the famous Du Bois–Washington debate in a slightly different light. Du Bois indeed favors struggling for political rights and a liberal education for the Talented Tenth, while Washington pushes for the acquisition of marketable skills and accumulation of property among Afro-Americans. But, in regard to Afro-American leadership, Washington preserves an important place for skilled workers and entrepreneurs, who have close contact with ordinary Black people. For Du Bois, at this stage in his long career, only the educated elite could provide leadership, an elite that easily falls prey to idealization of the Afro-American masses.

14. Du Bois, "The Talented Tenth," in *Seventh Son,* 1:385.

15. An important note should not be overlooked regarding Afro-American nationalist movements in the exceptionalist tradition, namely, their invariably authoritarian and sexist character. These movements—e.g., Garvey, Black Muslims, Congress of African People—delegate power from top to bottom within a highly rigid hierarchical structure wherein women are relegated to the lowest rungs, the most powerless positions. As Christopher Lasch has suggested, these movements may contain elements of a machismo complex and express assertions of masculinity heretofore ignored. Lasch's insightful essay "Black Power: Cultural Nationalism as Politics" is in his work *The Agony of the American Left* (New York: Vintage Press, 1969), 117–68. See also the provocative book by Michele Wallace, *Black Macho and the Myth of the Superwoman* (New York: Dial Press, 1979).

16. Despite ostensible gains during the past decade by the Black white-collar and stable blue-collar working class, the Black poor has increased, in numbers and percentage. In the US Census of 1972, the poor and near-poor represented a staggering 42 percent of all Afro-Americans. See Sar Levitan, William Johnston, and Robert Taggart, *Still a Dream* (Cambridge, MA: Harvard University Press, 1975), chap. 2, esp. 33.

17. Martin Kilson makes this acute observation in his article "Black Power: Anatomy of a Paradox," *Harvard Journal of Negro Affairs* 2, no. 1 (1968): 30–34. He writes: "Some professionals are adopting a Black Power ideological format not with the intent of preparing themselves for service to self-governing urban black communities but to make themselves more visible to the white establishment, which is not at all adverse to offering such persons good jobs as alternatives to Black Power. The more viable Negro businessmen are also simulating the Black Power phenomenon in this way. . . . The Black Power advocates have virtually no control over this use of their political style by the professional and business black bourgeoisie, which means the Black Power advocates will eventually lose the payoff potential of nationalist politics. If so . . . the Negro lower classes, whose riots legitimize Black Power, will be joined by the Black Power advocates in holding the bag—with nothing in it save a lot of therapeutic miscellany" (34).

18. Fortunately, there are no Afro-American strong assimilationalists, though there are still a few white ones around, e.g., Shockley and Jensen.

19. This viewpoint has been extremely influential in American sociological studies on Afro-Americans. For example, Gunnar Myrdal's renowned *An American Dilemma* (New York: Harper, 1944) states, "American Negro culture . . . is a distorted development, or a pathological condition, of the general American culture" (p. 928). Nathan Glazer and Daniel Patrick Moynihan's first edition of *Beyond the Melting Pot* (Cambridge, MA: MIT Press, 1963) reads: "The Negro is only an American, and nothing else. He has no values and culture to guard and protect" (53). And the list goes on and on, e.g., Stanley Elkins's Sambo thesis about slave personality in *Slavery* (1959), the Moynihan report on the Afro-American family (1965), Kenneth Clarke's *Dark Ghetto* (1965), etc.

20. E. Franklin Frazier, "Racial Self-Expression," in *Ebony and Topaz: A Collectanea,* ed. Charles S. Johnson (New York: Opportunity, 1927), 120.

21. In later life, like most active minds, Frazier makes claims inconsistent with his earlier views and engages in a fruitful exercise of self-criticism. Based on his earlier perspective, it is not surprising the Black middle class dangles in a world of make-believe since white society excludes them and they abhor their own culture; Afro-American intellectuals also would be hard put to project positive self-images if Afro-American culture is what the early Frazier suggests it is. For Frazier's later essay on Afro-American intellectuals, see "The Failure of the Negro Intellectual," *Negro Digest,* February 1962.

22. My treatment of Afro-American literary texts is intentionally truncated; it remains at the simplistic level of paraphrase, since such a treatment suits the purpose at hand. In the contemporary scene of Afro-American literary criticism, the major tendencies are the learned yet aloof cosmopolitanism of Nathan Scott Jr.; the impressive though flawed structuralisms of Robert B. Stepto and Henry Louis Gates Jr.; the refined Black Aesthetics of Stephen Henderson; the

equivocal hence mediating cultural anthropological viewpoint of Houston A. Baker Jr.; and the crude though pregnant Marxism of Amiri Baraka. I prefer a Marxist option that does not simply interpret texts, but, more important, provides a theory about the institution of literature (which makes literary texts possible, defines what it is to be "literary," and circumscribes the perimeters of meanings to be found in such texts) and accents the Afro-American participation therein. I present a sketch of this perspective in my extended critique of Fredric Jameson's trilogy—*Marxism and Form, The Prison-house of Language,* and *The Political Unconscious*—entitled "Fredric Jameson's Marxist Hermeneutics," in "Engagements: Postmodernism, Marxism, Politics," special issue, *Boundary 2: A Journal of Postmodern Literature* 11, no. 1/2 (Autumn 1982–Winter 1983): 177–200. See also my Marxist critique of both Gerald Graff's humanist realism and Jacques Derrida's deconstructionist poststructuralism in my essay "Beyond Realism and Anti-Realism: A Critique of Graff and Derrida," *Bucknell Review,* Special Issue on Literature and Philosophy (forthcoming). The pertinent texts of the aforementioned Afro-American literary critics include Nathan Scott Jr., "The Dark and Haunted Tower of Richard Wright," in *Five Black Writers,* ed. Donald B. Gibson (New York: New York University Press, 1970), 12–25; Scott, "Black Literature," in *Harvard Guide to Contemporary American Writing,* ed. Daniel Hoffman (Cambridge, MA: Harvard University Press, 1979), 287–341; Robert B. Stepto, "Teaching Afro-American Literature: Survey or Tradition, The Reconstruction of Instruction," in *Afro-American Literature: The Reconstruction of Instruction,* ed. Dexter Fisher and Robert B. Stepto (New York: Modern Language Association of America, 1979), 8–24; Stepto, *From behind the Veil: A Study of Afro-American Narrative* (Urbana: University of Illinois Press, 1976); Henry Louis Gates Jr., "Preface to Blackness: Text and Pretext" and "Dis and Dat: Dialect and the Descent," in Fisher and Stepto, *Afro-American Literature,* 44–69, 88–119; Stephen E. Henderson, "The Forms of Things Unknown," in *Understanding the New Black Poetry: Black Speech and Black Music as Poetic References,* ed. Stephen E. Henderson (New York: William Morrow, 1973), 1–69; Houston A. Baker Jr., *The Journey Back: Issues in Black Literature and Criticism* (Chicago: University of Chicago Press, 1980); Baker, "Generational Shifts and the Recent Criticism of Afro-American Literature," *Black American Literature Forum* 15, no. 1 (Spring 1981): 3–21; Amiri Baraka, "The Revolutionary Tradition in Afro-American Literature," in *Selected Plays and Prose of Amiri Baraka / LeRoi Jones* (New York: William Morrow, 1979), 242–51; Baraka, "Afro-American Literature and Class Struggle," *Black American Literature Forum* 14, no. 1 (Spring 1980): 5–14.

23. Nathan Huggins concurs with this observation in his book *Harlem Renaissance* (New York: Oxford University Press, 1971), 119, where, in discussing Rudolph Fisher's novel *The Walls of Jericho* (1928), he writes: "Joshua 'Shine' Jones, Rudolph Fisher's proletarian hero, has several walls to bring down. There is the

barrier of race, of course, which remarkably is the least of his concerns. His resentment is directed primarily against class distinctions and the pretentions of high-toned Negroes. Thus, Fisher wrote the only novel of the decade that exposed class antagonisms among Harlem blacks." See also Robert Bone's perceptive comments on Fisher's attempts to bridge the gap between other cleavages, e.g., rural vs. urban, artist vs. middle class, West Indian vs. southern black, in his short stories. Robert A. Bone, *Down Home: A History of Afro-American Short Fiction from Its Beginning to the End of the Harlem Renaissance* (New York: Putnam, 1975), 150–59.

24. My reading of Richard Wright is influenced by Martin Kilson's unpublished paper, "Nationalism and Marginality in Black Writers: The Case of Richard Wright." For his shorter treatment of Wright, see Martin Kilson, "Politics and Identity among Black Intellectuals," *Dissent,* Summer 1981, 339–49.

25. James Baldwin, "Everybody's Protest Novel," in *Notes of a Native Son* (Boston: Beacon Press, 1955), 17.

26. My reading of Baldwin is influenced by Stanley Macebuh's *James Baldwin: A Critical Study* (New York: Third Press, 1973).

27. Toni Morrison, *Sula* (New York: Alfred A. Knopf, 1974), 105.

28. For noteworthy treatments of this rich tradition, see Eileen Southern, *The Music of Black Americans: A History* (New York: W. W. Norton, 1971); LeRoi Jones, *Blues People: The Negro Experience in White America and the Music That Developed from It* (New York: William Morrow, 1963); Jones, *Black Music* (New York: William Morrow, 1969); Ralph Ellison, *Shadow and Act* (New York: Random House, 1964), 187–250; Albert Murray, *Stomping the Blues* (New York: McGraw-Hill, 1976); André Hodeir, *Jazz: Its Evolution and Essence,* trans. David Noakes (New York: Grove Press, 1956); Ben Sidran, *Black Talk: How the Music of Black America Created a Radical Alternative to the Values of the Western Literary Tradition* (New York: Holt, Rinehart & Winston, 1971).

29. Ralph Ellison, "Juneteenth," *Quarterly Review of Literature* 13, nos. 3/4 (1965): 276. For the first full treatment of Ellison's writing career, see Robert O'Meally, *The Craft of Ralph Ellison* (Cambridge, MA: Harvard University Press, 1980).

30. The other important stream of thought and behavior in the Afro-American humanist tradition is reformist. It extends from Frederick Douglass through Booker T. Washington to Benjamin Hooks. This stream is represented by those people who satisfy the cultural criteria of Afro-American humanism and advocate certain reforms in the capitalist system. They fail to promote structural change in society. The stream of thought and action mentioned above (p. 75) represents those people who satisfy the same cultural criteria, but support the replacement of the capitalist system with one that extends democracy into the institutions of production so that the government and economy are truly "of the people, by the people, and for the people." This replacement constitutes a structural change in society, especially a redistribution of its wealth.

Chapter 4: Prophetic Afro-American Christian Thought
and Progressive Marxism

1. For the classical Marxist claim concerning the impotency of religion, especially Christianity, see Karl Marx, "Contribution to the Critique of Hegel's Philosophy of Right," in Karl Marx, *Early Writings,* trans. and ed. T. B. Bottomore (New York: McGraw-Hill, 1964), 43–59. For an often-neglected Marxist treatment of the sheer historical character of religious belief, see "Private Property and Communism," in the Bottomore volume, 152–67. For a detailed Marxist treatment of the relationship between progressive Christians and moralists who have good intentions but little (or grossly inadequate) social analysis, see the rarely read critique of utopian socialists in *The German Ideology,* in Karl Marx and Frederick Engels, *Collected Works,* trans. Richard Dixon and others, vol. 5 (New York: International Publishers, 1976), 455–581.

2. My viewpoint is informed primarily by the work of Søren Kierkegaard, William James, and John Dewey. See Søren Kierkegaard, *Philosophical Fragments,* trans. David F. Swenson (Princeton, NJ: Princeton University Press, 1936); Kierkegaard, *Concluding Unscientific Postscript,* trans. David F. Swenson and Walter Lowrie (Princeton, NJ: Princeton University Press, 1968). See William James, *The Varieties of Religious Experience: A Study in Human Nature* (New York: William Collins, 1958), esp. 329–97; James, "The Will to Believe," in *Pragmatism; and Four Essays from "The Meaning of Truth"* (New York: Meridian Books, 1955), 177–93. Although I disagree with Dewey's adjectival approach to religion, I find his writings on the subject provocative. See esp. John Dewey, *A Common Faith* (New Haven, CT: Yale University Press, 1934). For a more direct theological confrontation with logical positivism and analytical empiricism, see my essay "A Philosophical View of Easter," *Dialog: A Journal of Theology* 19 (Winter 1980): 21–24, and my review of *The Grammar of Faith,* by Paul Homer, *Union Seminary Quarterly Review* 35, nos. 3 and 4 (Spring and Summer 1980): 279–85.

3. The major Christian critic of Marxism remains Reinhold Niebuhr. His most notable treatment is found in *Moral Man and Immoral Society: A Study in Ethics and Politics* (New York: Charles Scribner's Sons, 1960). For the claim of naiveté, see 142–68, 257–77; for the charge of narrowness, see 51–82, 169–99; and for the criticism related to shortsightedness, see 200–256. A more recent discussion on similar issues was initiated by the Polish philosopher Leszek Kolakowski in his famous essay, "Responsibility and History," in his *Toward a Marxist Humanism,* trans. Jane Zielonko Peel (New York: Grove Press, 1968), 87–157, and in his succinct piece, "Can the Devil Be Saved?," *Encounter* 43, no. 1 (July 1974): 7–13. A detailed reply was put forward by the influential Marxist historian E. P. Thompson in "An Open Letter to Leszek Kolakowski," in *The Poverty of Theory and Other Essays* (New York: Monthly Review Press, 1979), 303–402.

Kolakowski elliptically replied in his essay "My Correct Views on Everything," *Socialist Register* 11 (1974).

4. For the classic characterization of one-dimensional societies—societies ingeniously successful in absorbing, co-opting, and domesticating oppositional forces—see the most influential Marxist work in American academic Marxism, Herbert Marcuse's *One-Dimensional Man: Studies in the Ideology of Advanced Industrial Society* (Boston: Beacon Press, 1964). For a brilliant use of this perspective to the evolution of American culture, see Sacvan Bercovitch, *The American Jeremiad* (Madison: University of Wisconsin Press, 1978).

5. The best treatment of this crucial matter is found in Stanley Aronowitz's pioneering work, *The Crisis in Historical Materialism: Class, Politics and Culture in Marxist Theory* (New York: Praeger, 1981), 13–17, 123–36. For a brief characterization of this not yet digested book, see my review in *Village Voice,* January 6–12, 1982, 40.

6. See Hegel's lesser *Logic* (Part 1 of the *Encyclopedia of the Philosophical Sciences,* 1830), 3rd ed., trans. William Wallace (New York: Oxford University Press, 1975), 171–75. For elucidation, see J. N. Findlay, *Hegel: A Re-Examination* (New York: Macmillan, 1958), 189–94.

7. Quoted from Gayraud S. Wilmore, *Black Religion and Black Radicalism* (Garden City, NY: Doubleday, 1973), 49.

8. Wilmore, *Black Religion and Black Radicalism,* 76. See also Albert J. Raboteau, *Slave Religion: The "Invisible Institution" in the Antebellum South* (New York: Oxford University Press, 1978), 147.

9. Wilmore, *Black Religion and Black Radicalism,* 53–54.

10. Wilmore, *Black Religion and Black Radicalism,* 57.

11. Benjamin E. Mays, *The Negro's God as Reflected in His Literature* (Boston: Chapman & Grimes, 1938); Howard Thurman, *"Deep River" and "The Negro Spiritual Speaks of Life and Death"* (Richmond, IN: Friends United Press, 1975)—the first book was originally published in 1945, the second in 1947; Thurman, *Jesus and the Disinherited* (New York: Abingdon-Cokesbury Press, 1949); George D. Kelsey, *Racism and the Christian Understanding of Man* (New York: Charles Scribner's Sons, 1965).

12. Albert B. Cleage Jr., *The Black Messiah* (New York: Sheed & Ward, 1969); James H. Cone, *Black Theology and Black Power* (New York: Seabury Press, 1969); James H. Cone, *A Black Theology of Liberation* (Philadelphia: J. B. Lippincott, 1970); Cecil Wayne Cone, *The Identity Crisis in Black Theology* (Nashville: African Methodist Episcopal Church, 1975); Major Jones, *Black Awareness* (Nashville: Abingdon Press, 1971); Major Jones, *Christian Ethics for Black Theology* (Nashville: Abingdon Press, 1974); William Jones, *Is God a White Racist?* (Garden City, NY: Doubleday, 1973); Charles H. Long, "The Black Reality: Toward a Theology of Freedom," *Criterion,* Spring–Summer 1969, 2–7; Charles H. Long, "Perspectives for a Study of Afro-American Religion in the United States," *History of Religions* 11, no. 1 (August 1971): 54–66; J. Deotis

Roberts, *Liberation and Reconciliation: A Black Theology* (Philadelphia: Westminster Press, 1971); Roberts, *A Black Political Theology* (Philadelphia: Westminster Press, 1974); Joseph R. Washington, *The Politics of God* (Boston: Beacon Press, 1967); Washington, *Black Sects and Cults* (Garden City, NY: Doubleday, 1972); Leon Watts, "Transcendence and Mystery in Black Theology," *IDOC International Documentation* 71 (March–April 1976): 60–75; Preston Williams, "The Black Experience and Black Religion," *Theology Today* 26 (October 1969): 246–61, and "James Cone and the Problem of a Black Ethic," *Harvard Theological Review* 65 (October 1972): 483–94; Wilmore, *Black Religion and Black Radicalism.*

13. *Black Theology: A Documentary History, 1966–1979,* ed. Gayraud S. Wilmore and James H. Cone (Maryknoll, NY: Orbis Books, 1979), 618. James Cone's essay in this volume, entitled "Epilogue: An Interpretation of the Debate among Black Theologians," is the best available treatment of the discussion and dialogue among Black theologians of this stage. See 609–22.

14. Black Theology Project, "Message to the Black Church and Community," in Wilmore and Cone, *Black Theology,* 348.

15. James H. Cone, "Black Theology and the Black Church: Where Do We Go from Here?," in Wilmore and Cone, *Black Theology,* 355–56.

16. My first piece is found in Wilmore and Cone, *Black Theology,* 552–67. The second article appeared in *Witness* 63, no. 4 (April 1980): 16–19. See also my short piece "Socialism and the Black Church," *New York Circus* 3, no. 5 (October/November 1979): 5–8.

17. James Cone's important essay "The Black Church and Marxism: What Do They Have to Say to Each Other?" was jointly published by the Black Theology Project of Theology in the Americas and the Democratic Socialist Organizing Committee. This joint effort signifies neither James Cone's nor the Black Theology Project's support of DSOC's social democratic political stance.

18. Dialectical methodology is a complex procedure useful for grasping, comprehending, interpreting, explaining, or predicting phenomena. Aside from the foundation laid by Plato, this procedure was first fully developed by Hegel and deepened by Marx. Hegel's most succinct discussions of this approach can be found in his lesser *Logic,* no. 81, pp. 115–19, and *The Phenomenology of Mind,* trans. A. V. Miller (New York: Oxford University Press, 1977), 9–45. For Marx's brief formal presentation of this approach as it relates to his social theory, see Karl Marx, *Grundrisse: Foundations of the Critique of Political Economy,* trans. Martin Nicolaus (New York: Random House, 1973), 83–111.

19. The most explicit and extensive treatment of the social context of theological reflection by a Black theologian is found in James Cone's *God of the Oppressed* (New York: Seabury Press, 1975), chap. 3, 39–61.

20. The most sophisticated dialogue among Black theologians has focused on the status of this biblical truth. William Jones has claimed that Black theologians do not provide sufficient empirical evidence to warrant this truth. He

suggests that Black theologians have not taken seriously the possibility of a malevolent deity. For Jones, an acceptable Black theology must deal adequately with the problem of theodicy. James Cone has responded to Jones's argument by claiming that Jesus' victory over suffering and death constitutes the necessary and sufficient evidence for the belief that God sides with the oppressed and acts on their behalf. In short, Cone holds that empirical evidence is never a reliable basis of a biblical truth; the problem of theodicy is never solved in a theoretical manner, only defeated by one's faith in Jesus Christ. For Jones's incisive and insightful discussion, see his *Is God a White Racist?* For Cone's reply, see his *God of the Oppressed,* 187–94.

21. This conception of science pervades Marx's mature writings. For example, he states, "But all science would be superfluous if the outward appearance and the essence of things directly coincided." (Karl Marx, *Capital,* vol. 3, ed. Frederick Engels [New York: International Publishers, 1967], 817.) Notice also the demystifying aim of theory in the first few paragraphs of the famous section 4 entitled "The Fetishism of Commodities and the Secret Thereof" of chapter 1 in *Capital,* 1:71ff.

22. These figures come from the nearest thing to an official survey on the maldistribution of wealth in America conducted by the Federal Reserve Board in 1962. As one of its authors, Herman Miller, noted, "The figures were so striking as to obviate the need to search for trends." For a further exposition and elaboration on this study, see Gus Tyler, "The Other Economy: America's Working Poor," special issue, *New Leader,* May 8, 1978, 20–24.

23. This point illustrates the undeniable link of the orthodox Marxist view to the Enlightenment. More specifically, it portrays the inherent elitism and paternalism of such a view. We need only recall Vladimir Lenin's well-known claim (in *What Is to Be Done?* 1902; China Books, 1973) that the working class can achieve only trade-union consciousness on its own, thereby requiring a vanguard party to elevate it to revolutionary consciousness. For Lenin, this party brings enlightenment to the benighted proletariat.

24. This view is illustrated clearly in an essay by José Míguez-Bonino, a leading Latin American liberation theologian, entitled "Popular Piety in Latin America," in which he states: "From a theological as well as a political perspective the popular piety that used to exist and that still predominates in Latin America can only be considered as a profoundly alienated and alienating piety, a manifestation of an enslaved consciousness and, at the same time, a ready instrument for the continuation and consolidation of oppression. The intent to transform the mobilizing power of that piety to goals of transformation without radically altering the very content to the religious consciousness seems psychologically impossible and theologically unacceptable." This essay appeared in *Cristianismo y Sociedad* (Buenos Aires) 47 (first issue, 1976): 31–38, trans. James and Margaret Goff. Gustavo Gutiérrez, another prominent Latin American liberation theologian, understands popular culture and religion in a more subtle and sophisticated

way. I base this judgment on my cordial and provocative discussions with him during his visiting professorship at Union Theological Seminary in the fall of 1977. It seems to me his own cultural roots and his serious study of cultural Marxist thinkers, especially Antonio Gramsci and José Carlos Mariátegui (the father of Latin American Marxism), principally account for his sensitivity to popular culture and religion. I must add that Gutiérrez's viewpoint is now more widely accepted among Latin American liberation theologians.

25. This serious concern of Black theologians and religious scholars is exemplified best by Charles H. Long's highly suggestive essay, "Perspectives for a Study of Afro-American Religion in the United States," *History of Religions* 11, no. 1 (August 1977): 54–66; Gayraud S. Wilmore's solid study, *Black Religion and Black Radicalism,* esp. 298–306; and James H. Cone's speculative work, *The Spirituals and the Blues* (New York: Seabury Press, 1972). The "armors, forms, and products" of Afro-American culture I have in mind here are the spirituals, blues, gospels, jazz, folktales, and sermons. What is not sufficiently emphasized by Black theologians, religious scholars, or cultural critics is the radical potential embedded within the style of these art forms. The most important aspect of them is not what is conveyed, but how this "what" is conveyed. It is this "how" which bears the imprint of struggle and constitutes the distinctive imposition of order on chaos by Black people. It is this "how" or style that contains the real message or genuine content of these works of art. To my knowledge, only the essays of Ralph Ellison and Albert Murray explore this frontier of Afro-American art forms. See Ralph Ellison, *Shadow and Act* (New York: Random House, 1964), and Albert Murray, *The Omni-Americans: New Perspectives on Black Experience and American Culture* (New York: E. P. Dutton, 1971).

26. This point is best illustrated by the words of Hugo Assmann, one of the most radical Latin American theologians. "In my opening address I was sometimes aggressive because, as a Westernized Latin American, I don't feel at ease with my colour, my 'gringo' face, my German origin. I don't feel happy with the fact that my theological dissertation was written in German. I have a psychological necessity to say to you in Western language that I am not Western. We Latin Americans are still in the early stages of our search for a Latin American identity. If you look in my library you will find books by German authors, French authors, Italian authors, Marx, Moltmann etc. There is something false in this . . . Something which is not Latin American." This quote is from the publication *RISK* (p. 62), which is based on the Symposium on Black Theology and Latin American Theology of Liberation, May 1973, at the Ecumenical Center in Geneva, Switzerland.

27. It is not surprising that Gramsci comes from a degraded cultural region in Italy, namely Sardinia, and had intense experiences of ostracism owing to his hunchback, poor health, and short height (he was barely five feet tall). A sample of his writings can be found in *Selections from the Prison Notebooks,* trans. and ed. Quintin Hoare and Geoffrey Nowell Smith (London: Lawrence & Wishart, 1971).

28. The book by Raymond Williams I have in mind is his *Marxism and Literature* (Oxford: Oxford University Press, 1977), esp. chap. 2, 75–141.

29. Gramsci discusses this conception in his seminal essay, "The Intellectual Selections from the Prison Notebooks," *Prison Notebooks,* 5–23. Although he completely misunderstands the nature of the radical potential of Afro-American culture and Afro-American intellectuals, this does not harm his theoretical formulation of the notion of organic intellectuals.

30. I should add that this also holds to an important degree for white poor and Hispanic Pentecostal churches.

31. The best recent treatments of these issues I know are Peter Evans's *Dependent Development: The Alliance of Multinational, State, and Local Capital in Brazil* (Princeton, NJ: Princeton University Press, 1979) and the superb collection of essays in "Strategies for the Class Struggle in Latin America," special issue, *Contemporary Marxism* 1 (Spring 1980).

32. Raymond Williams, *Keywords: A Vocabulary of Culture and Society* (New York: Oxford University Press, 1976), 48–50, and his *Marxism and Literature,* 13–16.

33. My understanding of the Industrial Revolution follows closely the scenario painted by Eric J. Hobsbawm in his classic work, *The Age of Revolution: 1789–1848* (Cleveland: World Publishing Co., 1962), 44–73.

34. Hobsbawm, *Age of Revolution,* 57.

35. My information about George Washington Woodbey, a fascinating Black preacher, comes directly from Philip Foner's timely essay, "Reverend George Washington Woodbey: Early Twentieth-Century California Black Socialist," *Journal of Negro History* 61, no. 2 (April 1976). For Foner's treatment of Woodbey along with other Black socialist preachers in the United States, including Reverends George W. Slater Jr., S. C. Garrison, and George Frazier Miller, see his monumental work, *American Socialism and Black Americans: From the Age of Jackson to World War II* (Westport, CT: Greenwood Press, 1977), chap. 7, 151–81.

36. It is interesting to note that *The Bible and Socialism* was dedicated to "the Preachers and Members of the Churches, and all others who are interested in knowing what the Bible teaches on the question at issue between the Socialists and the Capitalists, by one who began preaching twenty-nine years ago, and still continues."

37. Foner, "Reverend George Washington Woodbey," 141–43.

38. Foner, "Reverend George Washington Woodbey," 143.

39. Foner, "Reverend George Washington Woodbey," 139.

Chapter 5: Afro-American Revolutionary Christianity

1. To attempt to account for this failure is to raise the question that constitutes the title of Werner Sombart's classic *Why Is There No Socialism in the United States?,* trans. Patricia M. Hocking and C. T. Husbands (White Plains,

NY: International Arts and Sciences Press, 1976). For a succinct treatment of this recently reissued work, see Jerome Karabel's review, "The Reasons Why," *New York Review of Books*, February 8, 1979, 22–27.

2. The significance of this historical inception is examined in Seymour Martin Lipset, *The First New Nation: The United States in Historical and Comparative Perspective* (New York: W. W. Norton, 1979), 15–98.

3. The classic statement on the impact of the absence of a feudal past on American life is Louis Hartz's *The Liberal Tradition in America* (New York: Harcourt, Brace, 1955).

4. Alexis de Tocqueville, *Democracy in America*, vol. 2, ed. Phillips Bradley (New York: Alfred A. Knopf, 1945), 123–44.

5. Stanley Aronowitz, *False Promises: The Shaping of American Working Class Consciousness* (New York: McGraw-Hill, 1973), 137–213.

6. This point is graphically put in Alan Dawley's well-known claim that "the ballot box was the coffin of class consciousness" in his *Class and Community: The Industrial Revolution in Lynn* (Cambridge, MA: Harvard University Press, 1976). See also Selig Perlman, *A History of Trade Unionism in the United States* (New York: Macmillan, 1922), 285–306, and Perlman, *A Theory of the Labor Movement* (1928).

7. The prohibitive role of American-style politics regarding class consciousness and class organization is explored in Seymour Martin Lipset, *Political Man: The Social Bases of Politics* (Garden City, NY: Doubleday, 1960), 303–31, and Richard Hofstadter, *The Idea of a Party System: The Rise of Legitimate Opposition in the United States, 1780–1840* (Berkeley: University of California Press, 1969).

8. For reliable studies that accent state repression of the Left, see James Weinstein, *The Decline of Socialism in America 1912–1925* (New York: Monthly Review Press, 1967), and Robert Justin Goldstein, *Political Repression in Modern America from 1870 to the Present* (Boston: G. K. Hall, 1978).

9. Lipset, *Political Man*, 27–86. The Western frontier, which partially served as a safety valve for urban conflict, was one of America's natural resources (after conquering indigenous peoples). This "natural resource" was the major focus of the influential essays of Frederick Jackson Turner reprinted in *Frontier and Section*, with an introduction by Ray Allen Billington (Englewood Cliffs, NJ: Prentice-Hall, 1961). The best brief treatment of Turner I know is Richard Hofstadter's chapter in his *The Progressive Historians: Turner, Beard, Parrington* (New York: Alfred A. Knopf, 1968), 47–164.

10. Aronowitz, *False Promises*, 178–83, 408–10. See also Harry Braverman's highly acclaimed *Labor and Monopoly Capital: The Degradation of Work in the 20th Century* (New York: Monthly Review Press, 1974).

11. James Weinstein, *The Corporate Ideal in the Liberal State, 1900–1918* (Boston: Beacon Press, 1968); Gabriel Kolko, *The Triumph of Conservatism: A Re-Interpretation of American History, 1900–1916* (Chicago: Quadrangle Books, 1967).

12. For fine historical treatments of Eduard Bernstein, major leader of the Second International, see Peter Gay, *The Dilemma of Democratic Socialism: Eduard Bernstein's Challenge to Marx* (New York: Columbia University Press, 1952), and George Lichtheim, *Marxism: An Historical and Critical Study* (New York: Frederick A. Praeger, 1962), 259–300.

13. For critical examination of Lenin's position, see Alfred G. Meyer, *Leninism* (New York: Frederick A. Praeger, 1962), 1–144, and Robert C. Tucker, "Lenin and Revolution," in *The Lenin Anthology,* ed. Robert C. Tucker (New York: W. W. Norton, 1975), xxv–lxiv.

14. For a superb analysis of Stalinism, see Stephen F. Cohen, "Bolshevism and Stalinism," in *Stalinism: Essays in Historical Interpretation,* ed. Robert C. Tucker (New York: W. W. Norton, 1977), 3–29. See also Robert C. Tucker, *Stalin as Revolutionary, 1879–1929: A Study in History and Personality* (New York: W. W. Norton, 1973), 292–367. For a gallant yet flawed defense of Stalin, see Bruce Franklin, introduction to *The Essential Stalin: Major Theoretical Writings, 1905–1952,* ed. Bruce Franklin (Garden City, NY: Doubleday, 1972), 1–38.

15. For a fair treatment of Trotsky's stance, see Irving Howe, *Leon Trotsky* (New York: Penguin Books, 1979), 61–128. See also Robert H. McNeal, "Trotskyist Interpretations of Stalinism," in Tucker, *Stalinism,* 30–52.

16. The Luxemburg essays can be found in *Selected Political Writings of Rosa Luxemburg,* ed. Dick Howard (New York: Monthly Review Press, 1971); the Pannekoek essay in *Pannekoek and Gorter's Marxism,* ed. D. A. Smart (London: Pluto Press, 1978), 50–73; and the Korsch essay in *Karl Korsch: Revolutionary Theory,* ed. Douglas Kellner (Austin: University of Texas Press, 1977), 124–35. For recent treatments of Councilism, see Stanley Aronowitz, "Left-Wing Communism: The Reply to Lenin," in *The Unknown Dimension: European Marxism since Lenin,* ed. Dick Howard and Karl E. Klare (New York: Basic Books, 1972), 169–94; Serge Bricianer, *Pannekoek and the Workers' Councils* (St. Louis: Telos Press, 1978); and Andrei Silard, "On the History of the Workers' Councils," *Telos* 48 (Summer 1981): 49–64.

17. Antonio Gramsci's "Workers Democracy" can be found in *Antonio Gramsci: Selections from Political Writings, 1910–1920,* trans. John Matthews (New York: International Publishers, 1977), 65–68; Gramsci, "The Modern Prince," in *Selections from the Prison Notebooks,* trans. and ed. Quintin Hoare and Geoffrey Nowell Smith (London: Lawrence & Wishart, 1971), 123–205. The best treatments of Gramsci are John M. Cammett, *Antonio Gramsci and the Origins of Italian Communism* (Stanford, CA: Stanford University Press, 1967), esp. (for our purposes) 65–138, 156–200; Carl Boggs, *Gramsci's Marxism* (London: Pluto Press, 1976), 85–126; and Walter L. Adamson, *Hegemony and Revolution: A Study of Antonio Gramsci's Political and Cultural Theory* (Berkeley: University of California Press, 1980), 105–246.

18. For an exhaustive examination of the first generation of Afro-American Marxists, see Philip Foner, *American Socialism and Black Americans: From the*

Age of Jackson to World War II (Westport, CT: Greenwood Press, 1977), 45, 73, 88, 95, 142, 151–81. See also his treatment of Hubert Harrison, 207–18. On Ben Fletcher's involvement with the Industrial Workers of the World, see Foner, *History of the Labor Movement in the United States,* vol. 4, *The Industrial Workers of the World, 1905–1917* (New York: International Publishers, 1965), 123–29.

19. For elaboration, see chap. 1, n. 26. Note also that *The Messenger* was the first *national* socialist magazine edited by and for Black people in the United States. The first Black socialist magazine was J. B. Reed's *American Negro Socialist* based in Butte, Montana, 1915.

20. For further information, see chap. 1, n. 27.

21. A major consequence of this Leninist captivity is the deep attachment of Afro-American Marxist-Leninists to the Black Nation Thesis. This Thesis—first put forward by the Communist International in 1928 and 1930 resolutions—holds that Afro-American oppression should be analyzed as a particular evolving historical form of national oppression; that Afro-Americans either have constituted or do constitute an oppressed nation in the Black Belt South; and that those Afro-Americans outside this Black Belt South comprise an oppressed national minority in the rest of the United States. This Thesis was propounded and propagated (in varying degrees) by the Communist Party U.S.A. until 1959. The Black Nation Thesis began as an honest yet misguided attempt by Marxist-Leninists to repudiate the racist reductionist perspective of the Bernsteinian Socialist Party which denied the specificity of Afro-American oppression by simply subsuming it under general working-class exploitation. This Thesis—formulated upon the heels of the Garvey movement—ingeniously captures the sense of cultural separateness among Afro-Americans, while ignoring the undeniable fact that Afro-Americans have never been nor are a nation. Neither adroit appeals to Stalin's definition of a nation (common language, territory, mode of production, and culture) nor historical examples of the Afro-American impulse toward a rhetoric of nationhood discredit this stubborn fact. In short, an ahistorical racial determination of a nation, a flaccid statistical determination of national boundaries, and an illusory distinct national economy for Afro-Americans provide the unacceptable grounds for the Black Nation Thesis. The overwhelming majority of Afro-Americans are a racially coerced section of the multileveled working class who suffer under specific forms of racist (and for Black women, sexist) oppression, cultural degradation, and class exploitation. The predominance of the Black Nation Thesis among Afro-American Marxist-Leninists ironically accounts for both the lure of radical young Black people with a healthy sense of cultural separateness to right-wing Marxism and the perceived irrelevance of Marxist-Leninist views on racism among the majority of Afro-Americans. In other words, the Black Nation Thesis has served as a sincere attempt yet poor excuse for the absence of a sophisticated Marxist theory of the specificity of Afro-American oppression. For recent noteworthy inquiries on this subject, see Stanley Aronowitz's insightful perspective in *The Crisis in Historical*

Materialism: Class, Politics and Culture in Marxist Theory (New York: Praeger, 1981), 89–112, and Linda Burnham and Bob Wing's provocative and often persuasive essays, "Toward a Communist Analysis of Black Oppression and Black Liberation, Part 1: Critique of the Black Nation Thesis," *Line of March: A Marxist-Leninist Journal of Rectification* 2, no. 1 (July–August 1981): 21–88, and "Toward a Communist Analysis of Black Oppression and Black Liberation, Part 2: Theoretical and Historical Framework," *Line of March* no. 8 (September–October 1981): 31–90. For the classical Marxist-Leninist defenses of the Black Nation Thesis, see James S. Allen, *The Negro Question in the United States* (New York: International Publishers, 1936), and Harry Haywood, *Negro Liberation* (New York: International Publishers, 1948). An interesting contemporary reformulation of the Black Nation Thesis is found in Nelson Peery's *The Negro National Colonial Question* (Chicago: Workers Press, 1978).

22. Wilson Record, *The Negro and the Communist Party* (New York: Atheneum, 1971), 54–183; Benjamin J. Davis, *Communist Councilman from Harlem: Autobiographical Notes Written in a Federal Penitentiary* (New York: International Publishers, 1969), 53–100; Harry Haywood, *Black Bolshevik: Autobiography of an Afro-American Communist* (Chicago: Liberator Press, 1978), 391–466. I also relied on my lecture notes of a near two-hour presentation by Harry Haywood (along with Victoria Garvin) at Holy Name Church on West 96th Street in New York City on March 20, 1981.

23. Robert Allen, with the collaboration of Pamela P. Allen, *Reluctant Reformers: Racism and Social Reform Movements in the United States* (Garden City, NY: Doubleday, 1975), 242–43.

24. Besides the Foner volume on the Industrial Workers of the World, *History of the Labor Movement in the United States,* vol. 4, see Melvyn Dubofsky, *We Shall Be All: A History of the Industrial Workers of the World* (New York: Times Press, 1969), and Elizabeth Gurley Flynn, *Memories of the Industrial Workers of the World (IWW),* Occasional Paper 24 (San Jose, CA: American Institute of Marxist Studies, 1977). To no surprise, there is no major study of A. J. Muste's American Workers Party nor of the pre-party and party formations headed by Paul Mattick. The best information available comes from the lively prints and reprints of *Living Marxism* and *Council Communist Correspondence.* On the crucial role played by the National Negro Labor Council in the early 1950s, see Philip Foner, *Organized Labor and the Black Worker, 1619–1973* (New York: International Publishers, 1976), 293–311, and Mindy Thompson, *The National Negro Labor Council: A History,* Occasional Paper 27 (San Jose, CA: American Institute of Marxist Studies, 1978). Root and Branch still publish their journal, with minimal visibility. The best books on the League of Revolutionary Black Workers in Detroit are Dan Georgakas and Marvin Surkin, *Detroit—I Do Mind Dying: A Study in Urban Revolution* (New York: St. Martin's Press, 1975), and James A. Geschwender, *Class, Race, and Worker Insurgency: The League of Revolutionary Black Workers* (Cambridge: Cambridge University Press, 1977).

25. Charges for American Marxist co-optation of Afro-American national-ism are put forward in Harold Cruse's influential work, *The Crisis of the Negro Intellectual* (New York: William Morrow, 1967). American Marxist attitudes toward populism are at the center of the controversial (yet first-rate) scholarship of Lawrence Goodwyn, *Democratic Promise: The Populist Moment in America* (New York: Oxford University Press, 1978), and James R. Green, *Grass-Roots Socialism: Radical Movements in the Southwest, 1895–1943* (Baton Rouge: Louisiana State University Press, 1978). For their lively debate and dialogue, see Lawrence Good-wyn, "The Cooperative Commonwealth and Other Abstractions: In Search of a Democratic Premise," *Marxist Perspectives* 3, no. 2 (Summer 1980): 8–42; Good-wyn, "Organizing Democracy: The Limits of Theory and Practice," *Democracy: A Journal of Political Renewal and Radical Change* 1, no. 1 (January 1981): 41–60; and James Green, "Populism, Socialism and the Promise of Democracy," *Radical History Review* 24 (Fall 1980): 7–40. For feminist responses to Marxist neglect, see Shulamith Firestone, *The Dialectic of Sex* (New York: William Morrow, 1970), esp. 1–14, and Batya Weinbaum, *The Curious Courtship of Women's Liberation and Socialism* (Boston: South End Press, 1978), 3–89. See also *This Bridge Called My Back: Writings by Radical Women of Color,* ed. Cherrie Moraga and Gloria Anzaldua (Watertown, MA: Persephone Press, 1981), and *Top Ranking: A Collec-tion of Articles on Racism and Classism in the Lesbian Community,* ed. Joan Gibbs and Sara Bennett (Brooklyn, NY: February 3rd Press, 1980).

26. The best recent treatment of the relative impasse of the Afro-American liberation movement is Adolf L. Reed Jr.'s "Black Particularity Reconsidered," *Telos* 39 (Spring 1979): 71–93.

27. For useful works on the Garvey movement, see Tony Martin, *Race First: The Ideological and Organizational Struggles of Marcus Garvey and the Universal Negro Improvement Association* (Westport, CT: Greenwood Press, 1976), and Randall K. Burkett, *Garveyism as a Religious Movement: The Institutionalization of a Black Civil Religion* (Metuchen, NJ: Scarecrow Press, 1978).

28. The best treatment of Bill Thompson is in Harold F. Gosnell's *Negro Politicians: The Rise of Negro Politics in Chicago* (Chicago: University of Chicago Press, 1935), 37–62. For his fine description of Oscar DePriest, see 163–95. The seminal essay on Black inclusion within mainstream electoral politics in American society remains Martin Kilson's "Political Change in the Negro Ghetto, 1900–1940's," in *Key Issues in the Afro-American Experience,* ed. Nathan I. Huggins, Martin Kilson, and Daniel Fox (New York: Harcourt Brace Jovanovich, 1971), 167–92.

29. For a general treatment of the civil rights movement, see Thomas R. Brooks, *Walls Come Tumbling Down: A History of the Civil Rights Movement, 1940–1970* (Englewood Cliffs, NJ: Prentice-Hall, 1974). For studies on Martin Luther King Jr., note David L. Lewis, *King: A Critical Biography* (New York: Frederick A. Praeger, 1970), and Hanes Walton, *The Political Philosophy of Mar-tin Luther King, Jr.* (Westport, CT: Greenwood Press, 1971).

30. The best commentary on Malcolm X remains self-commentary. See his *Malcolm X Speaks* (New York: Merit Publishers, 1965). For a fine attempt at highlighting the many dimensions of Malcolm X, see *Malcolm X: The Man and His Times,* ed. John Henrik Clarke (New York: Macmillan, 1969).

31. For a small taste of the Black conservative viewpoints, see *The Fairmont Papers: Black Alternatives Conference San Francisco, December 1980* (San Francisco: Institute for Contemporary Studies Press, 1981). The best Black conservative work remains Thomas Sowell's *Race and Economics* (New York: David McKay, 1975). For a noteworthy attack on the role of the state from the Left, see Lorenzo Komboa Ervin, *Anarchism and the Black Revolution,* Pages from Prison, No. 4 (New York: Anarchist Black Cross, n.d.).

32. Cornel West, "Prospects for the North American Christian Left," in *Theology in the Americas: Detroit II Conference Papers,* ed. Cornel West, Caridad Guidote, and Margaret Coakley (Maryknoll, NY: Orbis Books, 1982), 156–72.

Response to Chapter 1: Cultural Alienation and Intellectual Insecurity in the Modern West

1. See Barbara Ransby, *Ella Baker & The Black Freedom Movement: A Radical Democratic Vision* (Chapel Hill: University of North Carolina Press, 2003).

2. Erica R. Edwards, *Charisma and the Fictions of Black Leadership* (Minneapolis: University of Minnesota Press, 2012), 21.

3. Martin Luther King Jr., "Recommendations to the Dexter Avenue Baptist Church for the Fiscal Year 1954–1955," in *The Papers of Martin Luther King, Jr.,* ed. Clayborne Carson, vol. 2 (Berkeley: University of California Press, 1994), 287.

4. Cornel West, "The Prophetic Tradition in Afro-America," *Drew Gateway* 55 (1984–85).

5. Edwards, *Charisma and the Fictions of Black Leadership*, 16.

Response to Chapter 2: Reflecting on Modern Racism

1. Kate McGee, "Texas Bill to Ban the Teaching of 'Critical Race Theory' Spiked at the Last Minute on a Technicality," *Fort Worth Report,* May 28, 2021, https://fortworthreport.org/2021/05/28/texas-bill-to-ban-the-teaching-of-critical-race-theory-spiked-at-the-last-minute-on-a-technicality/.

2. Michel Foucault, "Nietzsche, Genealogy, History," in *Language, Countermemory, Practice: Selected Essays and Interviews,* ed. D. F. Bouchard (Ithaca, NY: Cornell University Press, 1977), 146.

3. Sharon Holland, *The Erotic Life of Racism* (Durham, NC: Duke University Press, 2012), 3–4.

4. Holland, *Erotic Life of Racism,* 6.

5. Holland, *Erotic Life of Racism,* 6.

6. Charles H. Long, *Significations: Signs, Symbols, and Images in the Interpretation of Religion*, Series in Philosophical and Cultural Studies in Religion (Aurora, CO: Davies Group, 1999), 202–10.

7. Theologian Mayra Rivera rethinks the category of flesh as creative, divine, and a conduit through which we encounter each other and the world. This challenges flesh within much of Christian theological traditions as base, perverse, and sinful. For Rivera, rethinking theology through flesh and the body has profound implications in reformulating the form, content, and end goals of theology. Rather than seeing theology as aimed toward transcendence, it is a discourse about immanence and carnality, helping to shed light on a number of this-world phenomena such as experiences of race, gender, and more. Mayra Rivera, *Poetics of the Flesh* (Durham, NC: Duke University Press, 2015).

8. Womanist theologian Monica Coleman explores the symbiotic relationship between God, humanity, and the ancestors in understanding divine reality and human action within this reality. Coleman is not interested in speaking of divine reality as something that sits above or over humanity and creation, like most traditional theologies. Instead, she writes about divine reality as something that emerges and enlarges, over and over again, in and through creation and the world's patterns and processes, which has implications for the way we talk about humanity, suffering in the world, and our action with God to effect justice. Monica Coleman, *Making a Way Out of No Way: A Womanist Theology* (Minneapolis: Fortress Press, 2008).

9. See Tamura A. Lomax, *Jezebel Unhinged: Loosing the Black Female Body in Religion and Culture* (Durham, NC: Duke University Press, 2018), 14–30.

Response to Chapter 3: The Four Traditions of Afro-American Response

1. Arguably the best introduction to the study of African American political thought is now Melvin L. Rogers and Jack Turner, eds., *African American Political Thought: A Collected History* (Chicago: University of Chicago Press, 2021).

2. E. Franklin Frazier, "The Failure of the Negro Intellectual," in *The Death of White Sociology*, ed. Joyce A. Ladner (Baltimore: Black Classic Press, 1973), 58.

3. Gunnar Myrdal, *An American Dilemma: The Negro Problem and Modern Democracy*, 3rd ed. (New York: Harper, 1944), 784.

4. Myrdal, *American Dilemma*, 786.

5. E. Franklin Frazier, *Black Bourgeoisie* (New York: Free Press Paperbacks, 1997), 173.

6. Myrdal, *American Dilemma*, 13.

7. Myrdal, *American Dilemma*, 746–49, 836.

8. Ralph J. Bunche, "Negro Political Philosophy," in *Selected Speeches and Writings*, ed. Charles P. Henry (Ann Arbor: University of Michigan Press, 1995), 27–34. Also, see Bunche, *A Brief and Tentative Analysis of Negro Leadership* (New York: New York University Press, 2005), esp. 47, and Rayford W. Logan,

introduction to *What the Negro Wants,* ed. Rayford W. Logan (Chapel Hill: University of North Carolina Press, 1944).

9. Harold Cruse, *The Crisis of the Negro Intellectual* (New York: William Morrow, 1967), 6–7; Cruse, "Negro Nationalism's New Wave," in *Rebellion or Revolution?* (New York: William Morrow, 1968), 68–73.

10. Rahel Jaeggi, *Critique of Forms of Life,* trans. Ciaran Cronin (Cambridge, MA: Belknap Press of Harvard University Press, 2018).

11. On the "ethics of the oppressed," see Tommie Shelby, "The Ethics of Uncle Tom's Children," *Critical Inquiry* 38, no. 3 (2012), 514.

12. Frantz Fanon, *The Wretched of the Earth,* rev. 60th anniv. ed., trans. Richard Philcox (New York: Grove Press, 2021).

13. Frazier, "Failure of the Negro Intellectual."

14. In later texts, written after 1987's *Beloved,* West appears to take Morrison as the exemplar of humanism. See Cornel West, "Black Strivings in a Twilight Civilization," in *The Cornel West Reader* (New York: Basic Civitas Books, 1999).

15. On cultural constructionism, see Chike Jeffers, "The Cultural Theory of Race: Yet Another Look at Du Bois's 'The Conservation of Races,'" *Ethics* 123, no. 3 (2013).

16. See, for example, the essays critiquing "racial reasoning," sexism, misogyny, and the politics of Black solidarity in Toni Morrison, ed., *Race-ing Justice, En-gendering Power: Essays on Anita Hill, Clarence Thomas, and the Construction of Social Reality* (New York: Pantheon, 1992).

17. See, for example, Farah Jasmine Griffin, "Zora Neale Hurston's Radical Individualism," in Rogers and Turner, *African American Political Thought,* 314–29, and Barbara Foley, *Wrestling with the Left* (Durham, NC: Duke University Press, 2010).

18. Some of this road has been traveled by Jack Turner, *Awakening to Race: Individualism and Social Consciousness in America* (Chicago: University of Chicago Press, 2012).

19. Robert Gooding-Williams, *In the Shadow of Du Bois: Afro-Modern Political Thought in America* (Cambridge, MA: Harvard University Press, 2009), 6–7.

20. Richard Wright, *White Man, Listen!,* in *Black Power: Three Books from Exile; "Black Power," "The Color Curtain," and "White Man, Listen!"* (New York: Harper Perennial, 2008), 690.

Response to Chapter 4: On Capitalism, Christianity, and Culture

1. William Strickland, "Whatever Happened to the Politics of Black Liberation?," *Black Scholar* 7, no. 2 (1975): 20–26.

2. See Gary J. Dorrien, *American Democratic Socialism: History, Politics, Religion, and Theory* (New Haven, CT: Yale University Press, 2021).

3. Michel Foucault, *Fearless Speech,* ed. Joseph Pearson, Semiotext(e) Foreign Agents Series (Los Angeles: Semiotext[e], 2001).

4. These texts are part of a broad rethinking of Marxist thought undertaken by a number of African American activists and organizations in the wake of the Black freedom movement. See Max Elbaum, *Revolution in the Air: Sixties Radicals Turn to Lenin, Mao, and Che* (New York: Verso, 2002).

5. Manning Marable, *Blackwater: Historical Studies in Race, Class Consciousness, and Revolution* (Dayton, OH: Black Praxis Press, 1981).

6. Angela Y. Davis, *Women, Race and Class* (New York: Vintage Books, 1981).

7. Albert B. Cleage Jr., *The Black Messiah*, Search Book ed. (New York: Sheed & Ward, 1968); C. Eric Lincoln, *Is Anybody Listening to Black America?* (New York: Seabury Press, 1968); Tom Skinner, *Black and Free* (Exeter: Paternoster Press, 1969).

8. Lerone Bennett Jr., *The Negro Mood, and Other Essays* (Chicago: Johnson, 1964).

9. James H. Cone, *Said I Wasn't Gonna Tell Nobody: The Making of a Black Theologian* (Maryknoll, NY: Orbis Books, 2018), 71.

10. Brandon M. Terry, "This Faith," *Los Angeles Review of Books*, July 15, 2020, https://lareviewofbooks.org/article/this-faith/. See also Andrew J. Douglas and Jared A. Loggins, *Prophet of Discontent: Martin Luther King, Jr. and the Critique of Racial Capitalism* (Athens: University of Georgia Press, 2021).

11. Cornel West, "Philosophy and the Afro-American Experience," *Philosophical Forum* 9, no. 2/3 (1977–78): 148.

12. John H. McClendon, "Eugene C. Holmes: A Commentary on a Black Marxist Philosopher," in *Philosophy Born of Struggle*, ed. Leonard Harris (Dubuque, IA: Kendall/Hunt, 1983), 37–50.

13. McClendon, "Eugene C. Holmes," 46.

14. Theodor Adorno, *Minima Moralia: Reflections on Damaged Life* (1951; repr., London: Verso, 2006), 247.

Response to Chapter 5: Afro-American Revolutionary Christianity

1. Eddie Glaude Jr., "The Black Church Is Dead," *Huffington Post,* April 26, 2010, https://www.huffpost.com/entry/the-black-church-is-dead_b_473815.

2. Eric L. McDaniel, Maraam Dwidar, and Hadill Calderon, "The Faith of Black Politics: The Relationship between Black Religious and Political Beliefs," *Journal of Black Studies* 49, no. 3 (2018): 257.

3. E. L. McDaniel, "What Kind of Christian Are You? Religious Ideologies and Political Attitudes," *Journal for Scientific Study of Religion* 55 (2016).

4. See Obery M. Hendricks, *The Politics of Jesus: Rediscovering the True Revolutionary Nature of the Teachings of Jesus and How They Have Been Corrupted* (New York: Doubleday, 2006).

Contributors

Cornel West is Dietrich Bonhoeffer Professor of Philosophy and Christian Practice at Union Theological Seminary in New York. He is the author or editor of more than thirty books, including *Race Matters, Democracy Matters*, and his memoir, *Brother West: Living and Loving Out Loud*.

Myisha Cherry is Assistant Professor of Philosophy at the University of California, Riverside. Among her publications is the celebrated book *The Case for Rage: Why Anger Is Essential to Anti-Racist Struggle*.

Keri Day is Associate Professor of Constructive Theology and African American Religion at Princeton Theological Seminary. She is the author of several books, including *Azusa Reimagined: A Radical Vision of Religious and Democratic Belonging*.

Brandon M. Terry is Associate Professor of African and African American Studies and Social Studies at Harvard University. He is the coeditor of *To Shape a New World: Essays on the Political Philosophy of Martin Luther King, Jr.*

Shatema Threadcraft is Associate Professor of Gender and Sexuality Studies, Philosophy, and Political Science at Vanderbilt University. She is the author of *Intimate Justice: The Black Female Body and the Body Politic*.

Corey D. B. Walker is Wake Forest Professor of the Humanities at Wake Forest University. He is the author of *A Noble Fight: African American Freemasonry and the Struggle for Democracy in America*.

Jonathan Lee Walton is Dean of the School of Divinity, Presidential Chair of Religion and Society, and Dean of Wait Chapel at Wake Forest University. He is the author of *The Lens of Love: Reading the Bible in Its World for Our World* and *Watch This! The Ethics and Aesthetics of Black Televangelism*.

Index

Printed in the USA
CPSIA information can be obtained
at www.ICGtesting.com
CBHW030148230124
3686CB00001B/9